Scandals,
Scamps,
and Scoundrels

Also by James Phelan

Howard Hughes: The Hidden Years

Scandals, Scamps, and Scoundrels

The Casebook of an Investigative Reporter

James Phelan

Random House New York

Portions of this work appeared in different form in the Las Vegas *Sun*, the Long Beach
Press-Telegram, *The Reporter* magazine, and the *Saturday Evening Post*.

Library of Congress Cataloging in Publication Data
Phelan, James, 1912–
Scandals, scamps, and scoundrels.
1. Phelan, James, 1912–
2. Journalists—United States—Biography.
I. Title.
PN4874.P47A37   1982   070'.92'4 [B]   79-4794
ISBN 0-394-48196-8

Manufactured in the United States of America
98765432
First Edition

To George and Kate McCullom

Contents

Foreword by Tom Wicker ix

Note to the Reader xi

1. *The Clifford Irving Hoax* 3

2. *Beginning* 40

3. *California Con Man's Cure-All* 52

4. *The Subterranean Lobbyists* 66

5. *Rehearsal for Watergate* 81

6. *The Case of the Duplicate Murder Confessions* 99

7. *Big Pearl* 120

8. *Jim Garrison* v. *Clay Shaw* 138

9. *My Life with Howard Hughes* 177

10. *The Assassin, the Impersonator—and Others* 210

Foreword

In his note to the reader, Jim Phelan calls himself a "puzzle addict." No doubt he's that. But this book is more significantly the confessions of a man doggedly devoted to the proposition that public disclosure is an important kind of justice that sometimes even prompts the real thing.

It's more fashionable these days to tax reporters with unwarranted invasions of privacy; the charge is fair enough against some, and in some cases. But too often "invasion of privacy" is intoned—as if in all cases privacy were the highest conceivable value—by solemn spokesmen to suggest that upstart reporters have no business looking under the surface of things.

Jim Phelan has other ideas about reporting—always has had, he tells us here, even in his cub days. He may have been born knowing that an "official secret" is usually more official than secret, that an "authorized statement" usually protects the authorizing party, and that "no comment" is an evasion most often justified by fear of public reaction.

Knowing all that, as well as more than he probably wants to about human nature and the condition of man, Phelan has the enduring conviction that it's therefore precisely a reporter's job to look under the surface of things (like most, he'd be embarrassed to call it "seeking truth"). And while such subterranean poking around may result occasionally in an unavoidable invasion of someone's privacy, it's far more likely to turn up deception, greed, fraud, graft, theft, waste, rape of the public interest, and rank injustice, private and official.

Phelan also appears to suffer incurably (it's surprising how many reporters do) from the notion that if Americans knew enough about it, they wouldn't tolerate so much deception, greed, fraud, graft, theft, waste, ineptitude, rape of the public interest, and rank injustice, private and official.

Here are accounts of a number of stories that resulted from these peculiar ideas—as well as from Jim Phelan's ingenuity, sound instincts, perseverance, integrity and not inconsiderable courage (he is the only reporter I have ever known who volunteered to take an enema just to get a story). It was Phelan's unfinished manuscript on Howard Hughes that Clifford Irving pirated; here's how he did it and how Phelan and others tracked him down. It was Phelan who untangled the web of the "Hughes loan" to Richard Nixon's brother—a story that as told here ("Rehearsal for Watergate") reflects small credit on anyone involved, including the Kennedy political apparatus. And if you'd like a primer on how law officers can and do railroad innocent people, even when they *know* they're innocent, read "The Case of the Duplicate Murder Confessions."

But all these are first and foremost good stories; for example, "Big Pearl," a description of an unconscionable private fraud, and especially "Jim Garrison vs. Clay Shaw," the best account I've read of an unconscionable official fraud.

Jim Phelan has solid roots; he is a veteran of the splendid magazine reporting—some of the best journalism this country ever produced—that used to appear regularly and at length in the *Saturday Evening Post*, *Collier*'s, *Life*, *Look* and other journals now mourned. That kind of reporting took time, experience, resourcefulness, and someone willing to foot substantial expense accounts. Jim Phelan had them all and became one of magazine reporting's top practitioners; he still is finding ways to tell the public that things are not always, perhaps not even usually, what they seem.

So Phelan may label himself, if he chooses, a mere "puzzle addict." But I'd call him a first-rate reporter, determined, indefatigable and idealistic. He'd probably deny the last charge, but the evidence of this book supports it.

—Tom Wicker
March 15, 1982

Note to the Reader

Some people become addicted to acquiring huge amounts of money, collecting scrimshaw, becoming the world's greatest figure-skater, or injecting themselves with heroin. I got hooked instead on seeking what lies behind the façade of camouflaged people and mocked-up events. Puzzles, real-life mysteries, masquerades, and charades fascinate me, and this led me into journalism, an occupation where one gets paid for scratching the intolerable psychic itch of curiosity.

This book is about some of the puzzles I undertook to unravel as a newspaperman and magazine writer. They deal with a gallimaufry of well-known and obscure people whose only common denominator is that they were involved in events that were not what they seemed to be. Most of them were dissemblers who fashioned their own masks, but a few, like the unfortunate airman who confessed two murders he did not commit, wore false faces that were put on them by others.

I spent a number of years as a reporter before recognizing that I was relentlessly drawn to unsolved journalistic jigsaw puzzles. The discovery intrigued me, because I had not been conscious of this tilt. When I realized how my journalistic tree inclined, I tracked back to where my twig had been bent. When I was a skinny-shanked youngster in a small Southern Illinois town, I caddied for a banker at the local country club. He was a good golfer, liked the earnest way I caddied, tipped generously, and I came to idolize him. He had a beautiful wife and drove a Pierce-Arrow, the only one in town, and once gave me a ride home when my bicycle had a flat tire. He had been educated in the East, was literate and witty, and did not seem to belong in a little Illinois town. Discontent was already stirring in me, and I looked on him as a superior foreigner from a distant land where I yearned to journey. Like Edwin Arlington Robinson's Richard Cory, who "glittered when he walked" and "one calm summer night, went home and put a bullet through his head," he had a secret flaw. One fine summer afternoon, I was passing his bank and saw two officers thrusting my hero into a police car. He was sent to prison for embezzlement, and I will always remember the stiff smile he gave me as the police took him away. This early loss of innocence altered the way I looked at the world.

Once I had acquired a press card, my curiosity led me into what is now called investigative reporting. I became an investigative reporter, on my own initiative and without anyone's urging or supervision, before I had ever heard of the term. It is a term that has always struck me as somewhat awkward and redundant, since inquiry is the core of all reporting. If an investigative reporter is one who investigates what he writes about, what do all the others do?

Pragmatically, the term provides a useful distinction because—to paraphrase Orwell—while all reporters are investigative, some are more investigative than others. As used here, the term refers to the true compulsives who keep poking at a stubborn story long after their more sensible colleagues have had their quick go at it and moved on. We curiosity addicts were aptly described by Douglas Kennedy, editor of *True* magazine in its heyday, when it specialized in this genre. "An investigative reporter," he said, "is one who doesn't know when to quit."

Full-time practitioners constitute only a small fraction of the national press corps. They work in a high-risk specialty, akin to the people who make a living walking a tightrope across Niagara Falls or defusing bombs. A single bad error and one disappears into a maelstrom of libel or is blown out of the business. Their ranks are also kept thin by the economics of journalism. True investigative reporting is brutally expensive, compared with the quick in-and-out of conventional deadline reporting. It requires an investment of a great deal of time and money. I once worked on one story for five months, during which my publisher put out more than $20,000 in expenses, plus my salary. All of this produced a single newspaper story that ran about 2,000 words and costed out to a horrendous $17 a word, as the paper's apoplectic official bean-counter pointed out. I learned early on that most publishers and editors prefer stories that can be assembled in a day or two with a few telephone calls.

Libel hazards have been sharpened in recent years by a series of multimillion-dollar damage awards to plaintiffs. A California resort sued *Penthouse* magazine for $522,000,000—more than ten times the net worth of the magazine—because of an article linking the resort and its owners to organized crime. *Penthouse* spent seven years and more than $6,500,000 in legal fees defending an article for which it paid the authors only $3,000. Such lawsuits have given rise to media complaints about their chilling effect on investigative reporting. Journalists tend to look upon libel suits with the same fear and loathing with which Don Juans view venereal disease, but both overlook the fact that such ailments, while painful, inspire salutary restraints and precautions. The chilling effect of libel suits would be substantially reduced if publishers and editors budgeted more for producing articles and less for lawyers to defend them. Such a reordering of priorities would raise the general quality of investigative reporting, which would benefit everyone (except the lawyers) —the public, the reporters, and their targets. Ultimately, the most effective and equitable defense against libel is the truth.

Since Woodward and Bernstein became national folk heroes by helping topple Richard Nixon, investigative reporting has seen an incursion of enthusiasts long on ambition and short on experience, as evidenced in the Janet Cooke case and similar disasters. There has also been an increase in hubris and elitism among the media, some of which confuse their constitutionally protected right to inform with an obligation to instruct or indoctrinate. Among the by-products of this elitism have been campaigns for state shield laws that give journalists the right to protect the identities of anonymous sources. Not all journalists support such legislation. Shield laws collide head-on with the venerable right of the accused to face his accuser. They also tempt reporters to manufacture quotations that fit the otherwise legitimate thrust of a story. Journalism functioned for a long time without shield laws and can survive—and probably improve itself—without them.

Apart from its other hazards, investigative reporting is an inherently chancy undertaking, much like drilling a wildcat oil well. The reporter may be seeking something that simply isn't there, or is buried beyond reach, and he may work diligently for weeks and produce nothing at all. Publishers and editors, like investors who finance wildcatters, get no pleasure whatever from learning that they have bought a dry hole. During my years on newspapers, I kept blunting my drill-bit on the hard economics of the newsroom. Again and again I would get onto a story with intriguing implications, great gaps in facts, and promising leads, only to get whistled off it for counting-house reasons.

The reluctance of newspapers to support my curiosity habit propelled me into writing for magazines. I found them a much more congenial home for the overly investigative reporter. There one could work on a story for weeks or even months without cocking the right eye on the clock and the left on an unhappy bookkeeper. I worked in these pleasant vineyards for a quarter century, and was blessed that this time coincided with the last golden years of the big national magazines—*Life, Look, Collier's,* the *Saturday Evening Post.* My happiest years were the six I spent as a staff-writer for the *Post* in the '60's. I share the nostalgia of Joan Didion, who wrote to me after the *Post* died, "It was the best place to be when we were there, and weren't we lucky to be there?"

Financed by the *Post* and other magazines, for years I was able to go wherever curiosity took me, across the U.S., to Europe, Mexico, the Caribbean. The magazines were such busy marketplaces in those days that I supported my family for a year in the south of France on free-lance assignments in Europe.

The rise of television withered the magazines. One by one, the national giants died, cut off by television from the advertising revenue that nourished them. After foreclosing on the magazine homes of investigative reporters, television gave few of us shelter. Television seems to fear the complexities of such reporting, and distrusts itself to cope with them. The outstanding exception is *60 Minutes,* which works so well that one wonders why it is all alone.

Specialty magazines still flourish, but publications such as *Golf Digest, Yachting,* and *Psychology Today* do not finance safaris of investigative reporters. The two top markets for us today are *Playboy* and *Penthouse.* I have written for both, but not with the comfort I felt at the *Saturday Evening Post.* I have no hostility toward naked ladies, but I do not approve of their rubbing against my prose and

distracting the readers. Norman Rockwell never did such things at
the *Post.*

Although most of my work was financed by magazines, this is not
a collection of reprinted articles. In each story, the events have been
expanded to include the reporter in the cast of characters. The intent
was to try to show how a reporter works, as opposed to the antics
he is put through in most novels, movies, and television shows. I
have never, the reader is warned, burgled an office, tapped a telephone, passed myself off as an FBI agent, or broken a story by
seducing the mistress of a senator. Nor have I ever punched out any
gangsters, although I once was knocked down and kicked into a
muddy ditch by two small-town thugs.

In retelling these stories I have updated them, given them a
broader perspective, and included new material or a missing de-
nouement. This is especially true of the chapter on the efforts of
New Orleans District Attorney Jim Garrison to convict Clay Shaw
of conspiring to assassinate President Kennedy. This chapter is
three times the length of my original *Post* article and contains new
material that recently came to light.

Some of the material in two chapters—on the grounding of Clifford Irving's high-flying hoax and on the last tragic years of billionaire Howard Hughes—was originally published as cover stories
in *Time* magazine, although I was not then and never have been an
employe of *Time.* In both instances, *Time* purchased my research
and processed it into print with its own group-journalism production line. These stories are recounted here in expanded form and in
my own language.

I owe especial thanks to Jim Silberman, who conceived the idea
of this investigative casebook, and to Robert Loomis, executive
editor at Random House, who shepherded it through a preposter-
ously long writer's block. I also owe thanks to the late Herman
Ridder, one-time head of the Ridder newspaper chain, who financed
me on two of these stories with a good-natured, to-hell-with-the-
expense insouciance that is rare among publishers.

I am grateful to many investigative reporters across the country.
When not competing head-to-head on a story, they are generous in
charting the pitfalls for a colleague venturing into a strange terrain.
There are too many to name, but they are headed by Wallace
Turner of the N.Y. *Times,* one of the very best in our business.

Among other favors, he helped me to understand my motivation as an investigative reporter by explaining his own. He said he worked on puzzling stories because of an internal imperative, rather than to punish wrongdoers, or see his byline on page one, or out of the notion that he would measurably improve the world.

"When a story logically goes from A to B to C, and then suddenly jumps to E," he said, "I can't relax until I've learned what happened to the missing D. When I find out, I'm ready to go on to something else. I'd be satisfied even if I didn't write what I've learned, but if I don't the *Times* won't pay me."

To approach a tangle of facts thus, as a puzzle to be solved rather than as an indictment to be prosecuted, is an effective safeguard against the journalistic hazards of partisanship or ideological distortion. In their fervor, partisans and ideologues sometimes hammer jigsaw pieces into holes they don't fit. That kind of solution affords a puzzle-addict no satisfaction whatever.

I owe a final thanks to Lew Gillinson, formerly managing editor of *Cosmopolitan*, for advice anyone contemplating investigative reporting also should keep in mind. Gillinson sent me to Denver long ago to check on a chiropractor who claimed he could cure cancer. Before I left New York, he told me to sit down and listen.

"This fellow sues everyone in sight if they even lift an eyebrow in his direction," he said. "He's got $90,000,000 in libel suits on file, so nail down everything you write and I mean *everything*. Don't even say he has one head and two arms unless you count them yourself."

I researched the cancer expert in Denver, and found that many of his "cured" patients subsequently died of cancer. When I wrote the article, I dutifully described him as a "one-headed, two-armed Denver chiropractor."

Gillinson struck this phrase from my copy, but thanked me for checking.

"After all," he said with a grin, "you never know what you'll find if you don't go and look."

This is a book about going and looking.

Scandals,
Scamps,
and Scoundrels

1

The Clifford Irving Hoax

December 7, 1971, was the thirtieth anniversary of the bombing of Pearl Harbor. It was also, by happenstance, the day McGraw-Hill announced its forthcoming publication of the autobiography of Howard Hughes, as told to Clifford Irving. Another happenstance put me in Las Vegas, which proved to be an early center of action in Irving's bombing of McGraw-Hill. I had flown out to talk to Hank Greenspun, editor and publisher of the Las Vegas *Sun*, and was walking into his office when an excited newsman, waving a long sheet of yellow UPI wire copy, almost ran me down.

"What's the matter," I asked. "Did the Japs attack Pearl Harbor again?"

"It's Howard Hughes," he exclaimed. "He's written his autobiography."

"You're kidding," Greenspun and I chorused, grabbing at the telecopy.

It was authentic, the announcement at least. McGraw-Hill said it had acquired the world rights to the life story of Howard Robard Hughes, billionaire, moviemaker, airline proprietor, number one gambling-joint owner in Nevada, and the least-seen human since H. G. Wells's Invisible Man. McGraw-Hill would publish his story, told in his own words, in March. *Life* magazine had bought the magazine rights, and would shortly print three long excerpts.

This project had been put together, the announcement said, by one Clifford Irving, a novelist from McGraw-Hill's stable. Mr. Irving had interviewed Mr. Hughes "throughout the Western hemisphere" in more than a hundred tape-recorded sessions conducted "in various motel rooms and parked cars." Prior to excerpting the autobiography, *Life* would publish an article by Mr. Irving relating how he had pulled off this incomparable journalistic coup.

"Clifford Irving," said Hank Greenspun. "Who he?"

"Never heard of him," I replied.

"A great Hughes-watcher *you* are," commented Mr. Greenspun. "For fifteen years you've been bird-dogging Hughes, and here a fellow comes out of nowhere and gets his autobiography."

"That's life," I said, shrugging.

Greenspun lit a large, black cigar and blew out a contemplative plume of smoke. "Don't feel too bad about it," he said. "That book's a fake."

Greenspun has an Olympian manner of taking a fast look at a complex issue and arriving at a firm opinion. He is a hunch-player extraordinary, a man who feels things in the marrow of his fibulae and acts thereupon with great confidence. Mere reporters, who are expected to acquire some facts before they come to a conclusion, resent Greenspun's oracle-of-Delphi approach. Greenspun is all the more irritating because he is correct more often than he has any right to be.

"How the hell do you know the book's a fake?" I challenged. "Maybe this Clifford Irving is the secret son of Howard Hughes, and Daddy's giving him a break in the writing game."

"It's a fake," said Greenspun again, pleased with the effect he was producing. "Hughes isn't in any shape to write a book. Tell you what. If that book is authentic, I'll kiss your butt a hundred and thirty times in the middle of the Las Vegas Strip."

"You've got a bet," I said, "with one provision."

"What's that?"

"If I win, I don't have to collect," I told him, heading for the door. "Talk to you later. Got things to do."

I hurried out to the Hughes headquarters on the grounds of the Sands Hotel to try to grub up some facts. Hughes had fled Las Vegas a year earlier to Paradise Island in the Bahamas, at the height of an internal brannigan that deposed his right-hand man, Bob Maheu. His functionaries, however, had remained in place to run his gigantic Nevada holdings. I looked up his Nevada spokesman, a bespectacled former L.A. *Times* newsman named Arelo Sederburg. He was sitting at his desk with a faintly stunned look, handling a flood of incoming calls.

"We have no comment at this time."

"No comment."

"No, Charlie, I don't know any more about it than you do. I'll get back to you if we have anything to say."

There was a lull in the calls and Sederburg waved and said, "Hello, and no comment to you, too. We don't know *anything* about this Clifford Irving thing, scout's honor. Maybe in a hour or so we'll have something."

"What do you think, Arelo?" I asked.

"No comment," said Arelo Sederburg, reaching for a buzzing phone.

I wandered over to the Sands casino, watched the people lose their money, and sorted out the pros and cons on whether Howard Hughes, at the age of sixty-six, had decided to Tell All.

Con: Hughes put an inordinate value on his privacy. Over the years he had spent a fortune suppressing and trying to suppress books and articles about his personal life. He had even set up a company, Rosemont Enterprises, and assigned to it all rights to his life story to inhibit would-be biographers. It made no sense that, after artfully dodging publicity for years, he would leap into the klieg-light glare with his own life story. *Pro:* The one predictable thing about Hughes was that he was unpredictable.

Con: Since Sederburg was "no commenting," Hughes's top people didn't know anything about the book. *Pro:* Hughes wouldn't necessarily have told them about it if he had written it.

Con: The timing of the book was atrocious. Nevada officials, offended by his departure to the Bahamas, were insisting that he show up in person in Nevada for questioning about a sweeping reorganization of his gambling interests. Hughes kept refusing. If Hughes indeed had been hopping about the Western Hemisphere dictating his memoirs to Clifford Irving, he was deliberately antagonizing Nevada officialdom. *Pro:* Hughes deliberately antagonized all sorts of people, whenever the whim moved him.

Con: Three separate sources had told me that Hughes suffered from internal loss of blood, and needed periodic blood transfusions. He lived in total isolation because, among other reasons, he never knew when he'd need another transfusion. I'd set forth this information in an article for *Playboy,* "Can the Real Howard Hughes Still Stand Up?" which was on the magazine stands at that very moment. If my information was right, Hughes couldn't chase around all over the place to rendezvous with Clifford Irving. *Pro:* My information was wrong, and I'd just been shot down as a Hughes expert.

Con: The McGraw-Hill release said Clifford Irving had put the autobiography together in the past year. Hughes was a procrastinator, a fiddler-with-details, notoriously unable to make up his mind. He had diddled with the design of a flying cargo boat and a photo-reconnaissance plane for World War II without getting them off the ground until the war was over. He drove plane contractors mad with design changes; Bob Gross, head of Lockheed, had his guards throw Hughes out of his office for this reason. *Pro:* McGraw-Hill and Time-Life were experienced publishing firms, two of the biggest in the business. *Time* had a top-flight Hughes expert right in its New York office—Frank McCulloch. McCulloch was the last journalist to interview Hughes in person, and the last journalist to have talked to him on the telephone, more than ten years ago. Nobody could get a fake manuscript past Frank.

I had once observed Hughes's detail-fiddling close up, and it had left a vivid impression. When he first came to Vegas, he issued a series of written public statements to the newspapers. In one of them, dealing with Las Vegas's need for a new airport, he had written and rewritten his statement four times, according to his aides. Each time, he would carefully write it out, have it typed, and then change a few words or punctuation marks and have it completely redone. He had gone over the next-to-final draft of the statement and decided that one sentence had too many commas. To remedy this, in a reference to "Houston, Tex." he had removed the comma between the city and the state. When the final draft was delivered to the Las Vegas *Sun,* a staff member had reinserted the comma. The Hughes emissary objected strenuously. "Mr. Hughes took that comma out *himself,*" he cried. "He doesn't *want* a comma there." To calm the emissary's fear and trembling, the staffer took the offending comma out again.

It seemed highly unlikely, and totally out of character, that Hughes could churn out his life story, 200,000 words long, in less than a year, and approve it for final publication without 3,974 revisions, rewrites, and comma-agonizings. This minor idiosyncrasy, in fact, was the most persuasive single argument that the book was a fake.

I added up the pros and cons. They canceled out, and I was back where I had started. I left the tourists exhorting the heedless dice, and went back to see Sederburg. He was visibly happier.

"We've got a statement," Sederburg exulted. "We're just giving it to the wire services now. Hughes Tool Co. is denying the existence of any Hughes autobiography."

"Toolco denies it?" I asked. "How come Howard Hughes doesn't deny it?"

Sederburg shrugged. "I relay official statements to the media. The official statement is that Hughes Tool Co. denies the existence of any Hughes autobiography."

I left his office and ascended the Hughes hierarchy to a Higher Figure. "Tell me, for my own burning curiosity," I asked the Higher Figure, "how come this book denial comes from Toolco, and not from the Man himself?"

The Higher Figure told me what had happened. Hughes officials had wanted to kill the McGraw-Hill story fast, but the Man was not "available." So they put together the denial without talking to Hughes.

The Toolco denial was based on three phone calls. One went to Chester Davis, the top Hughes lawyer; the second to Bill Gay, Hughes Tool vice-president; and the third—and most important—to Howard Eckersley, chief personal aide to Howard Hughes. Eckersley was head of the so-called palace guard, the six male secretary-nurses who were the only Hughes functionaries who ever saw or talked to the Man himself. On the basis of information from Eckersley, Gay and Davis had ordered the denial.

"Eckersley said there is simply *no way* Clifford Irving could have interviewed Hughes the way he said he did," said the Higher Figure.

"I don't think a Toolco denial will kill the story," I said. "Only Hughes can say whether or not he wrote a book."

"That's all right," said the Higher Figure. "We understand that Mr. Hughes sleepeth. In a few hours we'll lay his personal denial on top of the Toolco denial, and that will be the end of the McGraw-Hill book."

"I'm at the International," I told the Higher Figure. "When the Man awaketh and denieth, calleth me."

"It's a promise."

The Toolco denial, hot on the heels of the McGraw-Hill announcement, made it plain that there was an intriguing story beginning to simmer.

At the hotel, I phoned a New York friend knowledgeable in publishing circles, and routed out the home phone number of the McGraw-Hill publicist, Maury Hellitzer. I called him at his Princeton, New Jersey, home, complimented McGraw-Hill for scoring the publishing coup of the decade, and informed him of the Hughes Tool denial. It didn't seem to bother him. I then made a cheeky suggestion.

"If there's any question about this book being kosher," I said, "I can run a fast litmus test on it. I could have Noah Dietrich check it for you. He spent years with Hughes and knows more about him than any other living person."

There was a short, cool silence at my suggestion that McGraw-Hill might have purchased a lemon. But Mr. Hellitzer was unflaggingly polite and proper. He told me they had handwritten documents attesting to the authenticity of the autobiography.

"That's another problem," I said. "They've had all kinds of trouble out here in Nevada trying to verify a Hughes letter changing his casino management. Known specimens of his handwriting are rare. I have access to two unquestioned exemplars of his writing, if you'd like to match them against your samples."

He said he would buck my information up the executive ladder and get back to me. The next day he called and said that McGraw-Hill was grateful for my offer, but there simply weren't any problems. Thankyouverymuch.

I couldn't wait to talk to Frank McCulloch at *Time* magazine. We were friends going back many years. We'd worked parallel on a number of stories when he was managing editor of the Los Angeles *Times*. Frank resembles an egg-bald Buddha and has a mind like a razor. He's one of the best newsmen I've ever known—inquisitive, resourceful, totally honest. Since *Life* had put out $250,000 for the magazine rights to the Hughes book, Frank would have to know all about it.

I called him in New York the day after the McGraw-Hill announcement. He knows my gravel voice the minute I say "Hey, Frank."

"You're calling about the Hughes book," said McCulloch.

"Indeed," I said. "Tell me the whole tale."

Frank sounded—well—*miffed.* "I don't know anything, Jim," he told me. "All I know is what I read in the New York *Times* this morning. I even missed the story there, until someone pointed it out to me."

"You're kidding."

"Nope."

"You mean that *Life* put out two hundred and fifty thousand for the magazine rights to this book without checking the book with *you?*"

"Yep."

"I can't believe that," I said.

"Believe it," said McCulloch.

It looked as if everyone—Clifford Irving, McGraw-Hill, Time-Life—was finessing us Hughes experts.

"That story about how Clifford Irving got the autobiography, that's got to be a phony, right?" I said. I told Frank about the three phone calls that had preceded the Toolco denial, and what Eckersley had said.

"Sure it's a phony," Frank agreed. "The problem, though, is whether Irving faked the story about meeting Hughes all over the landscape, or whether Hughes instructed Irving to tell it that way, for his own devious reasons. The Man is devious."

"There could be a simple explanation for Irving's story about meeting Hughes in cars and motel rooms from here to Tuscaloosa," I said. "Maheu tells me that Hughes used to eat his heart out in envy because Maheu was bouncing all over the country in a Hughes plane while the Man had to stay glued to the ninth floor at the Desert Inn. Maybe Hughes is just promoting the idea that he travels wherever he wants, like Maheu."

"With Hughes, anything is possible," said Frank McCulloch. "Keep in touch."

At noon I checked back at the Hughes headquarters. There was still no denial from Howard Hughes. "Your leader sleepeth deeply," I told Sederburg.

Day Two of the mystery passed without word from Howard Hughes.

And Day Three and Day Four.

The stony silence from Howard Hughes had a major impact on both sides of the controversy. It bolstered McGraw-Hill and Time-

Life in their confidence that they had an authentic autobiography, and that Toolco had gone out on a limb in denouncing it. It was part of the Hughes legend that he slept at odd hours—but for *four days?*

As McGraw-Hill's confidence soared, that of the Hughes people in Las Vegas visibly sagged. Like a chorus line of Rockettes executing a precision pivot, they swung around in a 180° turn until by Day Four they were facing the opposite direction. They had expected an angry repudiation of the book by Hughes himself in a matter of hours after the Toolco denial. As the silence from the Bahamas lengthened, it grew more ominous. They knew, from long experience, that their billionaire boss, like Providence, worked in mysterious ways. They began to contemplate the awful possibility that Howard had gulled his own people, secretly assembled his autobiography with this Clifford Irving, and might well, at any moment, chop off the limb his high officials and spokesmen had imprudently raced out on.

Outwardly, they remained firm in their denial of The Book. Privately, they began to discuss the prospect that someone might have to eat that denial, a word at a time.

After all, Toolco—which meant Davis and Gay—had labeled the book a fraud solely on the word of Hughes's personal aide, Howard Eckersley. Their speculation that the book was authentic now took two tracks:

1. Eckersley had told the Toolco officials that the book was a fraud because Hughes instructed him to do so. "I can just see the Old Man," one Hughes official told me, "sitting down there in Nassau, laughing his head off at Chester Davis and Bill Gay."

2. Eckersley himself had been gulled by Hughes, who had put together his book with Clifford Irving without informing his chief personal aide.

Such speculation reflected the bizarre and unreal reality of the empire of Howard Hughes, where no one—except the billionaire proprietor—ever knew what the hell was actually going on. It was a world where the emperor played one segment of his court off against another, where today's prime minister is tomorrow's cast-out pariah. Fresh in everyone's memory was the recent convulsion in leadership, wherein Robert A. Maheu had been brought into the Hughes hierarchy, swiftly elevated past Bill Gay, officially designated chief honcho and alter ego of Howard Hughes, ensconced in a $650,000 Hughes-

built mansion—and then publicly cast back down overnight in favor
of Bill Gay. And cast down without warning or even a terse telephoned "bye-bye, Bob" from the emperor. If it had happened to
Maheu, it could happen to Gay, Davis, or Eckersley. So when Gay,
Davis, and Eckersley combined their voices and said, "Believe us,
fellows, Howard hasn't written any book," it did not necessarily
mean that Howard hadn't written a book.

The Las Vegas functionaries now began to take a closer and more
cautious look at the Clifford Irving opus. There was almost nothing
available for inspection. From beginning to end, McGraw-Hill held
the manuscript close to its corporate vest, like a canny poker player
in a high-stakes game in a strange town. But it had released a brief
passage from the preface, purportedly handwritten by Hughes:

> I believe that more lies have been printed and told about me than
> about any living man—therefore it was my purpose to write a book
> which would set the record straight and restore the balance . . .
>
> Biographies about me have been published before—all of them mis-
> leading and childish. I am certain that in the future more lies and rubbish
> will appear. The words in this book—other than some of the questions
> which provoked them—are my own spoken words. The thoughts, opin-
> ions and recollections, the descriptions of events and personalities, are
> my own. I have not permitted them to be emasculated or polished,
> because I realized, after the many interviews had been completed and
> transcribed, that this was as close as I could get to the elusive, often
> painful truth.
>
> I have lived a full life and, perhaps, what may seem a strange life—
> even to myself. I refuse to apologize, although I am willing now to
> explain as best I can. Call this autobiography. Call it my memoirs. Call
> it what you please. It is the story of my life in my own words.

I had coffee on the morning of Day Four in the office of Perry
Lieber, public-relations director for all the Hughes hotels. Lieber,
an unflaggingly cheerful man with sad eyes, had been with Hughes
since the late 1940's, when Hughes owned the RKO studio in Hollywood.

"Uncle Jim," said Lieber, "that passage in the preface where it
says 'I refuse to apologize, although I am willing now to explain'—
that bothers me. It bothers me deeply. That, my friend, is pure
Howard Hughes. If I've heard him say that once, I've heard him say
it twenty times."

Lieber's comment was fascinating. How could Irving have picked up Hughes's way of speaking if he had never met Hughes? The entire preface, in fact, sounded like authentic Hughes. I had read a large number of his memos, plus all his 1947 congressional testimony, plus some other documents that no other writer, to my knowledge, had ever laid eyes on. All this had given me a sense of Hughes's style. That McGraw-Hill preface had captured it superbly.

At the end of Day Four, I checked out of the International and flew home to Long Beach. There was a sheaf of call-back requests from reporters around the country, all with the same question: Do you know anything about this Clifford Irving book on Howard Hughes? I told them I had no information—which turned out not to be true at all, at all.

I had the whole answer to the hoax out in the work room behind my house, and didn't know it. It was an 85,000-word unpublished first draft of the memoirs of Noah Dietrich, the former $500,000-a-year right-hand man to Howard Hughes. Dietrich and Hughes had broken up in 1957, after thirty-two years. Some years later Dietrich had asked me to collaborate on his memoirs. The project had not worked out, but I had finished a first draft of his book. The manuscript had been gathering dust for eight months, ever since I had parted company with Dietrich.

After the McGraw-Hill announcement, I spent two months constructing theories (and then demolishing them), chasing false leads, plodding up blind alleys, and interrogating people who didn't know anything, in an effort to learn whether Howard Hughes had written, or Clifford Irving had faked, the autobiography of the billionaire.

And all along, the Rosetta stone that would solve the mystery lay ignored in my own files.

There were three reasons why I didn't connect my manuscript with the Irving hoax. First, I went for two months strongly inclined toward the belief that the Hughes autobiography was genuine, for persuasive reasons we'll examine. Second, I couldn't get even a peek at Irving's manuscript. Third, I had never heard of Clifford Irving, and wasn't aware that I even knew anyone who knew him. He lived and worked on the island of Ibiza, one third of the way around the world, and I couldn't conceive of any way he could have laid hands on my manuscript.

Ironically, a Long Beach friend—Judge Kenneth Sutherland—figured out the Irving mystery at the very outset. Sutherland knew I had worked on the Dietrich memoirs. After I came back from Las Vegas, he told me—half in jest—that Irving must have got hold of my manuscript and used it to construct the Hughes "autobiography."

I poured scorn all over his suggestion. "You've been reading too many cheap mystery stories, Judge," I told him. "I've kept that manuscript locked in my file. There is no way Clifford Irving could have got his hands on it."

It turned out there was a way. It had been handed over to Irving, without my knowledge, by an ex-Hollywood producer named Stanley Meyer. Stanley had once been an associate of Jack Webb in the TV series *Dragnet*, but he had fallen on bad days and turned desperate. How Helpful Stanley Meyer had got *his* hands on my manuscript is a small, unpleasant story replete with chicanery. It would have made a good little script for Sergeant Joe Friday.

I'd signed on with Noah Dietrich to ghost his memoirs in 1970. He sought me out because he had liked a long cover story I did on Howard Hughes for the *Saturday Evening Post* back in 1963. It dealt with Hughes's massive money problems with TWA, and the article blamed Howard's woes on his breakup with Noah Dietrich, and his loss of Dietrich's financial genius. Noah wrote me a complimentary little note, and then, seven years later, telephoned me out of the blue and asked me to work with him on a book about his life with Hughes. I jumped at the chance. Dietrich was a Comstock Lode of unique, unpublished material about the invisible billionaire, and such sources were exceedingly rare.

Noah and I turned out to be the oddest couple of the year. The project went badly from the start. Dietrich was an energetic little octogenarian with an awesome amount of energy and a penchant for snapping out decisions like a Gatling gun. He lived in a handsome mansion high in Benedict Canyon in Beverly Hills, with a swimming pool, three cars, a gardener, a maid, and a former Goldwyn Girl for his wife. But alas, Noah complained, no ready cash. He could not afford an advance for his ghost writer, or even the expenses of assembling his memoirs. My long fascination with Hughes overcame my business sense, which at best is minimal. Noah was eighty-two, and would not be available forever, so I undertook his memoirs without a penny in advance—and agreed to finance the project myself.

Noah brought in Stanley Meyer, an old friend from the movie world, as a sort of vice president in charge of everything. Meyer was a smooth, affable fellow who resided in a magnificent estate called Four Oaks in suburban Encino. Four Oaks was originally the home of Stanley's father-in-law, Nate Blumberg, one of the earlier and more successful of Hollywood's great studio nabobs. When old Nate died, Stanley had inherited Four Oaks—but not his father-in-law's genius for making money. Four Oaks was a stunning show-place, valued at $1,250,000 and decked out with an additional $500,-000 in furnishings, paintings, and antiques. But Stanley—like Noah—complained that he was strapped for cash. No matter. If merchandised properly, Noah's memoirs would fetch in millions, said Stanley, and Stanley had just the right high-powered merchandiser to turn the trick. He was a New York literary agent named Paul Gitlin, and Gitlin was the hottest agent in the big time book biz. Gitlin handled the two greatest money writers in the world—Harold *(The Carpetbaggers)* Robbins and Irving *(The Word)* Wallace. Stanley would persuade Gitlin to take Noah on as a client.

The duties and responsibilities were apportioned fairly. Noah would provide the memories, Stanley would supervise, expedite, and serve as something he termed "referral agent"; Gitlin would package and merchandise the product, and I would do the work and pay the bills. It occurred to me that a large number of egos were clustering around a somewhat modest book, and that the projection of profits was overly euphoric. My colleagues brushed aside my demurrers on the grounds that this was a project in a big league that I wot not of. This was true. Like most working journalists, I don't really believe in any sum of money larger than a twenty-dollar bill.

It took me five months to talk Noah's memoirs out of his head and onto my tape recorder. We put over one hundred hours on tape, and it took a stenographer two months to transcribe the tapes. I'm a slow writer, and Noah was impatient to get those Robbins-Wallace–type royalties rolling in. I spent too much time, in Noah's view, cross-checking Noah's stories. He had a remarkable memory, but it was human and had some bare patches and flaws. My caution offended him, and he was not mollified when I caught a few whopping errors. I started writing late in the summer of 1970, and by the following

February had the first draft finished except for the final three chapters.

We had a Rube Goldberg procedure for handling the manuscript. Noah demanded each chapter as I finished it, then he edited it, had it retyped, and handed it on to Stanley Meyer for forwarding to Gitlin. I protested that this was no way to write a book. "Occasionally I want to shift material from one chapter to another," I said. "Let me write a full first draft," I pleaded. "Then we'll sit down and go over the draft from start to finish, agree on what needs to be done to put the book in final shape. When it's in final shape, *then* we'll send it to Gitlin."

In February I took a weekend off and read the 75,000 words written so far in first draft. I didn't like the draft, and wrote Noah a long memo telling him why. I took most of the blame myself, laid out my suggestions for a revision, and told him I could give him a final and better draft in three months. But I also told him that the book was too much Dietrich and not enough Howard Hughes, and that, as they say in southern Illinois, tore the door off the barn.

In February, *Look* magazine called me and wanted to see the draft with the idea of bidding on the magazine rights. I flew to New York to talk to *Look.* On arrival, I made a courtesy stop at Gitlin's office to tell him what I was doing. We had met only once, and got along together like oil and water. He is a small, paunchy, bearded man with hooded eyes and a reputation as a negotiator. "Books are just like any other merchandise, Phelan," he told me. "You get a hot item, package it right, and then it's just like selling soap or deodorant."

Gitlin objected violently to my showing the draft to *Look.* His resistance astonished me; agents normally consider it a coup to have a book excerpted in a major national magazine. Gitlin argued that the manuscript was not in proper shape, and I readily agreed. "But the material is all there," I said, "and in three months we'll have a decent final draft." Gitlin was adamant, and I canceled the preview at *Look.* A major publishing firm was intensely interested in the Dietrich memoirs, Gitlin told me. All he needed to lock down the deal was my transcript of Noah's tape-recorded interviews. He wanted to show it—that very weekend—to the publisher's editor-in-chief. Meanwhile, I was to go back and finish up the last three chapters of the first draft.

"That doesn't make any sense, Paul," I protested. "It's a bad first draft. I don't like it and I've told Noah I don't like it. In fact, I wouldn't let my name go on it as collaborator. I want to get on with the revision. It's a waste of time to finish a first draft that I don't like myself."

He reached over and patted me, sincere as Pal Joey, on the knee. "Let me give you some good legal advice," he said, plainly concerned with my welfare. "If you don't finish the draft, Noah can charge you with breach of contract. Finish it up, and meanwhile give me your transcript. I'll arrange for you to do the final version under the supervision of the best editor in New York City. Trust me, Jim. I'd never screw you."

So I turned over my transcript of the tape sessions to Paul Gitlin. He swiftly had it Xeroxed, and triumphantly shot a copy off to Stanley Meyer to use in recruiting a new writer. I flew back to Long Beach, finished the final three chapters, and turned them in to Noah. He accepted them graciously. Then he reached into his desk and drew out a letter, dated the day before, discharging me as collaborator.

I had to admire the efficiency of the operation and blush at my own gullibility. Noah said he was sorry that things hadn't worked out, but business was business. When the book was finished and made a fortune, Noah even planned to pay me something for time and expenses. I looked down at him at his desk, and tried to rein in my anger. He had spent thirty-two years advising one of the great voracious sharks of American capitalism, and, as he said, business is business.

So we settled our differences like two businessmen. I had $15,000 of my own money and a year of unpaid labor in the project. I had an airtight contract with him, and demanded a written settlement. We hammered one out—again no cash, but $40,000 off the top of the royalties if and when the book was published—with a proviso that the publisher would pay the $40,000 directly to me. I tossed the settlement and my copy of the manuscript into my file, and never gave it another thought. I went back to magazine writing, with a mental note that ghostwriting for big business executives—and dealing with high-powered agents like Paul Gitlin—was a line of work for which I possessed no talent whatever.

Some months later I heard that Noah had lined up Bob Thomas, an AP movie columnist, to rewrite his memoirs. Still later, I heard Thomas had finished his version, and they couldn't find a publisher. Noah called me one day and complained, "Hell, Jim, this guy isn't any better at writing a book than you are." I told him that such excessive flattery was embarrassing. I wrote off my expenses to experience, discounted my $40,000 pie-in-the-sky down to zero and busied myself writing for people who paid in real money.

Then along came Clifford Irving and his is-it-or-isn't-it autobiography of Howard Hughes. The subject of Hughes heated up with the book-buying public and Noah called me again. He'd finally had an offer for his memoirs and was of a mind to sign a contract. He and Gitlin had parted ways, and he was about to accept a $5,000 advance from a paperback house. I told him that wasn't worth uncapping his fountain pen for, but he complained that the rewritten manuscript had been turned down by ten publishing houses. "I'm going East, Noah," I told him. "Let me make a pass at some of the publishing houses. With all the uproar about Hughes, we ought to do better than a five-thousand-dollar advance."

En route to Florida on a magazine assignment, I stopped off in New York and obtained for Noah an offer from Fawcett Publications for a $65,000 advance. I jubilantly phoned Noah and caught him ten minutes before he was to sign up with the other house for $5,000. Noah happily signed with Fawcett, and his twice-written memoirs finally moved toward print.

Meanwhile, down in the Bahamas, Howard Hughes had stirred from his sleep and broken his silence. On the seventh day after the McGraw-Hill announcement, Hughes telephoned Frank McCulloch at *Time* magazine and loudly cried foul. He had never heard of Clifford Irving, he told McCulloch, never collaborated with him on a book, never met him in any motel or parked car. And he certainly had not got any money from McGraw-Hill for his life story. He was very explicit about the money and that continued to outrage him. McGraw-Hill had paid a total of $750,000 for his story and *who had got the money?*

Hughes's phone call to McCulloch had one inexplicable and typically Hughesian aspect. At the outset of the call, Hughes put Frank off the record. Frank was to make no public disclosure that Hughes had called him, or that Hughes had repudiated the autobiography. Hughes counted on McCulloch informing the Time-Life brass of the repudiation and thus quietly killing the book. For some reason Hughes wanted to kill the book without appearing in the dread public arena—even as a voice over a long-distance phone.

The phone call didn't work. In fact, it had exactly the opposite of its intended result. Frank dutifully reported to his superiors that Hughes had labeled the book a fake. But instead of canceling the project, the Time-Life brass decided only to take a harder look at it, and unleashed McCulloch for a belated investigation of Clifford Irving. Like Hughes, they put McCulloch under wraps. He was to function as their investigator, not as a newsman. He was to report his findings directly to the Time, Inc., executive offices. With Time-Life's prestige at stake—particularly its long-cultivated air of Olympian omniscience—the facts in the controversy had become of too heady moment for mere journalism.

McCulloch honored the restrictions. He didn't breathe a word of the Hughes call to me, although by now we were in touch almost daily. I didn't learn that Hughes had telephoned him until a week or so after the call, when that story was leaked to the press by members of the Hughes camp, disgruntled over *Life*'s failure to scuttle the autobiography.

McCulloch went eagerly to work, assisted by two crack Time-Life reporters, Bill Lambert and Sandy Smith. For more than a month he went steadily down the wrong trail, and working independently, I went the wrong way also. We were both led astray by the disciplines of investigative reporting. Briefly put, these require that you 1) keep your options open, 2) disbelieve your own saintly grandmother unless her story checks out independently, and 3) accept no solution that does not accommodate all controverting evidence. It was point 3 that kept us going south on a trail that led north.

Cliff Irving had produced an impressive array of communications purportedly handwritten by Howard Hughes. There were several short letters from "Hughes" to Irving, plus a nine-page letter to Harold McGraw, plus dozens of interlineations in the margins of the autobiography manuscript. In addition, McGraw-Hill had canceled checks totaling $650,000 endorsed with the signature "H. R. Hughes." At the behest of *Life*, McGraw-Hill had specimens tested by two New York authorities on questioned documents, as handwriting experts call themselves. Both stamped Irving's "Hughes" samples as authentic, and both spoke forth with the certainty of the Holy Father making a pronouncement *ex cathedra*.

The first, Alfred Kanfer, declared:

It can be stated that the two handwriting specimens were written by the same person. Both handwriting samples show full identity in regard to the strongest and most outstanding characteristic, the very wide and almost disintegrating spacings between words. There is furthermore full identity in the way the margins to both sides of the writing are handled. The ratios between height and width of the letters are identical, and so are the ratios between down and upstroke pressures, all letters written with the same force and one could almost say the same vehemence, and what is most characteristic, even the irregularities and fluctuations of size and pressure in both writings are identical. To this can be added the identity of letter forms.

The chances that another person could copy this handwriting even in a similar way are less than 1 in a million.

In a second and independent examination, the nationally known firm of Osborn & Osborn was almost equally authoritative. It stated that "the questioned documents accurately reflect in every detail the genuine forms and habit variations thereof which make up the basic handwriting identity of the author of the specimen documents. Moreover, in spite of the prodigious quantity of writing contained in the questioned documents, careful study has failed to reveal any features which raise the slightest question as to the common identity of all the specimen and questioned signatures and continuous writing." Osborn concluded:

These basic factors, we believe, make it impossible as a practical matter, based on our years of experience in the field of questioned handwriting and signatures, that anyone other than the writer of the specimens could have written the questioned signatures and continuous writing.

This was insurmountable evidence—to McCulloch and me—that Irving had indeed dealt with Howard Hughes. Forging a signature is one thing; forging a nine-page letter is something quite different. A skilled forger, given enough samples to work from and enough time, can reproduce a signature so well that no expert can spot it. But forging an extended holograph (continuous writing) is enormously difficult. It is a rule of thumb among experts that, given a single doubtful page of continuous writing, and one page of authentic writing for comparison, they can declare with certainty whether the questioned page is forged or genuine. Both Kanfer and Osborn had the nine-page letter from "Hughes" to Harold McGraw for examination, and both had several pages of a recent Hughes letter to Gay and Davis for comparison. To fool two experts with nine pages of writing is comparable to a runner turning in a three-minute mile: It may be theoretically possible, but no human has ever come close.

Therefore, we reasoned, Howard Hughes had written the letter to Harold McGraw authorizing publication of his memoirs, and endorsed the checks for $650,000 made out to "H. R. Hughes." And therefore, his phone call to McCulloch terming the book a fake had to be squared with this "scientific" finding.

Separately, we formulated the same theory to accommodate the seemingly irreconcilable Hughes phone call to McCulloch, repudiating the work, and the Hughes letter to Harold McGraw, approving its publication. Our scenario went like this:

Hughes had collaborated with Clifford Irving on his memoirs, but had kept the project secret from his entourage and the Toolco executives. Hughes had written the letter to McGraw, and cashed the $650,000 in checks. When McGraw-Hill announced the book, Howard Eckersley had correctly reported that Hughes never left his Nassau hotel suite and hence couldn't have met Irving in those cars and motels. The Toolco people jumped to the conclusion that the book was a fake, and issued their denial. Then Hughes had broken the dismaying news that he *had* collaborated with Clifford Irving, while never leaving his Nassau hotel room. He either (we reasoned) had Irving slipped into his hotel room under a fake name, or had spirited out his tape-recorded memoirs to Irving without Eckersley's knowledge. Upon learning the awful truth, our scenario continued, Hughes's lawyers had pointed out the terrible consequences. A candid autobiography would bring a deluge of libel suits running into the hundreds of millions of dollars. It would offend potent politicians, upon whose good will Hughes depended for vast federal contracts. It would destroy what little good will the Hughes empire still retained in Nevada, where he owned six high-priced casinos vulnerable to license cancellation. Dismayed at the impending havoc he had engineered, Hughes had said, "Okay, fellows, what do I do *now?*" "Repudiate the book!" chorused his lawyers in our script. "Let Clifford Irving take the rap. Call your old friend McCulloch at *Time* and tell him Cliff's a phony."

This ingenious script explained everything—even the long delay between the McGraw-Hill announcement and Hughes's angry phone call to Frank. Hughes and his lawyers, we reasoned, had spent that time arguing and deciding on their course of action. McCulloch and I basked in our ingenuity. We were further encouraged when Noah Dietrich, analyzing the situation independently, came up with the same explanation out in Beverly Hills. He told the Associated Press that Hughes had gone off on "an ego trip," written the book, and then had second thoughts.

It was a great scenario, with only one flaw. It was dead wrong.

McCulloch had another persuasive reason to believe Irving's manuscript to be authentic. The *Life* executives had permitted Frank to read the first half of it, and it was full of unpublished anecdotes that Frank knew were true. Then one day, while cross-examining Cliff Irving, McCulloch had got a glimpse of the second half of the manuscript. McCulloch began reading the top page, which was upside-down. (Reading copy upside-down—and backwards—is a trick most newsmen learn early in life.) He saw a passage where he, McCulloch, was quoted, and it pricked his curiosity. He asked Irving if he could read it. Irving pretended to demur, on the grounds that "Hughes" had stipulated that no one—except the highest McGraw-Hill and *Life* executives—should have even a prepublication peek at his opus. But then Irving locked the door of the room and let McCulloch read the passage.

It dealt with a long telephone call from Hughes to McCulloch more than a dozen years earlier. Hughes had appealed to McCulloch to try to kill a *Fortune* magazine article about his TWA money troubles. McCulloch made detailed notes on the phone call, and sent a top-secret memo to the Time, Inc., executives.

And here, in Irving's manuscript, was a "Hughes" account of this phone call, remarkably accurate.

"Man, that shook me up, right down to the cellar," McCulloch told me later. "I could think of no way Irving could have got the details of that phone conversation, except from Hughes."

There was another way. Irving had got a copy of Frank's confidential memo from helpful Stanley Meyer. Stanley had got it from Noah, and Noah had got it from me. Where I got it is a secret, sealed in concrete, that I have explained only to Frank McCulloch. I had intended to summarize the memo in the final draft of Dietrich's memoirs, only after getting McCulloch's approval. But I had given a copy to Dietrich, who gave a copy to Stanley Meyer, who later handed it over to Cliff Irving without letting either Dietrich or me know what he had done.

After Irving was shot down and I told McCulloch this story, he was convinced that Cliff Irving had tricked him into reading the passage. "I think he opened his manuscript, the day I quizzed him, to the page that had my name in it," Frank said. "He figured I'd scan it and spot the reference to that Hughes phone call. It was a great trick, and it worked.

"But then, Cliff is a great con man, one of the best. Here's an example. When we cross-examined him, trying to break down his story, he never made the mistake of telling his story the same way each time. There would be little discrepancies in it, and when we'd catch him up, he'd freely admit them. The average con man will have his story down letter-perfect, so he can tell it over and over without deviation. An honest man usually makes little mistakes, particularly in relating a long, complex story like Cliff's. Cliff was smart enough to know this, and gave a superb impersonation of an honest man. When we'd catch him up on something that looked incriminating, he'd freely say, 'Gee, that makes it look bad for me, doesn't it? But that's the way it happened.' He conveyed the picture of being candid, even to his own detriment—while he was turning out lie after lie after lie."

But at the time, Irving's accuracy on such matters as the Hughes-McCulloch phone call, plus the handwriting evidence, made a believer out of Frank. He executed an affidavit supporting Irving and his manuscript:

> I am convinced beyond reasonable doubt as to the authenticity of the Howard Hughes autobiography. This conviction is based upon my long-standing personal familiarity with Howard Hughes, my readings of the manuscript, and my interviews with Clifford Irving. My belief in that authenticity is not shaken by denials of that story, nor is my belief in the authenticity of the autobiography shaken by the denials which I have heard from a man I believe to be Howard Hughes. Such actions are perfectly consistent with the Hughes I know."

McCulloch's affidavit embittered the Hughes camp. "Frank has Hughes's own word that the manuscript is a fake," one publicist told me. "He's just trying to save *Life*'s two-hundred-and-fifty-thousand-dollar investment."

"You don't know McCulloch," I told him. "If Frank thought that manuscript was phony, he'd walk out on his job at *Time* before he would support it—and he's been there almost twenty years."

"*You* fellows have to believe Hughes," I told the publicist. "But he's been digging a credibility gap for years, playing one person off against another. Now he's fallen into his own ditch."

At the eventual showdown, McCulloch was out in front in exposing Clifford Irving. When I brought him the clinching evidence, he didn't drag his feet or try to talk around it or worry about how it affected his Time-Life career. He swung around with the facts, the way a compass needle swings back to the north after someone has flipped it into a dizzying spin.

Johnny Goldman of the Los Angeles *Times* was the first newsman to knock a leg out from under Irving. He located the Baroness Nina van Pallandt, who had gone trysting in Mexico with Cliff when Cliff claimed to be meeting Howard Hughes. Nina had just told all to the postal inspectors in Nassau, and she told enough on the phone to John to impeach Cliff's story. Cliff couldn't have interviewed Howard in Mexico, she conceded to Goldman; he wasn't away from her side long enough to interview anyone.

By this time, Hughes had deployed all his forces to prove Irving was a fraud. He had Chester Davis and his law firm working frantically on the case, and had enlisted the professional talents of Intertel, a glossy, high-priced intelligence outfit in Washington. Intertel, founded by two former Department of Justice officials, supposedly had topflight connections in the federal establishment. In addition, Hughes had his long-time public relations firm, the Carl Byoir agency, at work on the Get Irving assignment. They set up the highly publicized telephonic interview with seven selected newsmen, who solemnly posed questions for two hours to an electronic box purportedly carrying the voice of Hughes from the far-off Bahamas to an L.A. television studio. The voice again denounced Irving as a fraud, this time on the record, and the seven newsmen all agreed that it was Hughes's voice coming out of the box. Nina's disclosure that Cliff couldn't have met Hughes in Mexico had more impact on the public than on McCulloch or me. Our own expertise betrayed us. We both had known from Day One that Cliff hadn't met Hughes in the way the McGraw-Hill announcement set forth. So when that part of his story fell down, we congratulated ourselves on our insight—and continued down the path of error. There was still the authenticity of Cliff's manuscript and the "Hughes" handwriting. As Frank put it, "Until that holographic chain is broken, I have to go with Irving." Hughes's public repudiation of the book, via the seven newsmen, carried no more weight with McCulloch than did Hughes's private repudiation.

The public response to the telephonic interview was an interesting commentary on the mythology that enveloped Hughes. The big question with the man on the street turned out to be: Was that *really* Howard Hughes talking? Hughes had been the Invisible Man for so long that his voice, certified by seven newsmen who had once known him in the flesh, convinced hardly anyone. There were many people who firmly believed Howard Hughes was dead and had been replaced by a skilled Doppelgänger. Others believed that he was incapacitated, or had been frozen like a gigantic TV dinner for a Buck Rogers-like defrosting in the twenty-first century.

On the day after his telephonic interview, I made three phone calls to people who in the past had talked extensively to Hughes, including Maheu. All three affirmed their conviction that it was indeed Howard on the horn. All their assurances were categorical. "No question," said Maheu. "No one could fake that reedy voice; I've heard it a thousand times."

The next person to knock a leg out from under Cliff (he turned out to have more than the normal number of legs) was Robert Peloquin, founder of Intertel. By devices that he did not reveal, Peloquin learned that the "H. R. Hughes" who had endorsed the McGraw-Hill checks and deposited them in a Swiss bank was a woman using the name "Helga R. Hughes." Peloquin was also the first to conclude that the woman was Cliff Irving's wife, disguised with a wig and dark glasses.

The dreadful news that the check-cashing H. R. Hughes was a woman calling herself Helga R. Hughes leaked out to the Time, Inc., and McGraw-Hill people shortly after Peloquin ferreted it out. Irving got wind of this—but not of Peloquin's zeroing in on Edith Irving. Cliff then wrote McCulloch a letter in an attempt to ease the impact of the distressing news. He wrote it on a plane bound from New York to Ibiza, where he was rushing to bolster up Edith for what he accurately anticipated to be an impending ordeal. The letter told more about the essential Clifford Irving than all the articles, books, and television interviews devoted to him. One needs to keep

in mind only that none of the events he described so meticulously
ever occurred.

Dear Frank—I've been sitting on the plane thinking and thinking about
our discussion this afternoon, and playing detective, and a lightbulb has
exploded in my brain—triggered by some of your questions, particularly
about the room and the house in Florida on the last trip. I'm not sure
of the significance; and memory can play tricks especially when you're
forcing it as hard as I am now.

But for whatever it's worth—

I remember some more details of the bedroom in which I last saw
Hughes. I think I told you there were blinds on the windows. There
were also, I believe, flowered curtains—or at least patterned chintz-type
curtains. The bedspread, I believe, matched them, or was similar. The
furniture was relatively light in color and appearance, and in good taste
but not showy. The easy chair in which I sat was not a big chair, or so
I remember it. In other words, what I'm trying to say is: in retrospect
it does not strike me as being a *man's* bedroom.

Also: and maybe even more important—on both the Dec. 3rd and
Dec. 7th meetings, I'm sure that Holmes left the room for several minutes prior to my final departure. On both occasions he came back to get
me and lead me into the hallway, blindfold me and guide me out of the
house. On the second occasion (Dec. 7th), I'm almost positive the car
was not in front of the steps where Holmes had originally parked it. I
remember his having to guide me some distance along gravel or concrete. I got in first; then he got in behind the wheel. He muttered
something I didn't catch and then *shoved the seat back.* The sound is
unmistakable. As I've told you, Holmes is about six feet tall. Also he
turned the air-conditioning on full blast (as he always had it) and as it
must have been when we originally arrived at the house.

The conclusions, unless I'm really losing my memory or fishing
blindly, are obvious. I don't know what significance they have, but I'm
zeroing in on this curious hint that the person opening the account in
Zurich may have been a woman.

My conclusions are that the house in which Hughes was staying in
what I assume to be the Palm Beach vicinity (a) most probably belonged
to a woman or (b) he was staying in a woman's bedroom. Secondly, after
Holmes parked the car in front of the house, a woman (or short man)
moved it into a garage or out of sight, then returned it to the front of
the house when Holmes was ready to drive me away.

(I wish I could go further and say that I smelled perfume but I didn't.)

I don't really know if this will aid our manhunt (or womanhunt), but
that's it, for what it's worth. You can give this information on a need-to-

know basis to anyone at Time Inc. or McGraw-Hill's . . . I have to say I'm getting more and more tranquilly pissed off at Mr. Hughes and Sherlock Holmes. Or maybe I'm wrong and I should feel sorry for them . . But there's more to this tale than told and my loyalty, whatever the hell that is, is damn near strained to the snapping point.

Bill Lambert, a seasoned veteran at investigative reporting who was working with McCulloch, kicked another leg out from under Cliff Irving. What Lambert did was a superb example of an ingenious reporter at work. Irving claimed to have seen Hughes for the last time in Florida in December, when Irving said he was met at the Miami airport by the mysterious (and fictional) Hughes aide, George Gordon Holmes. Holmes blindfolded Irving, then drove him for "an hour and a half" to the residence described in the above letter. From the elapsed time, Irving reported the house was probably in the Palm Beach vicinity. Irving said he got a receipt from Hughes for the final McGraw-Hill check, and picked up Hughes's corrections of the manuscript. He spent about forty-five minutes with Hughes, Irving claimed, and then was driven back to Miami by Holmes. Irving picked up a car he had rented upon arrival, he said, and then drove to the Newport Hotel and checked in.

Lambert flew to Florida and meticulously back-tracked Irving. He checked the car rental agencies at the airport until he found the record of Irving's car. He then went to the Newport and determined when Irving had checked in. By Irving's account, the round trip to the Hughes residence had taken three hours; he had spent forty-five minutes with Hughes, and the drive from the airport to the hotel took another half-hour. The car-rental records showed that Irving received the vehicle at 2:37 P.M. The earliest he could have checked into the hotel was around 7:00—if he had in fact been driven by "Holmes" to see Hughes. But the hotel register showed Irving had checked in at 4:51 P.M. Lambert had caught Irving in a small but crucial lie. Said Bill Lambert: "God bless auto renters and hotels for using time-stamps."

Early in February, I finished up my magazine work in Florida and flew home to Long Beach. Irving's story was now leaking like a riddled sieve. The Baroness Nina's disclosures, the unmasking of Edith Irving as "Helga R. Hughes," the billionaire's telephonic interview repudiating his Boswell, Bill Lambert's ingenious investigation—all this had opened up a credibility chasm that began to take on the dimensions of the Grand Canyon. Irving frantically churned out new fictions in an effort to close the gap; now he claimed, for example, that Edith had posed as "H. R. Hughes" on instruction from Hughes, and that Hughes had provided her with the fake passport with which she opened the Swiss bank account. When he had no explanation, he put on his cryptic look, or tried to bluff. "There is much more to all this than meets the eye," he warned McCulloch as his story was falling apart. "Watch your step, Frank —you're not to the bottom line yet."

He lashed on his horses of invention, a sort of literary Dracula from Ibiza, desperately racing for an unknown sanctuary before the sun rose. Publicly at least, McGraw-Hill continued to support him. They insisted that, whatever the flaws in his account of how he got the material, his manuscript had come from Hughes. *Time* and *Life* treated the story as an unresolved mystery. *Time* dutifully ticked off all the possible explanations, including the far-out theory that Clifford Irving himself had been hoaxed by a cunning cabal of Hughes's enemies, including someone impersonating the invisible billionaire. The public simply sat back, hugely enjoyed the whole spectacle, and happily awaited the next chapter. As reporter Theo Wilson of the New York *Daily News* commented, "Gee, it's years since we've had such a wonderful *Daily News* kind of news story!"

Up to the very end, the same two obstacles that deflected McCulloch and me the wrong way in the beginning continued to obscure the truth:

The authenticity of Irving's material.

The handwriting evidence.

We went up and down the hill, around Robin Hood's barn, and off through the mulberry bushes—and couldn't get past those two roadblocks. I called Frank when I got back to California, and we chewed on the dilemma. Frank said that Cliff's story was leaking at every seam.

"But if he faked the manuscript," I argued, "how the hell did he get a letter in Hughes's handwriting authorizing publication?"

"And the checks with Hughes's endorsements," said Frank.

"The checks don't bother me," I said. "A signature can be forged —but not a nine-page letter."

"And he could never have invented that manuscript without a pipeline straight to Hughes," Frank insisted.

That hung up Frank more than it did me, simply because Frank had read portions of Irvings manuscript and I hadn't. As Irving's story deteriorated, I asked McGraw-Hill six times for permission to examine the great work, and six times they said no. Their refusal was understandable, given their faith in Cliff Irving. He had warned them that Hughes would withdraw the manuscript if they showed it before publication to any outsider. They would have saved themselves time, trouble, and embarrassment if they had fudged on Irving's "commitment to Hughes." But they honored his fictitious pledge and their rectitude played straight into Cliff's hands.

What finished him off was a journalistic triple play. The New York *Times* began printing excerpts from Cliff Irving's opus. Their Hughes expert was Wallace Turner, a Pulitzer-Prize winner who headed their San Francisco bureau. I'd not met Turner at that time, but we'd consulted each other on the phone in the past when Hughes stories broke. Early in February, Turner tapped a leak somewhere and printed a couple of passages from *The Autobiography of Howard Hughes*. He wouldn't say where he got them. But by blind luck, one of the passages he printed pointed me directly to my dusty manuscript of the Dietrich memoirs.

It was a long-ago story about cheerful, sad-eyed Perry Lieber, the veteran Hughes publicist. It was an offbeat little tale, exactly the kind of dyed-in-the-wool Hughes anecdote that had made an Irving-believer out of Frank McCulloch.

Here's the way Irving wrote it, quoting "Hughes":

Some smart guy, one of my publicity men, was visiting one of those Hollywood columnists one time—Hedda Hopper, I think it was—and I called him and told him to get out to a public phone and call me back. A few minutes later—this was Perry Lieber, a publicity man at RKO —he called. I asked him his number and he gave it to me, and right away I knew something was wrong.

I checked my book, and the number he'd given me was Hedda Hopper's unlisted number.

So I got back on the wire and said, "What the hell are you trying to pull, Perry? When I want you to call from a public phone I mean a public phone, because that's private. Hedda Hopper's private phone is about as public as you can get, and I mean public in the worst possible way. What are you doing?"

Before he filed this little tale with the New York *Times*, Turner called Perry Lieber in Las Vegas and read it to him. Lieber was dumbfounded. The incident had happened just the way *The Autobiography* related it, and Lieber couldn't explain how Cliff Irving could have picked it up. Turner's article, in the February 10 *Times*, quoted Lieber's consternation:

"You've shaken me," Lieber said. "I don't want to lend any credence to that book, but that story was never published. I have never used it in a speech and I cannot remember ever telling anyone. How could Irving have learned of it?"

Despite the way TV and the movies portray reporters, in real life newsmen are almost never struck by instant, blinding revelations. They gather one little fact after another and put them on the scale until it slowly tips this way or that. But on February 10, Turner's story brought me an instant revelation. I was sitting in the kitchen, having an early-afternoon cup of coffee, when I read the Hedda Hopper phone story and Turner's account of Lieber's bewilderment. I smashed my fist down on the table and the coffee cup leaped a foot into the air and shattered on the floor.

I filled my lungs and scared the hell out of the neighbors.

"*Eureeeeeeeka!*" I bellowed, and grabbed the telephone and called Frank McCulloch.

Perry Lieber's memory had a small bare spot. He had told that Hedda Hopper story to me eleven years earlier—and forgotten he had told me. I'd told it to Noah, and not even Dietrich had ever heard it before. Noah suggested we include it in his book to illustrate Howard's security fetish.

Frank came on the phone. He had read Turner's story in the *Times*, and he was as baffled as Perry Lieber. How could Cliff have picked up the incident except from Hughes?

"Perry told the story to me, Frank," I said. "It's in the draft I did on Dietrich's memoirs. We've been busting our asses for two months now trying to figure out Cliff, and the answer is in my filing cabinet. Don't ask how, but Irving got hold of my Dietrich manuscript."

There was a short silence. "Man," Frank said, "that explains everything."

"Everything except Hughes's handwriting," I cautioned.

"I'll talk to the people upstairs and call back," Frank said. "Can you fly in with the manuscript?"

"Next plane," I said. He hung up and I called McGraw-Hill and got Hellitzer. He said he'd also talk to his people upstairs and call back.

I dialed L.A. International and booked a seat on the next flight. Frank called back and said, "Come on in." Ted Weber, vice-president at McGraw-Hill, called and said, "Come on in."

Weber said, "Phone when you get in and we'll have the Irving manuscript and its editor ready."

I rode the red-eye special, sleepless all the way. I went to *Time* from the airport. Frank was waiting for me when their offices opened. He looked at me and grinned and said, "Boy, you and I are stupid! You told me you were doing the Dietrich memoirs a year ago, and neither of us made the connection with Irving's manuscript."

"How could we? You never read the Dietrich manuscript and I've never laid eyes on the Irving manuscript."

We went down to the office of a *Time* lawyer, Jack Dowd, and Dowd called McGraw-Hill. He listened, frowned, covered the phone and looked at us unhappily. "Problems," he said.

McGraw-Hill's lawyer didn't want to let me look at their $750,000 manuscript. They just wanted to examine mine. I turned to Frank, and the blood was flushing up his neck angrily. He shook his head.

"No way," I told the *Time* lawyer. "Tell them it's a two-way street or no traffic."

Frank pulled me out in the corridor. "Hang in," he told me. "I'm sick of all the high-level maneuvering. We're trying to get to the bottom of a story and everyone's getting in the way. I can't let you have the *Life* copy of Cliff's manuscript, because McGraw-Hill controls it. But I know where we can buy a bootleg copy for a hundred dollars. If McGraw-Hill won't budge, you and I will move outside the corporate structures this afternoon, get our own copy and blow it out of the water by ourselves."

"That would be great," I said enthusiastically. "I never was an organization man."

We went back into Dowd's office ready to tell McGraw-Hill to flake off, but someone at McGraw-Hill had overridden their lawyer. They told me to come on over. I took a cab alone, with my manuscript in its old manila envelope. Hellitzer escorted me up to the executive conference room. Their editor-in-chief, a young, bespectacled, solemn-looking fellow named Robert Sussman Stewart, was

Dietrich memoirs and Cliff had them all. We just nailed a lulu that clinches it. Cliff has his Hughes telling another story that I dug up myself. You can tell *Life* that the autobiography is a certified fake."

"Grab a cab and come on over," Frank said. "We got a lot of work to do."

"I can't," I told him. "McGraw-Hill isn't convinced."

It took another four hours. The McGraw-Hill will to believe in Clifford Irving died hard. I began to feel like Ug, the lonesome caveman, trying to beat a forty-ton dinosaur to death with a stick.

We ticked off twenty-six parallel passages, and didn't cover one-tenth of Irving's manuscript. Throughout, Irving had rewritten and reworded almost everything he stole, but every now and then he got tired and picked up a few passages verbatim. There was other incontrovertible evidence of Irving's piracy. In one spot, Noah had told me a political story, and I'd fleshed it out with some background information of my own. Irving had the story, reworded, but he had used the same background context that I had supplied. In another spot, Irving had Hughes using a series of technical aeronautical terms, in describing some damage to the *Spruce Goose*. Irving had lifted the terms, *in the same sequence,* out of the Dietrich memoirs.

"Take a look at this," I said, handing over the passage from my draft. "You'll notice that those obscure terms, and the order in which Irving has Hughes reciting them, is from a conversation where Howard Hughes wasn't present."

At this point we were joined by Harold McGraw, president of the book division, and Shelton Fisher, president of McGraw-Hill. Mr. Fisher fixed me with a stern glare and loosed an executive zinger.

"I hope I don't offend you," he said, "but how do we know that you didn't somehow lift *your* material from *our* manuscript?"

The question stunned me, and knocked the logical answer out of my head. *The reason I couldn't have stolen from Mr. Irving, sir, is that I finished my manuscript before he started his. It is not possible to steal material from a writer before he writes it.* "You don't offend me, Mr. Fisher," I said. "You've been taken in by one fast-talking con man and it's proper to exercise caution that you're not being taken in by another. I'll give you a list of references and maybe you better check them before we go on."

Someone cleared a vice-presidential throat and we went on. On the next comparison, Stewart spotted a whole sentence where Irving had grown weary of rephrasing and had plagiarized word for word. With that, everyone shrugged and we quit.

"I have one question," Robert Sussman Stewart asked. "Did you ever hear of Hughes getting together with Ernest Hemingway?"

"*Hemingway?*" I asked. "Does Irving claim Howard Hughes met Hemingway?"

"He has a long section on Hughes visiting Hemingway at his place in Cuba," Stewart said. "And another section on Hughes meeting Dr. Albert Schweitzer in Africa."

"My guess is that those passages are fiction," I said. "But you could check the Hemingway story with his widow, Mary. Doesn't she live here in New York?"

McGraw-Hill hadn't checked with Mary Hemingway. Neither had Time-Life, although Mrs. Hemingway was a one-time staff writer for the Luce publications.

On my way out, I stopped in Harold McGraw's office. I said I was sorry to come as the bearer of bad news, and that it would have been more pleasant to have been able to authenticate the manuscript.

Incredibly, McGraw-Hill still was not ready to declare Clifford Irving's work a fraud. They issued a press release that left the fake's fakery unresolved. The statement said:

> As part of our continuing investigation into the Howard Hughes autobi-ography, McGraw-Hill has discovered additional information concern-ing a possible source of the material in that book. The new information was provided by James Phelan, an investigative reporter who was a collaborator on a manuscript about Howard Hughes written by Noah Dietrich. We have informed the U.S. Attorney and the New York District Attorney of this new information.

It seemed odd that they persisted, after that five-hour session, in referring to the Irving work as the Howard Hughes autobiography.

A short time later, something odder came to light. The day before our conference at McGraw-Hill, the Osborn handwriting firm had withdrawn its authentication of the "Hughes" handwriting. The Osborns had sent a messenger to McGraw-Hill, hand-carrying a new finding: they now labeled the "Hughes" letters and signatures a clever forgery. Before I showed up with evidence that Irving was a plagiarist, the final evidentiary prop under Cliff's fraud had been kicked down. Two of the people at the conference table had known this and kept silent while we laboriously matched up examples of Cliff's pocket-picking.

Time and *Life*, however, squarely bit the bullet. An hour after I left McGraw-Hill and was debriefed by McCulloch, *Life* issued a statement branding the Irving book a hoax and canceling plans to excerpt it. With only thirty-six hours to press time, *Time* scrapped its cover on Richard Nixon's imminent trip to Red China, substituted Clifford Irving as "Con Man of the Year," and announced it would tell the whole story of how Cliff had carpentered his flimflam.

Time was yanked up short the next morning by a weird assortment of opponents—McGraw-Hill, Clifford Irving, the Hughes forces, and Noah Dietrich. McGraw-Hill raced into court early Saturday, joined by attorneys for Irving and for Rosemont Enterprises, Hughes's corporate book abortionists. *Time* planned to publish 1,000 words of Cliff's fake parallel with excerpts from my Dietrich draft, and the outcries of "Don't you dare!" were deafening.

There ensued a short, bitter legal battle over the property rights to Irving's fake. McGraw-Hill invoked its contract, citing *Life*'s promise to pay $250,000 for permission to excerpt the Irving opus. But *Life* already was demanding back its $250,000, so if *Time* excerpted samples *free*, Time-Life would be violating its contract. *Time* argued that the Irving book had become news, and the newest news was that Cliff had stolen great chunks of his book, and they wanted to show their readers specimens of his thievery.

Rosemont stood on its traditional grounds; Hughes didn't want *anything* published about Hughes except by Rosemont. To discourage other publishers, Hughes had sold to Rosemont, which was headed by a Hughes executive and a Hughes attorney, all rights to his life story. Rosemont was the ideal publisher, from the viewpoint of Howard Robard Hughes; it had an unsullied record of never having published a single word about Howard Robard Hughes.

Irving's joining up with McGraw-Hill and Rosemont needed no explanation. Making the cover of *Time* is a writer's dream, but not a cover labeled "Con Man of the Year."

Judge Gerald P. Culkin granted an injunction restraining *Time* from comparing Irving's manuscript with mine. *Time* rushed immediately to an appellate court, and overturned the injunction.

There was a final roadblock. Noah Dietrich had fired off a wire warning *Time* against quoting from my manuscript, on the grounds that he owned all rights to it. But Dietrich neglected to mention that *he* had sold the rights to Fawcett Publications. So I called an old Fawcett friend, Ralph Daigh, at his home out in Rye, and Ralph cheerfully gave me permission to give *Time* permission to quote from my own handiwrok. And thus, after a long, acrimonious, and wearying day of sorting out everyone's claims, contentions, and property rights, the way was cleared to drive the final stake through Irving's fake.

Time's cover story finished off Irving's long, gaudy hoax. In dispatching Irving, *Time* also unaccountably skewered me. Midway in its story, *Time* commented that Irving was a much livelier writer than I am. The passages *Time* quoted from his fake tended to support this judgment. They had a free, easy style, unhobbled by any concern for accuracy. Whenever the facts slowed his narrative, Irving simply changed them or spiced them up with fiction. It struck me that *Time*'s comment was an exercise in the self-evident; fiction usually reads better than fact.

Before quitting New York, I went up to the tip-top *Time* executive suite and had a few words with Hedley Donovan, who had inherited the mantle of Henry R. Luce. I told him that I had brought my evidence of Irving's plagiarism to *Time* out of respect for Frank McCulloch, not love for *Time*.

"When flying out here," I told Donovan, "the thought came to mind that *Newsweek* would be delighted to have my evidence that Time-Life had been conned. I came here instead, and I can't understand why *Time* took a gratuitous swipe at me while I was in the process of helping *Time*. So I decided to present my bewilderment to someone in authority, and I presume that to be you."

The editor-in-chief of *Time* said, "What can I say, except that it was regrettable?"

It took months to sweep up the debris from the collapse of the great hoax. The two major remaining mysteries—who forged Hughes's handwriting, and who handed over my Dietrich draft to Irving—were swiftly resolved. Cliff himself had executed the remarkable forgeries that had fooled two sets of experts. He admitted being the penman—and then found that the prosecutors didn't believe him. He had acquired a peculiar status where no one believed anything he said, even when he was willingly incriminating himself. He had to sit down and dash off a convincing specimen of the Hughes holograph before the authorities accepted his confession.

His most lasting accomplishment may well be that he set back the science of handwriting verification by a hundred years.

When the *Time* cover story went to press, I lurched off to my hotel, groggy from sixty straight hours without sleep. Instead of landing in bed, I wound up being interrogated by federal postal inspectors who wanted to know how Irving had acquired my manuscript. The postal sleuths had got the case because Irving had used the mails to transport forged checks. All I could tell them was that the manuscript had passed through four sets of hands—mine, Dietrich's, Stanley Meyer's and Paul Gitlin's. I told them that I hadn't given the manuscript to Irving, and was reasonably sure Noah hadn't.

The interrogation lasted three hours, and ended at dawn. It was my first encounter with the postal inspectors. They comprise one tiny segment in the vast, lethargic federal bureaucracy that is dedicated, hard-working, and highly competent. There was a certain pleasure in being put over the jumps by true professionals. Using the device of double-teaming, they smoothly ran me over my story twice, with separate agents taking separate notes for later comparison. By the time the thin light of Sunday morning was filtering into the room, they had zeroed in on Stanley Meyer, although they didn't say so.

The head agent, a polite, soft-voiced Irishman named Lex Callahan, asked me a final question. "If you were going after the guy who took your manuscript, who would you work on?"

"Meyer and Gitlin," I said. "Meyer first, because Gitlin is rich, doesn't need the money, and has more to lose."

Callahan smiled, folded his notebook, and they went away. Shortly after, Stanley Meyer was subpoenaed out of California to the New York grand jury. He came indignantly protesting his total innocence—up to the threshold of the jury room. Yes, he'd known Clifford Irving back in Hollywood in the 1960's. Yes, he'd bumped into Clifford Irving by accident last summer in Palm Springs. Yes, he had acquired a copy of my manuscript and Noah's tape-recorded interviews. No, he had never given them to Clifford Irving. The notion was utterly ridiculous. Did people think he carried that damn manuscript around with him wherever he went? He had not—repeat NOT—given any of my material to Clifford Irving, and that's what he was going tell the grand jury.

Then he went into the jury room, and under the penalty of

perjury, told the truth. He admitted he had handed over everything to Clifford Irving and his researcher, Richard Suskind, when he was trying to find a writer to replace me.

Irving fleshed out the rest of the story before the grand jury. On acquiring the fruit of my year's work, he had whooshed it through a Xerox machine and returned the originals to helpful Stanley. Euphoric with his windfall, he had advised McGraw-Hill that Howard Hughes had decided to convert what was originally labeled by Irving as an authorized biography into an autobiography. And with this irresistible bait, Irving had jacked up the price at McGraw-Hill from $500,000 to $750,000.

Why Irving attempted the hoax and how he thought he could pull it off remain unanswered questions. Many people have posed these questions to me, but the answers lie outside the field of journalism. The late George Hunter White, a legendary undercover agent for the Federal Narcotics Agency, used to shunt aside similar questions about the men he nailed as major drug traffickers. "What makes them tick?" people would ask him.

White had a standard answer. "That's a question for the psychiatrists or the sociologists. I'm concerned only with the end product of drug trafficking. I don't think a street sweeper who pushes a broom in the wake of a parade is qualified to lecture on the digestive system of the horse."

Irving gave his own answers in a paperback, *What Really Happened*, that he wrote about the affair. He portrayed himself and his colleague, Suskind, as merry pranksters, a pair of Till Eulenspiegels or middle-aged Katzenjammer Kids out for a magnificent jape. The motive, he said, was above and beyond "the vulgarity inherent in the amounts of money involved."

"Dick had once said to me that it was an act of anarchy," Irving wrote. "We were showing up the Establishment, he said, in all its corporate myopia, in all its craven worship of the golden calf ... I had indeed demonstrated ... in the most graphic way I could find, a cool contempt for the underpinnings of American society."

Irving successfully burnished this romantic image in a series of talk-show appearances after he pleaded guilty and before he went off to jail. He kept stressing that he had no real interest in all that vulgar money. He made such an incessant point of this that it occurred to me he protested too much. His book had too many references to "our fifteen-room finca" in Ibiza and to "my Mercedes-Benz" to square with his pose as the cool hipster who despised money-grubbing. So I checked out what ultimately had happened to the McGraw-Hill loot.

Cliff came up almost $300,000 short, after all that talk about "full restitution." McGraw-Hill paid him a total of $716,000, and a year after the caper had recovered only $450,000. It got that $450,000 not from a penitent Irving, but by seizing one of his Swiss bank accounts. What really happened to the rest of the money is a secret he kept to himself when he wrote *What Really Happened*.

His book was billed as the true account of his hoax. But where it dealt with what I knew firsthand, it was heavily spiced with fiction. He seemed compelled to fantasize, much as old confidence men embellish the truth even when the embellishment serves no purpose other than to hone their skills. He quoted me as saying he had written "a very great book on Hughes" and as sympathizing with him because he "was knifed by some of the great corporations of this country, because he'd shown them the truth." Those quotes came out of Irving's head, not my mouth.

To this day I've never read his Hughes hoax, but I did handle it once. When *Life* declared it a fake, it send the manuscript back to McGraw-Hill for a refund of the $250,000 *Life* paid for the magazine rights. I happened to ride down the elevator at Time, Inc., with the lawyer who was returning the manuscript. He offered me a ride in a *Time* limousine, and when we got to the McGraw-Hill building a whimsy flew in the car window and tickled my fancy.

I asked the *Time* lawyer, "May I?"

He smiled and said, "Why not?"

I got out, he handed me the huge thousand-page bundle, and I carried the corpse of Irving's hoax back over the threshold into McGraw-Hill.

2
Beginning

A hard-headed hillbilly plumber named Bill Douthit elbowed me prematurely into investigative reporting back in the 1940's, before I had ever heard of investigative reporting, and almost got me killed. I was working on my first newspaper and he came knocking on my door with the kind of story every young, ambitious, inexperienced newsman fantasizes about getting his hands on. It was a case of assault and battery, of denial of due process, of bribery and corruption and malfeasance of office centering on a major law-enforcement official. With visions of righting a gross injustice—and getting a front-page byline story—I took up his cause, went off covertly on my own without my newspaper's knowledge, and fashioned a spectacular fiasco. I got beaten by two thugs, kicked into a roadside ditch, and never got a line of the story into print.

By an odd turn of events, this disaster convinced me that I had found my true calling and led me into the kind of reporting I have pursued ever since.

The newspaper was the Alton *Evening Telegraph* in southern Illinois. Alton is a somnolent old Mississippi River town that sprawls on the bluffs some twenty miles north of St. Louis. South of Alton, reaching to East St. Louis, lies a grimy industrial plain much like the New Jersey flats across the Hudson River from New York. The plain is odorous with steel mills, stockyards, brass mills, tanneries, and oil refineries that belch smoke by day and flames by night. These plants are manned by the descendants of European immigrants and Kentucky and Tennessee hill people lured to the area by the industrial booms of two world wars. Like New Jersey, it is an area of industrial domination, machine politics, and a long history of entrenched vice and corruption. Its foremost contribution to Illinois politics was Orville Hodge, a state auditor who looted the public treasury of two million dollars by forging state checks payable to nonexistent contractors.

I was born in Alton but raised on a daily diet of the St. Louis *Post-Dispatch*, the dominant newspaper in eastern Missouri and southern Illinois. The *Post-Dispatch* enjoyed a national reputation as one of the best newspapers in the country, and I grew up thinking of it as a misty Camelot staffed by fearless and incorruptible white knights. From the time I was ten, I was determined to become a newspaper reporter, preferably on the *Post-Dispatch*, and I never seriously contemplated any other line of work. When I finished high school, I raced up to the University of Illinois School of Journalism to learn the trade. I lasted five semesters before I was driven out by lack of money into the Great Depression. Newspaper offices in those days had long queues of experienced, jobless newsmen, and I spent seven years in the wasteland of a series of nonjournalistic jobs, mainly in Chicago. Then, in 1941, the golden door swung open back in my home town of Alton. I quit a $250-a-month job in Chicago and went gratefully to work as a twenty-nine-year-old cub newsman at nineteen dollars a week, on my way at last.

I served what seemed an interminable apprenticeship on the lowest level of the Alton *Evening Telegraph*, covering village board meetings, Rotary Club speakers, Moose and Elk Lodge elections, and the other minutiae of small-town journalism. The *Telegraph* was a better-than-average small-town paper, and made no pretense at being more than that. It prospered in the shadow of the St. Louis *Post-Dispatch* by diligently reporting the local happenings in its circulation area and leaving the big-time stories to the *Post-Dispatch*.

I began to chafe at my dull routine and grumble at the way the *Telegraph* closed its eyes to what was going on in Alton and in the river towns stretching south to East St. Louis. This is a familiar syndrome among reporters, I have learned over the years. Reporters march to a different drum than most publishers, and tend to consider themselves purer in heart than the men who meet their payrolls.

The latter have to concern themselves with editorial budgets, union contracts, the price of newsprint, and the cost of libel insurance, and they understandably are more restrained in going after difficult stories that entail a high financial risk. But from my impatient viewpoint, the *Telegraph* carried its caution and restraint to the point where its function as a newspaper was crippled.

The two counties across the Mississippi from St. Louis—Madison County on the north, which included Alton, and St. Clair County on the south—were notorious for wide-open vice. East St. Louis for years was the home of one of the best-known red-light districts in the nation. It was called the Valley, and consisted of a five-block congeries of whorehouses that were within hailing distance of the East St. Louis police station. In its heyday, the Valley rated with New Orleans's Storyville and San Francisco's Barbary Coast as a national institution. The streets of the Valley were unpaved and pocked with chuckholes, which slowed down the curious tourists and gave the girls a chance to solicit business. Periodically, street crews would invade the Valley and fill in the chuckholes. When the workmen departed, the doxies would swarm forth with shovels and restore the holes. Throughout its long years of notoriety, the local police force resolutely looked the other way. The Valley was finally closed by federal pressure in World War II, when its VD rate began to undermine the military effort.

Madison County had its share of brothels but specialized in illegal gambling. It harbored a dozen or more joints that offered craps, poker, and bookmaking and ran unmolested by the forces of law and order. In addition, there were two big-time casinos, the Mounds Club and the Hyde Park Club. The Mounds was the class joint, where a tie and jacket were mandatory, with a showroom with such entertainers as Sophie Tucker and Ted Lewis and a fully equipped casino.

The Hyde Park Club was more sinister. It was housed in an ominous-looking building in Venice, Illinois, near the foot of a bridge connecting with St. Louis. Surrounded by a high board fence, it had no identifying signs and its windows were bricked up so no light leaked out. Entrance to the club was via two locked doors equipped with peepholes. After passing scrutiny through the outer peephole, the customer entered a small room that served as a kind of decompression chamber. The door was locked behind the customer, and he was patted down for weapons before being passed on to the games inside. Other joints in Madison County were occasionally knocked over by rival mobsters, but no one ever penetrated the Hyde Park. The local police and the sheriff's men never tried.

The St. Louis *Post-Dispatch* looked upon the rowdy Illinois East Side as a wayward and intransigent distant cousin whose disreputable life-style was a constant embarrassment, irritant, and challenge. With its strong political clout and staff of good reporters, the *Post-Dispatch* kept St. Louis itself free of the more flagrant vices. This pleased the whorehouse and gambling entrepreneurs across the Mississippi, because anyone looking for action could indulge himself after a short cab ride across the river.

The Hyde Park Club was the special *bête noir* of the *Post-Dispatch*. The club cheekily provided free limousine service from a number of stations in St. Louis to whisk residents and visiting conventioneers across the bridge to its gambling tables. To counter this intolerable intrusion of "East Sideism" into its fiefdom, the *Post-Dispatch* assigned its top crime reporter, Ted Link, to monitor what the *Post-Dispatch* called "the notorious Hyde Park gambling establishment."

Link was a dark, good-looking, deceptively soft-spoken newsman who scourged mobsters and crooked politicians with skill and effectiveness for years. I immediately adopted him as a model of what a reporter should be, and followed his coverage of East Side corruption with awe and envy. His reporting on the Hyde Park Club produced what I considered a flawless gem of investigative reporting. He disclosed on the front page of the *Post-Dispatch* that a newly elected sheriff of St. Louis County and two other public figures—one an ex-sheriff of Madison County and the other a candidate for mayor of Venice—were sharing in the Hyde Park's gambling profits. He spelled out in exact detail, down to the penny, the cut each had received from the club in their most recent payoff. The story used none of the journalistic hedges such as "reportedly" or "according to informed sources," and nobody sued. Later Link told me how he had obtained such exquisitely precise information. As with most good stories, there was no magic involved. One of the Hyde Park partners had got miffed at the cut the politicians were taking out of the club's pie. He had quietly got in touch with Link and gave him a look at the club's books.

What *was* akin to magic was the access Link had to such unusual sources, in high and low places on both sides of the law. He had acquired them over the years because he had an uncompromising integrity that people of all sorts—whores, gamblers, mobsters, pimps, lawyers, cops, and honest public officials—recognized and respected. He was trusted even by mobsters he pursued with relentlessness. He was on good terms for years with the Shelton gang, a colorful family of strong-armed racketeers and slot-machine operators in Illinois. Link had learned they were being set up on a rigged charge and tipped them off. Later, when one of the brothers, Bernie Shelton, was gunned down from ambush in Peoria, the mobster's widow delivered to Link a secret recording the Sheltons had made of a shakedown threat by an Illinois politician. Bernie had put the recording in a safe-deposit box and instructed his wife to give it to Link if anything terminal happened to him. Link's stories precipitated a scandal in the Illinois Republican state administration and helped bring about the election of Adlai Stevenson as governor. With political evenhandedness, Link went on to bare a national scandal involving the Internal Revenue Service under the Democratic administration of President Truman.

When the *Post-Dispatch* would periodically front-page a story on East Side corruption, the Alton *Evening Telegraph* would either ignore it or carry a toned-down version attributed to the St. Louis paper, with no follow-up on its own initiative.

I found this puzzling in view of the character of the publisher of the *Telegraph*, a stern, churchgoing Scottish Presbyterian named Paul B. Cousley. He was obviously a man not given to tolerance of whorehouses and crap games. Indeed, he was of such high moral rectitude that he even frowned on beer drinking by his reporters. Most of us, after a hard day of newsgathering, would retire to the Knights of Columbus bar, where Mr. Cousley never intruded. And yet there were three wide-open gambling joints that had run for years in Alton, one only two blocks from the *Telegraph*'s offices.

After I had been on the paper a while, I cautiously raised the issue of the *Telegraph*'s passive tolerance of rampant vice with some of the older reporters. They told me a story that explained why the *Telegraph* persisted in sitting on the East Side compost heap and smelling only roses. Some years earlier Mr. Cousley had launched a *Telegraph* crusade against gambling at the instigation of a woman named Irene Kite. She had sought him out and offered to play the role of a latter-day Carry Nation, the Kansas temperance reformer who had chopped up bars with an ax. Mrs. Kite had proposed to fare forth with her own ax against the slot machines that were illegally gulping workingmen's wages. Mr. Cousley had rallied church groups and unleashed Mrs. Kite, trailed by his reporters and photographers. Then it had developed that Mrs. Kite was not a true spiritual descendant of Carry Nation, but the angry wife of a local gambler who had been fired from his job. Her motive had been pure revenge, and the crusade had collapsed into low comedy. Thereafter the *Telegraph* had shunned investigative reporting and had restricted itself to reporting only formal raids against the joints and the arrests of gamblers. Since the law officials never raided the joints, the wide-open gambling was not "news."

Under this journalistic Catch-22, vice had flourished for years on the East Side and the key offices of sheriff and county prosecutor had become prizes sought by a series of shoddy political hacks. It was a cynical political axiom that a single term in either office could enable a man to retire in comfort for the rest of his life. In southern Illinois I learned a rule of thumb that can be applied to measure the honesty of law enforcement anywhere: If the whorehouses and gambling joints operate in the open, the law is corrupt. Both of these vices depend upon public access to keep going, and if the cabdrivers and bartenders can tell you where the joints are open, the police have to know. And if the police know and hold off, the fix is in.

This was the situation when Bill Douthit showed up one night with a huge lump on the back of his head, an angry story of the collapse of law enforcement in Madison County, and his insistent demand that the free American press—meaning me—do something to set things right.

Douthit had been beaten up by two brothers who ran a busy gambling joint in East Alton. The Jones brothers were related by marriage to the Shelton family, a connection that inspired caution, if not respect, among their customers. The brothers had owed Douthit a long-overdue plumbing bill, and Douthit had encountered them in a roadhouse while they were drinking with some friends. When he had approached them about their bill, they had taken this as a social insult and assaulted him in a drunken rage. One of them had pinioned the plumber's arms while the other zapped him from behind with a blackjack.

The next day Douthit had gone over to the county seat to swear out a warrant for the arrest of the brothers. Although he had witnesses to the assault, and an egg-sized lump on his skull, the county prosecutor had refused to issue a warrant. When Douthit had grown insistent, the prosecutor had summoned a couple of deputies and had Douthit thrown bodily out of his office.

The county prosecutor was a tall, handsome, deep-voiced Democrat named William Burton. He had a townhouse in Edwardsville, the county seat, and a gentleman's farm out in the country, where he bred horses and cattle. I asked Douthit why Burton had refused him a warrant. Douthit gave me a look of deep scorn. "Everybody in the county knows that Burton is on the take from the gambling joints," he said. "I got nothing against gambling, but when they bought off Bill Burton they didn't buy up my legal rights. I'm entitled to a warrant and Burton's breaking the law to protect his crooked friends."

There was something touching and rather magnificent in his faith in equality under the law, his view that the prosecutor was the hired servant of the sovereign people, and his belief that the American press was a court of last resort when things didn't work the way they were supposed to. His indignation put me on the defensive, because in my heart I agreed with him.

I made some notes and said I'd get back to him. I went around to the roadhouse and talked to the owner and some customers and verified his story. Douthit was well known as an honest, hard-working plumber and the assault on him had angered the people who had witnessed it.

Then I took his story to a county judge who was a close friend of mine. He was one of the few straight political figures I knew, a Democratic maverick, and a practicing Catholic with deep-seated principles he had acquired studying under the Jesuits at St. Louis University. He also had no love for the county prosecutor. He was upset and intrigued with Douthit's story, and curious about my interest in it. He commented that it wasn't the kind of journalism that the *Telegraph* usually got into. He thought things over and suggested that Douthit file a sworn complaint with the Illinois attorney general and see what might happen. I sent Douthit to the judge and together they drafted an affidavit charging that law enforcement had broken down in Madison County, and sent it off to the state capital at Springfield. Douthit was delighted with all this, and envisioned the attorney general rushing down from Springfield and personally taking up his case. I was more doubtful.

It was at this point that I made a serious misjudgment. On the basis of what I had, and given the restricted view of the *Telegraph* on what constituted news, I was certain that the paper would not turn me loose on the story. On the other hand, if I nailed down some more facts and got something out on the legal record—such as a response from the attorney general—I knew the *Telegraph* would not ignore the story. So I decided to pursue the story on my own initiative and on my own off-duty time with the notion that I would present the paper with a *fait accompli* in the form of some St. Louis *Post-Dispatch* type of reporting. Dreams of glory.

I explained to Douthit that it was one thing for worldly fellows like us to know that wide-open vice implied a payoff, but that didn't constitute proof. He told me that he had a friend who had run a back-room crap game for years and had been quietly shut down after a falling-out with the prosecutor. He said if I approached him carefully, there was a lot the fellow could tell me. A few nights later he took me around to meet an Italian roadhouse owner. He was a short, broad-shouldered fellow named Domenick, and he was simmering with hot-blooded hostility toward the county prosecutor. After some sparring around and the drafting of some ground rules about what I would do with the information he gave me, he agreed to talk. And when he did, the scruffy troubles of Bill Douthit began to open up into a scandal of a much greater magnitude. Dom told me a sensational story about a wealthy heir to one of Alton's industrial fortunes, a tale of life and death and greed and money that was worthy of Dashiell Hammett or Raymond Chandler.

The heir had died a few months earlier, and I knew his name and had heard some stories about him. He had retired when he was in his fifties, with five or six million dollars as his share of the family enterprises. He had then embarked on a playboy career of drinking, partying, and compulsive gambling until his heart gave out. That much I knew, but Domenick knew much more.

He told me that the man had lost two million dollars in East Side joints in a couple of years. "He was a terrible crap-shooter," Dom said. "He'd get sore when he was losing, ask the house to take off the limit, and then he'd throw the money away in chunks. But when his luck turned good, he'd get nervous and pinch back on his bets, so he'd lose his money in thousands and win it back in tens. Every joint in the county was panting for a shot at him, and they all got him eventually. He dropped forty thousand in my back room here one night.

"His family got word of what was going on, and they read him the riot act. They told him he had to put his money in a trust fund run by the bank, or they were going to declare him incompetent. So they set up the fund and doled him fifty thousand dollars a year to live on. Then they went away, and the old boy started hitting the tables again. When his allowance ran out, he'd write checks and ask the house to hold them, or he would give them promissory notes. When he died, he had four hundred thousand dollars in paper around the county. The Hyde Park Club has most of his paper, but we all got some. I've got fourteen thousand myself."

Dom said that since the playboy had died there were some delicate negotiations going on with the bank over the checks and notes. The bank was balking at paying on the ground that the paper represented gambling debts and wasn't collectable.

"But there isn't anything on the paper that says they are gambling debts, and the guys are claiming they advanced him money out of friendship because they knew he was good for it," Dom said. "Nobody wants to go to court: the family because of the embarrassment and scandal, and the guys because of the heat all the publicity would bring down. So they are talking about so much on the dollar in a quiet settlement. And now get this.

"The bank is consulting confidentially with the county prosecutor about how the law reads. And *that* fellow is advising his buddies at the Hyde Park on how to squeeze the most out of the bank. He meets with the chief owner regularly. When I tell you this, I'm not giving you bar talk. I got friends in certain places. If they try to cut the rest of us out and settle with the Hyde Park there are some people who are ready to blow the prosecutor out of the water. If it goes that way, maybe we can arrange something with you. Right now everything is up in the air and nervous. What I want is to collect on the paper I'm holding, but I don't give a shit what happens to that guy in the county seat. He had no call to do what he did to Bill Douthit, but that's the kind of guy he is."

My friend the honest judge was also a friend of the bank's lawyer; they both belonged to the same Catholic parish. I took the bare bones of Dom's story about the dead playboy to the judge and ran it past him, leaving Dom out of it all the way. He said he would try to get a reading on the story from the lawyer. A couple of days later he told me that the story was true, that the negotiations over the playboy's debts were under way, and that the lawyer was upset that the story had leaked out. Then I put the judge on his word of honor, and told him what I had heard about the prosecutor's covert connection with the Hyde Park Club. The judge offered the opinion that things were getting very gamy in Madison County and that something was bound to bust loose. He also suggested that I was getting in over my head, and that I ought to be careful.

A couple of nights later the roof fell in on me. I stopped off in the evening at Douthit's combination plumbing shop and bachelor's quarters in East Alton. He was euphoric about what we had dug up, and I kept trying to calm him down. All we had was some sensational information without any way to get it into print. He didn't understand the niceties of journalism and the differences between allegation and provable fact. He just knew that the prosecutor was a crook and had done him wrong and ought to be brought to justice by the press, and on that simple basic premise it was hard to argue with him.

I left his place late and headed up the dark street to catch the last bus home. I had gone about a block when I heard feet running behind me and turned around. Two men piled into me. One grabbed my necktie and began to choke me with it, and the other put a gun to the back of my head.

"Listen, smartass," the man with the gun said. "We know what you're doing with Bill Douthit. Knock it off and stay away from him unless you want your fucking brains blown out." The fellow behind me kicked my legs out from under me, and the two of them booted me into a muddy roadside ditch. Then they ran back down the dark street and I was alone, with ditchwater seeping through my clothes.

It was the only time I have ever had a gun put on me in a lifetime of pursuing stories that people of various sorts didn't want pursued. I was outraged and terrified. But overriding the shock and fear was a strong exultant surge that is incontrovertible evidence that reporters are a little crazy. As I lay in the muddy ditch and listened to the two fellows run off into the night, I thought, "Boy, I'm really *onto* something."

The next morning, after wrestling with myself for a couple of hours, I decided I'd better let my publisher know what his reporter had been up to, and went in for a show and tell session with Mr. Cousley. I tried to make it easy on myself by assuring Mr. Cousley that I had not represented myself as working on an assignment. I told him I had just looked into the story on my own time to see if there was anything to it. I told him what had happened to Bill Douthit and what had happened to me the night before, but left out everything Dom had told me because I couldn't have told Mr. Cousley where I had got that story if he had asked me. I wound up relating what the gunman had told me about staying away from Bill Douthit.

Mr. Cousley was not pleased with me. He heard me out and then told me, "In that case, I would stay away from Bill Douthit." Then he dismissed me by going back to what he was doing. And that was that.

With hindsight, I don't fault him. He was entitled to run the kind of newspaper he wanted. Even a much bolder publisher, with a different concept of the news, would hardly have entrusted a story of that magnitude to an inexperienced neophyte operating on his own initiative.

Being Irish and reckless and full of resentment, I went and saw Bill Douthit again. I gave him a fair description of the two fellows who had jumped me, particularly the one who had choked me, who was in his early twenties and had red hair. Douthit nosed around and came up with the name of a young stickman who worked on the Jones crap table.

I went over to the county seat the next day and saw Mr. William Burton, the county prosecutor. I told him what I knew about Douthit and what had happened to me, and gave him the name of Dee Jones's red-haired crap dealer. I told him I had put it all in a memorandum and that if anything happened to Douthit or to me, the memo would be turned over to the St. Louis *Post-Dispatch*. Unlike Bill Douthit, I was not thrown out of the prosecutor's office, a courtesy that I interpreted as a tribute to the free American press. Burton played all this as if it was news to him, and said that what I told him was "shocking" and "deplorable" and would be looked into promptly. I did not go along with this charade. I told him that his friends in East Alton ought to pray every night that some hunter didn't shoot at a squirrel and hit me by mistake. Then I got up and walked out.

About a week later I was brooding over a beer at a place called Forkeyville Tavern, and Dee Jones sat down on one side of me and his brother on the other. Without any prelude, Dee told me he was sorry about what had happened to me and that "a couple of my young guys had gone off on their own." He said they didn't have very good sense, and probably had gone to too many bad movies. I said that such things happened, and he offered to buy me a drink and I let him do it.

We never heard from the Illinois attorney general, and Bill Douthit never got his day in court. His faith in the press as a court of last resort suffered a sad decline. The joints kept running wide-open and Bill Burton continued to preside over law enforcement in Madison County. I dropped the story of the playboy's estate and the gamblers and never found out how they came out. After a while I quit the *Telegraph* and took a job on a California paper.

Several years later I got a series of clippings from my friend the honest judge. Somebody had got angry at the county prosecutor and blew in the side of his townhouse with a bomb. The prosecutor had gathered up his wife and literally gone on the lam. He was in such a state of panic that he left almost everything behind, including $52,474.43 on deposit at an Edwardsville bank and 252 shares of corporation stock. After his disappearance, the Internal Revenue Service came in with an $80,000 tax lien for income he had neglected to report, and sold off his gentleman's farm to pay the bill. Burton became a southern Illinois version of New York's well-known Judge Crater, who simply vanished off the face of the earth one day. He never returned to retrieve his bank account or his stocks, apparently from a deep-seated distrust of the state of law enforcement in Madison County. Years later, a nephew filed a court action to settle his estate, on the presumption that he was dead.

In the clippings from the Alton *Evening Telegraph* were two short paragraphs.

"Near the end of his second full term as state's attorney his home was bombed. The case was never solved.

"Friends interpreted the bombing as a warning from area gambling overlords whose ire the prosecutor had aroused."

The honest judge had attached a little note to the clippings. "I remembered your story about Burton and the Hyde Park Club, and thought this would interest you."

When I read that I thought back to the night I had wound up in an East Alton ditch. I had been onto something, all right, but I was onto it with too little, too soon. But in the end it had all washed up into print and with that, inside me, an old wound healed over.

3

California
Con Man's Cure-All

The busiest doctor in California in 1952—and quite possibly the busiest private practitioner in the nation—was a forty-six-year-old man named Dr. Lynn A. Brinkley. His meteoric rise to such preeminence was, on the surface at least, the stuff that *Reader's Digest* and *Time* magazine sagas are made of, but before I became involved with him, hardly anyone outside of Los Angeles had heard of Dr. Brinkley.

Dr. Brinkley, a former fire-truck driver, did not become a doctor until he was forty. A few years later, without the benefit of any internship, he became titular head of an establishment in downtown Los Angeles that employed twenty associate doctors, a hundred nurses, attendants, and clerical workers, and treated more than 7,000 patients a month. His practice, in terms of patient load, outstripped that of the nationally known Mayo Clinic in Rochester, Minnesota.

I became aware of Dr. Brinkley soon after arriving in California from the Middle West. His presence was impossible to ignore; it thrust itself upon one like the palm trees, the used-car lots, and the endless sunshine. His red-and-yellow signs—BAD HEART? DR. BRINKLEY (D.C.)—assailed the eye from building walls and billboards throughout Los Angeles. Newspapers carried his full-page ads, proclaiming UNBELIEVABLE—$10,000 AVAILABLE FOR PROOF—PROVEN

METHOD—TRIAL TREATMENT $3, and his commercials were on radio and television wherever you flipped the dial.

From the outset, Dr. Brinkley intrigued me. Back in the Middle West doctors did not advertise, under pain of losing their licenses for unethical conduct. No doctors I had ever encountered provided treatment, trial or otherwise, for three dollars. But the Middle West also did not have flowers that bloomed riotously in February, so I attributed Dr. Brinkley's huckstering to a strange local custom in a strange new land. I had more immediate problems, such as finding a job, so I tucked Dr. Brinkley and his three-dollar trial treatment on a back shelf as something to look into some day.

In 1952, after I had gone to work for the Long Beach *Press-Telegram*, my attention was refocused on Dr. Brinkley. A Long Beach doctor I had become friendly with invited me to lunch and poured out a story full of outrage and indignation. He had encountered a woman who had a young daughter suffering from epilepsy. On the advice of one of her neighbors, the doctor said, the woman had taken the girl to Dr. Brinkley's establishment, where she had been treated for several months, until the mother's money ran out. The treatment had consisted of giving the epileptic girl a series of daily colonic irrigations.

I told the doctor I had never heard of a physician treating epilepsy with enemas.

"Dr. Brinkley isn't a physician," the doctor said. "He's a chiropractor."

I said that I didn't know that chiropractors treated epilepsy, that in the Middle West they gave people spinal adjustments for backaches.

"In California they do a lot of things they don't do anywhere else," said the doctor. "Out here they can treat you for anything, just so long as they don't perform surgery or prescribe pharmaceutical drugs."

He told me how this had come about. In most states, medicine and chiropractic coexisted uneasily under separate licensing laws passed by legislatures, where the state medical associations had considerable political clout. As a result, chiropractors were usually severely restricted. But in California, the chiropractors had executed an end run around both the legislature and the California Medical Association. They had employed the referendum process, written their own chiropractic law, and enacted it by statewide popular vote. This was the same process that Howard Jarvis, years later, utilized in passing his drastic tax-cutting Proposition 13. Such laws cannot be amended by the legislature, but only by another statewide popular vote. The chiropractors had written the most permissive practice act in the United States, and set it in concrete where the medical-dominated legislature couldn't touch it.

The law explained Dr. Brinkley's ubiquitous billboards and newspaper ads, the doctor said. Their code not only permitted chiropractors to advertise, it encouraged them. It also explained how Dr. Brinkley could treat epilepsy with a series of enemas.

"He could treat a case of acute appendicitis by soaking his patient's feet in chicken-noodle soup," said my medical friend. "And I mean that literally."

I found all this fascinating. But aware that medical men look on chiropractors much the way a bulldog views an alley cat, I thought it prudent to check my friend's apoplectic complaints. I got a copy of the chiropractic act, and it was as loose as an old shoe. It authorized licensees "to use all necessary mechanical, and hygienic and sanitary measures incident to the care of the body," but didn't define any of these "measures." It did not even require a chiropractor to spell out that he was a chiropractor. He could advertise himself as a "doctor" so long as he put the initials D.C. after his name. The D.C. stood for "Doctor of Chiropractic," but if the patient didn't know this, that was the patient's problem.

The code had attracted to California the densest concentration of chiropractors in the United States. In 1951, there were 5,306 of them in the Golden State, roughly one-fourth of the world's supply. Their ranks were policed by only two inspectors from the autonomous California Board of Chiropractic Examiners. I interviewed the inspector assigned to the 4,000 chiropractors in Southern California. He was a mild-mannered fellow who volunteered that he was "a real bug on cleanliness" and that "we have the cleanest chiropractic offices" in the country. He said he inspected about twenty offices a week. At that rate, he got around to each chiropractor once every four years.

I talked to the woman with the epileptic young daughter. She was a department store clerk, and had spent all her meager savings on Dr. Brinkley and his proven method. When her money was gone, she had unsuccessfully tried to kill her daughter and herself. "I know now that I was foolish," she told me. "But I was desperate when my neighbor showed me that ad, and I grabbed at a straw."

My medical friend had been right about the latitude chiropractors had in what they could do. I came upon a court case involving a Hollywood woman chiropractor. She operated a little black box that she claimed could broadcast cures to patients anywhere in the world. All she needed was a drop of blood from the patient, which provided the right wavelength to send the healing radiotherapy waves to the right person at the right place, a sort of inverse laser beam that would zap you into health. The box was also capable, she claimed, of diagnosing distant patients. Someone in Florida could mail her a drop of blood on a blotter, and the machine would determine what ailed him and shoot the cure across the continent without the patient's ever leaving home. Her trial produced some bizarre testimony, including that of a cynic who had sent the healer some blood from a male dog. Her diagnosis was that the patient was afflicted with cancer of the womb. The case against this lady Merlin had been filed not by California authorities, but in federal court under the Pure Food and Drug Act, on a charge of selling the magical black box in interstate trade. After her conviction, she was free to continue broadcasting cures from Hollywood to male dogs with malignant wombs.

Given the huge volume of Dr. Brinkley's practice and his peculiar treatment for epilepsy, I suggested to the managing editor of the *Press-Telegram* that I research the place in a newspaper series. He asked how long it would take me, and I estimated two or three weeks. He said that was too much time and money for one story. He was a native Californian and accustomed to offbeat healers, the way outback Australians are accustomed to kangaroos.

I took the idea over to the West Coast office of *Life* magazine. The station chief there, who had a Boston accent, thought Dr. Brinkley might make a good story, checked it with New York, and gave me a provisional go-ahead. Since it was my first try at magazine writing, I would have to do it on speculation. If it made print, $2,000; nothing if I struck out. When I left the office, I did a couple of euphoric entrechats and set off to look into Dr. Brinkley and his proven method. On assignment for *Life,* no less.

I expected that the prestige of *Life* would open up the Brinkley establishment like a can-opener. I would tell Dr. Brinkley that *Life* was interested in doing a major article about his prosperous establishment—which was literally true—and I'd be given the Class A grand tour and maybe even a free trial treatment. I was dead wrong.

I presented myself at Dr. Brinkley's on the morning of my next day off from the *Press-Telegram*. The offices, on the second floor at 355 South Broadway, looked like a large clinic or the wing of an exceptionally busy hospital. Doctors and nurses in crisp white uniforms bustled about and everything was spotlessly clean and businesslike. Off to one side, in a bottle-lined room marked "Laboratory," a bespectacled technician poured a liquid into a test-tube and studied it against the light. Now and then a call box clicked on, summoning some doctor. Soothing music wafted throughout the busy place from a hidden record player.

A smiling receptionist asked if she could help me. I told her I was a writer on assignment from *Life* magazine and would like to talk to Dr. Brinkley. If the doctor was not available, I would like to talk to his secretary and make an appointment.

The receptionist, instead of appearing pleased, looked uneasy. She said I would have to talk to Mr. John Osborne. "He's our director of advertising," she explained, "and handles these things."

I said that *Life* was not trying to get Dr. Brinkley to advertise in its magazine and that I was a *writer*. She said she understood that, but I would still have to talk to Mr. Osborne. She picked up her phone, cupped the mouthpiece, and spoke briefly in a low voice. She told me to follow her, led me to an office marked "Advertising Director," and introduced me to John Osborne.

It was a one-man office, without a secretary, but with a squawk box tied into the office call system. John Osborne did not rise to greet me, or invite me to sit down. He was a chunky, one-armed man in his fifties, with an empty right coat sleeve. He had an impassive face and very cold blue eyes. He asked me, brusquely, what it was that I wanted, and he did not smile. I knew I was in trouble.

I told him I was a writer on assignment from *Life* magazine, and that I wanted to arrange an interview with Dr. Brinkley.

He asked why *Life* was interested in Dr. Brinkley. He was a man who got to essentials quickly.

I told him that *Life* had learned that Dr. Brinkley had one of the busiest practices in the nation, that this was an achievement of considerable magnitude, and that we would like to recount the how and why of his success. Put that way, it sounded good and, more-over, was the truth.

John Osborne looked at me with his cold eyes and I had a distinct feeling that he wanted to spit.

"We don't want any articles in *Life* magazine," said Osborne.

In the forlorn hope that he did not know the difference between a magazine article and magazine advertising, I explained that this would not cost anything and all I wanted was to interview Dr. Lynn Brinkley.

"Dr. Brinkley isn't going to talk to you," said John Osborne. "Now I have to get back to work."

Five minutes after I had walked into the Brinkley office, I was back out on the street, stonewalled, but with my curiosity aboil. Who was John Osborne and why was he so mean to a writer from *Life?* This was Los Angeles, where *Life* had awesome clout. If Lynn Brinkley had been an actor or a studio executive, we would be purring on our way in a chauffeured limousine to the Polo Lounge, with John Osborne on the phone fetching in the girls. How could an advertising director be so certain that his boss wouldn't talk to a *Life* writer? Why didn't the receptionist put me through to Dr. Brinkley in the first place?

I retreated to a nearby coffee shop and contemplated. On the receptionist's desk there had been a printed notice about the new office hours. To serve its "growing number of clients," the doctor's office had extended its hours to 9:00 P.M. Monday through Saturday. Since John Osborne had spurned me as a *Life* writer, I would look the place over in the role of a patient. Only the morning receptionist and Osborne could recognize me, so I would come in, wan and ailing, on the evening shift.

Dr. Brinkley's billboards made a strong pitch for BAD HEART victims, so I would have a bad heart. But first I would establish clinically that I had a good heart. I went to a heart specialist and had a full battery of tests, including an electrocardiogram. The doctor gave me the medical equivalent of an A-plus, and to this day I have never suffered any cardiac problems.

The second time around, I went to Dr. Brinkley's early in the evening and looked it over from the entrance. There was a new receptionist, and John Osborne's office was dark. I went in with a melancholy mien, told the receptionist that I had read Dr. Brinkley's ad about heart trouble and wanted help. She sent me over to a friendly nurse who took a quick history. Just in case John Osborne had red-flagged my name, I gave the name and address of a Long Beach neighbor and complained of pain in my chest and irregular heartbeat.

The nurse took me back to a dressing cubicle and told me to take my clothes off and put on a hospital gown. Then she led me to the Heart Department, where a fellow strapped something on my arm and punched a button on a machine. "This is the Heartometer," he explained. "It records the functioning of your heart." "Oh," I said. Whatever the Heartometer did, it did it in about thirty seconds.

The nurse took my heart graph and led me to a darkened room and introduced me to a handsome doctor of about forty, with a touch of gray at his temples. I asked hopefully if he was Dr. Brinkley, but no luck. He was Dr. Mulroney, "an associate," and he was going to give me "a head-to-toe examination." He positioned me against a fluoroscope screen and scanned me with the view-plate. I did not get the full head-to-toe examination, because when he reached my abdomen he made a sound of dismay and called the nurse.

"Look," he told her, "you can see it even without the barium."

Whatever it was, the nurse said she could see it too.

"Good thing we caught this when we did," said the doctor. "Take him in and put him on the table. I'll be right in."

He sounded as if he was going to perform emergency surgery, and the table she helped me onto had some odd technical equipment. I lay there, reassuring myself that they could not legally cut me open. The doctor came in and told me to lie on my right side and relax.

"This is our Dierker table," he explained. "You have a severe intestinal impaction that is affecting your heart, and I'm now going to start the reduction process." With that he inserted a tube in my behind and turned on the water. And left it on.

I have been, all my life, a—well—regular fellow, and only once had I had an enema. This was different, a sort of Niagara Falls. It went on and on. I distracted myself by telling myself little jokes. *This is what an editor means by getting to the bottom of a story. They call this in-depth reporting.*

The doctor finally turned off the sluice. I asked him a plaintive question. Why he was treating my bad heart in such a roundabout manner?

He smiled patiently and said he would explain. My intestines were in dreadful shape and swollen way out of the ordinary. This condition had affected my liver, also, which was "like a sponge and much too large."

"All this has displaced your stomach upward, so that it presses on the diaphragm," the doctor recited rapidly. "That in turn pushes against your heart, squashing it out of its normal position."

He took out a pen and drew me a quick, crude sketch of my skewed interior. His drawing showed my heart arteries, which he labeled "heart arteries," with kinks in them, like a twisted garden hose. Anyone who has ever watered a lawn could understand a kinked heart artery.

He showed me my graph from the Heartometer. "You can see from your graph how this has affected you," he said. "Your heart is laboring under unnatural conditions. With the blood flow reduced, it is beating much too fast and the valves are no longer closing properly. Your heart is going BANG, BANG, BANG and rapidly wearing itself out."

I looked at my Heartometer reading. It was a piece of paper with some squiggles on it. I said, "Gee."

"Don't you be upset," said the doctor. "We've handled thousands of cases like yours. This is one of the things that Dr. Brinkley's treatment does best. We correct the intestinal condition and the heart automatically and quickly returns to normal. We just assist Mother Nature and Mother Nature doesn't make mistakes."

When I had dressed, he sat me down at his desk and tried to sign me up for a month of daily colonics for $400. After that, he thought everything would be fine if I would just come in periodically "so this terrible condition will never build up again." He said the treatment would also include a daily session on the "Battle Creek Health Builder."

I thanked him for saving my life, but side-stepped signing the contract. I had to explain things to my wife, who managed our finances, and I'd be back the next day.

"Well, okay, if that's how you have to handle it," he said. "But be sure you come back in tomorrow. I've left the treatment fluids in your colon and we'll have to take care of that without fail."

I wanted to ask if he had put a cork in me, but I didn't want to inject any levity into our doctor-patient relationship. I paid him the three dollars for my trial treatment, and he gave me a booklet entitled *The True Cause of Disease*, which he advised me to read.

Dr. Brinkley gave you a lot for that initial trial treatment. I had got a Heartometer reading, a fluoroscopic examination, an instant diagnosis, a session on the Dierker table, all that tap water, and a free booklet. What was most impressive was how fast they ran you through. Unlike most medical offices, where you made an appointment with the doctor at 2:00 P.M. and sat around reading back issues of the *National Geographic* until 3:30, at Dr. Brinkley's you could walk in off the street and they would service you as efficiently as a well-run carwash.

On the way out, I asked the nurse to show me the Battle Creek Health Builder. It was one of those reducing machines, with a belt that you put across your middle, that shimmies you vigorously when you flip the switch.

The True Cause of Disease explained the proven method in 120 pages of simple language that anyone could understand.

"There is only one cause for disease," it asserted. "This may sound strange, for the majority of people imagine that there is a different and specific cause for every ailment, and physicians generally do not combat this opinion. But as a matter of fact, there is only one disease, although its manifestations are various . . . and that is the retention of waste matters in the system.

"The presence of a grain of sand in a watch will retard its movements," the booklet went on. "What, then, must be the result of an accumulation of impurities in the human system? . . . Here, in a nutshell, lies the secret of disease."

To restore health, one needed only to flush out the internal swamp and then keep it flushed out. This would enable the body's natural healing processes to swat hostile microbes and germs before they established a beachhead. There was one exception. Dr. Brinkley warned that he did not treat cancer once it had bloomed into malignancy, although any tendency toward cancer could be fended off "by colon hygiene."

Patients were sternly warned against relying on the medical profession when stricken. It quoted an array of "eminent authorities" and "noted practitioners" to the effect that physicians, surgeons, and pharmaceutical drugs were the enemies of true health. "All medicines are poisonous," said one. Another, identified only as a Dr. Ramage of London, declared, "I fearlessly assert that in most cases the sufferer would be safer without a physician than with one." A Dr. Frank charged that "thousands are annually slaughtered in the quiet of the sickroom" and called on all governments to "banish medical men." The most sweeping charge was leveled by someone named John Mason Good, identified as the author of *A System of Nosology*. The eminent nosologist said the medical profession had "destroyed more lives than war, pestilence, and famine combined."

The booklet acknowledged that colonic irrigation as a cure-all was not an original discovery by Dr. Brinkley. He credited Charles A. Tyrell of New York. It required a full day of archaeological research at the Los Angeles library to exhume Dr. Tyrell. He was a peddler of nostrums, born over a century ago, who had acquired a degree late in life from something called the Eclectic Medical College in New York, now long defunct. Along with the true cause of disease, he had promoted the Ideal Sight Restorer "for near sight, far sight, old sight, astigmatism, cataracts, glaucome, cross-eye and paralytic blindness." It consisted of a rubber cup, like a miniature plumber's plunger, for producing a vacuum over the eyeball.

By his own account, Dr. Tyrell had not been the Columbus of colonic irrigation. He attributed the discovery to the ancient Egyptians, who in turn had picked it up from observing a bird called the Ibis, a species of snipe.

"The Ibis was observed, by the earliest naturalists, to suck up the water of the Nile river and, using its long bill for a syringe, inject it into its anus," Tyrell wrote. "Pliny says this . . . first suggested colonic irrigation to the ancient Egyptian doctors, known to be the first medical practitioners of any nation."

To research the invisible and inaccessible Dr. Lynn Brinkley (D.C.), I had to rely upon the records of the Board of Chiropractic Examiners and some legwork. He had been born in Little Rock, Arkansas, in 1906, and from 1929 to 1944 had worked as a Huntington Beach fireman. When the job of fire chief became vacant and he was passed over for it, he decided to switch occupations. He enrolled at the Los Angeles Chiropractic College on September 16, 1943, and emerged less than three years later as a full doctor of chiropractic, although such a degree normally required four years of study. The college recorder explained that Brinkley had cut this almost in half by carrying a heavy course load and attending summer classes. He had adjusted vertebrae for two years in Long Beach, and then the golden door of opportunity had swung open for him at 355 South Broadway in Los Angeles. And the man who had opened it was John Rothery Osborne, a.k.a. "Solo Wing."

Just as the Egyptian ibis, not Charles Tyrell, had discovered the cure-all qualities of colonic irrigation, it had been John Osborne, not "Bad Heart" Brinkley, who had discovered Charles Tyrell and his true cause of disease. According to the files of the State Board of Medical Examiners, Osborne had opened his cure-all mill in Los Angeles in 1945, using a worthless "naturopathic physician" certificate from a Texas diploma mill. In the three years before the medical examiners caught up with him, he had billed himself as Dr. Osborne and treated some 30,000 ailing Angelenos. Although he conceded that he did not know the symptoms of erysipelas from those of measles, he protested that he was simply providing "the oldest treatment known to man." Arraigned on five counts of practicing medicine without a license, he agreed to get out of the healing business, and plea-bargained to a single count of guilty and a $200 fine. He would dispose of his business, he told the judge, and "will not be in a position wherein I could even come in contact with the public. The offense I am charged with here could thus never be repeated."

He had then struck a deal with chiropractor Brinkley and returned to the colonics mill as advertising director. Although he had promised to get out of the cure-all business, he had said nothing about the cure-all *advertising* business. Under his watchful eye and using the same ad that had built his prosperous practice, the establishment had continued with the holistic discoveries of the Egyptian ibis, with one significant change. It was now protected by the Gardol shield of Dr. Brinkley's chiropractic license. By the time I came in with my kinked arteries, the place had treated 400,000 patients.

I made a trip up to Sacramento, where I learned that there had been an extensive assembly investigation of the Osborne-Brinkley operation. It had gone unreported in the press, which seemed odd, given the nature of the testimony.

One former Brinkley staff member, Dr. Leo Calloway (D.C.), testified that Brinkley was a front for Osborne. "He (Osborne) said that it would be very little trouble to get rid of Brinkley," Calloway said. "All he would have to do was take a twenty-minute walk around the block and see a lawyer and cancel Brinkley's contract. He said that he had been against the wall before, and had perfected his means of operation . . ."

He testified that Brinkley instructed his doctors to find colonic problems in all patients, to find that their blood pressure was either too high or too low, that after the first series of irrigations, "as a matter of standard policy, the patient was told that he had made progress, that he was not completely well, and that he needed another series of treatments." Continued treatments were to be prescribed whether the doctor believed the patient needed them or not. "No patient was ever discharged," Calloway testified. A second staff member, who said he was briefed by "Solo Wing" Osborne, supported these charges.

"This is a racket," said Calloway, who had quit the Brinkley operation in revulsion. "Those people are brought in and they are pounced upon from the minute they enter. The vultures leap at them. The doctor comes in and grabs the large colon. If there is nothing wrong with it he says it is impacted and they are going to die if they don't get it corrected."

In Los Angeles, I interviewed public health officers and staff doctors at County General Hospital. They told me there were instances of former Brinkley patients turning up with untreated tuberculosis and other contagious diseases. County General also got many Brinkley patients as charity cases after Brinkley had pumped their bank accounts dry.

Since John Osborne was the true rediscoverer of the true cause of disease and the pioneer of its renaissance in the Golden State, I trudged off on this new lead. The adroit manner in which he had snookered the Board of Medical Examiners had the aura of experience, so I visited the L.A. police bunco squad. They had a thick file on "Solo Wing." His career as a self-appointed healer was just the latest chapter in a lifetime of flimflam.

He had come to California in the twenties, when he was seventeen, drifted from job to job, sold real estate and used cars, and lost his arm while working briefly for the Santa Fe Railroad. He had discovered his true talent, as a promoter, at the age of thirty-two, when he had served as impresario of an imaginative venture that became known as The Affair of the Double-Decker Cemetery.

With only $5,000 in capital, he had acquired an option to buy a rundown sixty-five-acre orchard in the San Fernando Valley, just over the hills from the expanding city of Los Angeles. He had made a $1,000 down payment, with the remaining $64,000 due in four months. He rechristened the old orchard "Valhalla Cemetery," divided it into 70,000 burial plots and projected a lavish resting place with a great marble arch, statuary, fountains, and winding walks, a conceptual forerunner—all on paper—of the famed Forest Lawn of today.

He poured his remaining $4,000 into newspaper ads and a sales crew. The selling of cemetery lots is normally a low-pressure operation, but Osborne, faced with raising $64,000 in four months, had no time for such restraint. He devised a sales pitch aimed, not at a bargain for the Hereafter, but for a fast buck in the Now. Los Angeles was growing rapidly, his story went, and was desperately in need of cemetery space. A shrewd investor could get in on the ground floor at Valhalla, buy ten, twenty, or more burial plots, and clean up by reselling them to bereaved families with a body on their hands and no place to put it. Profits as high as 400 percent were in the offing within a year. Angelenos came running, seized with a fever for speculating in burial plots. Osborne paid off the orchard owner and expanded his sales crew until they were holding their rallies in an auditorium. He was so busy raking in the money that he had no time to build the great marble arch, the fountains, and so on. Then he ran out of cemetery plots, and began selling the same ones over and over. The project inevitably collapsed. Osborne was indicted by a federal grand jury for using the mails to defraud, sentenced to ten years in Leavenworth, and imprisoned on December 1, 1927. It took a brigade of accountants several years to unscramble the tangle. They discovered that he had sold the same cemetery plot to as many as six people and had even sold the site of the unbuilt marble arch. The cemetery eventually was developed by more sober entrepreneurs and today, under the same name, is a respectable burial ground, ranking with Forest Lawn.

Osborne conducted himself as a model prisoner and was released after three and a half years. He returned to Los Angeles, went into the numbers racket, and then organized the biggest bookie joint west of the Mississippi River. He ran it for several years with the help of a deputy sheriff, who would tip Osborne on upcoming raids. When the sheriff's office caught onto this, the deputy was indicted on sixty-one counts of accepting bribes from a bookmaker. In exchange for immunity, Osborne turned state's witness and testified against the officer, whose attorney excoriated Osborne as "an ex-convict, stool pigeon, and bookmaker." In the end, everyone walked away unscathed. Osborne then attached himself to a civic reform movement as an experienced authority on civic corruption. When the ticket won, they had no further use for him and he cast about for a new line of work. It was at this point that he encountered the writings of Charles Tyrell and went into the healing business until his arrest swept him to his rendezvous with ex-fireman Lynn Brinkley.

Putting all this together, on my days off, took four months. The West Coast editor of *Life* liked the article, but the New York office thought things over for a month and then "reluctantly" turned it down. They explained that it had limited picture possibilities, and given what went on at the busy colonics mill, they had a point.

This setback, however, turned out to be a disguised blessing that liberated me from the newspaper business. I took the manuscript to Dick Mathison, editor of the California newsmagazine *Fortnight*. Mathison bought it and put it on the cover. The California Medical Association reprinted it as a pamphlet and blanketed the state with it. *True* magazine saw a copy and commissioned me to do a long profile of "Solo Wing" Osborne. The NBC radio network, assembling an hour documentary on U.S. quacks, hired me to do a fifteen-minute segment on Dr. Brinkley's proven method, and flew me to New York to write and narrate it. This in turn caught the attention of *Cosmopolitan* magazine, which assigned me to explore the operation of a Colorado chiropractor who claimed to cure cancer.

The *Fortnight* article and its reprint brought a surprising number of complimentary letters from chiropractors. To conventional spine-adjusters, Brinkley's garish ads and unrestrained claims were an embarrassment and ammunition for their medical critics. "I hope you shut off his water," one wrote. Nothing happened to him legally, because what he was doing was well within the elastic limits of California's peculiar law. But with the magazine and network attention I gave him, he began to encounter difficulty in recruiting "associates," and after a while the place dried up and blew away.

Dick Mathison, who later became bureau chief for *Newsweek* and a prolific book-writer, delighted in telling people how he had bought my first article and started me as a magazine writer. He told how I had wound up on the Dierker table and the doctor had warned me to come back because he had left all that water in me.

"It was a weird story, but I knew that it was true," Mathison said. "When he came in with his manuscript, he gurgled when he walked."

4

The Subterranean Lobbyists

"Long Beach and its oil money is like a rich fat boy wandering through the slums with a big bag of candy," Herman "Hank" Ridder, a Long Beach newspaper publisher, complained. "The Supreme Court took away half of the money and now we may lose the rest of it. This time we don't even know who is trying to mug us. There's a new organization that calls itself the California Tidelands Protective Association, pushing a bill in Sacramento to take all the city's oil revenue and give it to the state. It has no dues or other visible sources of money. It's a well-financed, professional operation and we don't even know who is bankrolling it. That's why I called you. I want you to find out."

We were sitting on the patio of Ridder's handsome French Regency house overlooking a country club. Two years earlier I had quit his newspapers without ever having met him. Until he had telephoned me that afternoon, I wasn't aware that he knew I existed. He was a tall, elegantly dressed man in his late forties, with an urbane air that comes from a moneyed background and an Ivy League education.

He had come out to California in 1952 and cut a wide swath through the newspaper industry, buying up and merging competing newspapers in Long Beach, Pasadena, and San Jose for his family's national newspaper chain. He had then settled in as the publisher of the Long Beach newspapers, the *Press-Telegram* and the *Independent*. I had been swept up in the merger there and thrust under a new editorial management that I didn't get along with. At the age of forty-one, with a wife, two young daughters, a dog, and two cats, I had quit and gone free-lancing for magazines. I was keeping busy, had doubled my newspaper salary, and was delighted with and fiercely attached to my new independence. When Ridder had telephoned me and invited me out to his home, I had gone out of curiosity.

I told him that I appreciated his offer, but that I had quit his paper and had no wish to go back to work for it. He brushed aside my objections and set about changing my mind. He warmed me up with some flattery and punched my competitive buttons. He told me that he'd had his news staff work on this matter for a month, and that they had got nowhere.

"I need someone who can think for himself and work on his own. If you take this on, you'd be working for me, not the news department, and you'd find that somewhat different.

"I don't normally intervene with the news operation," he went on, "but this is more than just a news story. If the city loses the rest of its oil money, it will be an economic disaster that will have a serious effect on our newspapers. So I have a personal stake in what's going on, and I want to be up front with it. On the other hand, there is a matter of principle involved that I hoped would interest you. I strongly disapprove of a false-front organization trying to influence legislation while concealing its motives and its financing."

He sipped on a large beaker of Scotch. "You know, I used to be a reporter myself, a long time ago, and I enjoyed it. There are times, believe it or not, that I miss it.

"Before you give me your answer, let me tell you a couple of things. I've got my back up on this, and I'm committed. You'll be well paid. You'll have only this one assignment, and whatever time you need. And whatever money. You'd have an unlimited expense account."

In fifteen years in the newspaper business, no one had ever said that to me. I had never even *heard* of any reporter who had an unlimited expense account.

I asked him when he wanted me to go to work.

"How about right now?" he said.

We negotiated a salary without any haggling, and he got up and shook my hand. The entire conversation had taken about fifteen minutes, and two years after I had quit the *Press-Telegram* forever, I went back to work for its publisher.

"I'm leaving tomorrow for a vacation in the Caribbean," Ridder said. "Go down to the paper and draw whatever money you need to get started. I'll arrange things with the business manager so there will be no problems." Then he walked me out to my Plymouth, which was parked next to his Bentley.

The next day I went to the newspaper and drew $3,000. When I had quit, in 1953, I had been making Guild scale of $138 a week. The business manager did not tell me he was happy to have me back aboard. And when he counted out the money—twice—he looked like a sullen bear with a sore paw.

Long Beach and its tidelands oil was a story of geological serendipity and an unintentional blunder by the state legislature. Eons ago, Providence had deposited a huge subterranean lake of oil under the beach front of Long Beach. In 1911, not knowing that the tidelands contained an enormous petroleum fortune, the state legislature had granted them to Long Beach. The gift was made under a state program to encourage the construction, by selected cities, of local harbors along the coast.

In the ensuing years, Long Beach had a slow, almost somnolent growth, unaware of the riches under its civic mattress. The city had a pleasant site, with a magnificent stretch of white beach, palm trees galore, and a climate so mild that snow has fallen only four times this century. In its early years, it had no industry. Because there was nothing much to do there—and because it was a pleasant place to do nothing—it became a little mecca for retired Midwesterners fleeing winter. Before World War II, they migrated in such numbers that some anonymous wit pinned Long Beach with the enduring nickname of "Des Moines-by-the-Sea."

After receiving its tidelands grant, Long Beach set out dutifully to construct a small harbor. It had little money for the project, and the work proceeded slowly on a modest scale.

Then, in 1941, a wildcat driller thrust his steel straw down on the ocean front and into the underground lake of oil. Drilling crews poured into town, and overnight Des Moines-by-the-Sea found itself converted into a West Coast Saudi Arabia. The delighted city fathers commissioned a geological survey and learned that the legislature had given Long Beach what was then the greatest proven oil reservoir in the nation. It contained—by niggardly pre-OPEC pricing—more than two billion dollars' worth of oil.

The city scrapped its plans for a little harbor and went happily to work on a port to match its new-found wealth. It built a great man-made island, breakwaters, docks, warehouses, bridges, all financed with the tidelands oil money. On the filled land of Terminal Island, new wells were sunk, increasing the flow of oil and money. The Navy Department moved in and built its own shipyard, with the largest repair drydock on the West Coast. Long Beach wound up with one of the biggest and busiest harbors in the world.

But when the port was finished and flourishing, the oil money kept flowing in and the city, like the Sorcerer's Apprentice, couldn't keep up with the flood. As one envious official at the adjoining Los Angeles harbor complained, "They did everything at the Port of Long Beach except gold-plate the piers."

The incoming tide of money posed a peculiar problem for the city because of a restriction in the original tidelands grant. By the terms of the grant, the tidelands could be used only for commerce, navigation, and fisheries which benefited the state as a whole—and a court had ruled that the same restriction applied to the oil revenue. With its coffers overflowing with money, the city was forbidden to use any of it for local purposes, such as repairing streets or building hospitals or schools or parks. To make things worse, the city had to dig down into its own funds to provide schools and civic services for the thousands of new workers brought in by the harbor, the Navy shipyard, and the oil industry. Local taxes went up, the retired farmers complained and voted against bond issues, and the city took on a shabby, run-down look. Meanwhile, hundreds of millions of dollars piled up in the tidelands oil account.

Then a new problem developed. As the oil was pumped out of the tidelands, the city began to sink. Oil deposits usually occur under firm geological structures, but the tidelands were like a great layer of sand over the underground lake of oil, and when the oil was taken out, the land above it went down. At the center of the oil field, the surface eventually sank more than forty feet at the deepest point in a great bowl of subsidence. The Long Beach Naval Shipyard tilted, water mains occasionally snapped, and the downtown business streets sprouted cracks. Des Moines-by-the-Sea, which had been rechristened "The City with Too Much Money," became known nationally as "The Sinking City."

In consultation with their legal advisers and the two Long Beach state assemblymen, the city fathers arrived at what they thought was a solution, but proved a disaster. They drafted new legislation revising the tidelands grant. The bill declared that one-half of the tidelands oil revenue was not needed or spendable for the original purposes—promotion of navigation, commerce, fisheries—and was freed from the state restriction. The assumption of those who drafted the bill was that the oil money thus freed would become the property of Long Beach to use as it wished. The bill sailed through the legislature with surprising ease, but then was challenged in court. To the dismay of Long Beach, the Supreme Court ruled that the freed one-half of the oil money properly belonged to the original grantor, the state, and not the grantee, Long Beach.

From a detached view, the court decision had a certain comedic irony about it. The city had acquired its oil fortune by an unintentional act of charity by the state, and had now given away half the money by a similar blunder. But with half of its fortune evaporated and its port and business area sinking, Long Beach did not take a detached view of this irony. Cries of outrage and anguish rent the air, the city official who had drafted the disastrous legislation committed suicide in despair, and some civic hot-heads talked bitterly about seceding from the state of California.

By ruling that any "surplus" oil revenue reverted to the state, the court opened a whole new Pandora's box. All the legislature had to do to recover the rest of the unintended oil gift to Long Beach was pass another bill declaring the remaining oil income "excess." Into the legislative hopper went such a bill, and out of nowhere the California Tidelands Protective Association had sprung full-blown into being to promote the bill's passage.

In view of this convoluted history, I had no strong partisan opinions about who was the true and rightful owner of this oil fortune. What intrigued me was who was hiding behind the trees and covertly bankrolling the Protective Association. I read their pamphlets, which bore such titles as "The Long Beach Story and Your Pocket Book," and "Long Beach Has Its Hand in Your Pocket." They seemed excessively righteous for an organization that insisted on hiding its own pocketbook.

So I converted the first $3,000 of the *Press-Telegram*'s money into traveler's checks, and drove north to Sacramento to tilt a lance against the invisible dragons.

Ridder's news staff had compiled a thin folder on the California Tidelands Protective Association. Its state chairman was a San Diego man named Charles Forward, and the secretary was a Vincent Garrod from Saratoga. Neither was very active in the CTPA, the report said. The workhorses were three professional public relations men spotted around the state: one in the north at San Francisco, one for central California, at Fresno, and a third in Fallbrook, for southern California. Their campaign was tailored to obtain passage of an assembly bill written by Bruce Allen of San Jose, which would take Long Beach's remaining half of the tidelands oil money and put it in the state general fund. Allen, the report said, was a bright young legislator with a good record and no known connections with any oil interests. The association was busy lining up support for his bill from newspapers, envious cities, and farm organizations. The CTPA pitch was simple and effective: Long Beach had too much money and didn't need it, and the rest of the state did. It had recruited strong support for the bill among farmers, particularly in the water-short Central Valley and the south, who had been clamoring for years for a comprehensive project to irrigate the southern half of the state with water from the north, which had far more than it needed. Chief roadblock to the water project was money, and the CTPA solution was to take the money from Long Beach. The alternative was higher taxes, and most of the state was balefully closing in on the rich fat boy with the big bag of candy.

On the way north, I talked to some farm association officials the CTPA had lined up. None of them knew who was financing the association and the question didn't bother them. But they confirmed that they had been asked only for moral support, not for any money.

In Sacramento, I put in at the Senator Hotel and wasted a month or so trying to learn what oil interests would be most likely to profit from enactment of the Allen bill. It was a line of research for which I was poorly equipped; big business has always baffled me, and the politics of oil was incomprehensibly Byzantine. I concluded that the oil industry was made up of sovereign forces that behave like the great powers described in George Orwell's *1984*. A and B team up against C one year; then their economic interests change and B and C combine against A, or they all go it alone against one another.

Two oil companies could be bitter rivals in one oil field and loyal partners in another, or they would battle over a field for years and then reach an accommodation and join forces.

I gave up and decided to work backwards. Instead of trying to deduce who would profit from the CTPA's project, I'd start with the CTPA and try to backtrack to its Daddy Warbucks.

In the state capital, where political sophistication was more sensitive than among downstate farmers, the question of who was bankrolling the CTPA aroused more interest. Money is the mother's milk of politics, and among the legislators, lobbyists, and state officials the well-financed campaign to pass the Allen bill was the subject of considerable curiosity. The curiosity was heightened when a search of the state records disclosed that the CTPA had not been incorporated. It had just materialized with money for which there was no overt source.

None of the CTPA names rang any political bells among the pols until I talked to an old cow-county senator. He knew Vince Garrod, the CTPA secretary.

"He's former president of the California Farmers Inc., and does some lobbying for the Apricot and Prune-Growers Association," the senator told me. "Comes up here each session to keep his eye on farm bills. Fine old boy and a real straight arrow. He stays at the Senator Hotel."

I telephoned Garrod, told him I was a Long Beach newspaperman, and made a date for dinner. He was a pleasant, blunt, weather-beaten native Californian, and he talked like a man without guile. He said he couldn't tell me who was financing the CTPA because no one had told him and he hadn't asked.

He said he had been recruited as secretary by the CTPA public relations agent in San Francisco, James Friedman. "They wanted to open up the issue of all that Long Beach money and wanted to use my name," he said. "They told me Long Beach had more money than they needed and the state could use it. The farmers need a water project, and that's my only interest."

I asked what he knew about Friedman.

Garrod said he hadn't known Friedman. "He was sent to me by a San Francisco lawyer named Neil Cunningham. I've known Cunningham for years."

What did Cunningham have to do with the CTPA?

"I don't know," said Garrod. "But Neil wouldn't put me into anything that wasn't OK."

I asked if it bothered him to lend his name to an organization that concealed its source of money. He thought about that. "When you put it that way, it bothers me. You got any idea who is backing this outfit?"

I told him I didn't know and couldn't find out. "I'll be frank with you. That's all that bothers me and that's all I'm interested in, personally. What Long Beach and the legislature do about the tidelands oil money is something they can work out. But the Protective Association has an odd smell. If they're just trying to help the farmers, why the cloak-and-dagger business about where their money is coming from?"

Garrod agreed that didn't make much sense.

"Maybe they're after something else, and are using you and the other people who want a water project," I said.

Garrod said that he wouldn't like that, and asked me to let him know if I found out where the CTPA money was coming from.

I told him I was going to San Francisco to talk to Friedman, and asked if he minded if I told him about our dinner conversation.

"Hell, no, I don't mind," said Garrod.

I drove down to San Francisco, put in at the St. Francis, and ran into Dick Mathison, editor of *Fortnight* magazine, in town to talk to some San Francisco writers. He asked what I was doing, and I gave him a short summary. He offered me condolences. "We got into a Los Angeles oil story once and almost went broke," he said. "You've got a better chance of finding out who killed Bugsy Siegel. I'm glad you're not doing this story on speculation."

The next day I telephoned Friedman, told him why I wanted to see him, and asked for an appointment. He said he didn't think he could do anything for me, but that I could come over to his office in the DeYoung Building.

He was a bright professional publicist, courteous and nonresponsive. "I'm a PR man doing a job, and you're a newsman doing a job, and our interests bump up against each other. There just isn't much I can tell you."

He said that his client "inspired the formation of the California Tidelands Protective Association" and that its primary purpose was enactment of the Allen bill. He said he wouldn't name his client because his client didn't want to be identified, and he didn't know why his client wanted to remain anonymous.

I asked how Vince Garrod had become secretary of the association. Friedman said he'd probably got into it because he was interested in the tidelands money for a water project.

"That's why he took the job" I said, "but he took it because you recruited him and he told me you looked him up because Neil Cunningham told you to."

"You've been doing some work," said Friedman.

I asked if Cunningham represented his client, and Friedman said he didn't. Then how come Cunningham was giving him names to recruit as officials of the CTPA?

"You'll have to ask Mr. Cunningham," said Friedman.

I asked for Cunningham's telephone number.

Friedman opened his desk drawer and took out a black address book. He leafed through it and then became aware that I was sitting alongside him and peering over his shoulder. He swiveled his chair so I couldn't see into his black book. He gave me a number for Cunningham and put the address book back in his desk.

I dialed Cunningham on his phone, asked him some questions, and got nothing. Lawyers never tell newspapermen anything unless it serves their purpose.

I prodded Friedman a little about his shy client. "I hope you're not working for an international oil cartel headed by a group of ex-Nazis," I said. He said he was pretty sure that he wasn't.

"So am I," I told him. "But I also have a notion you don't know who your client really is."

He said he had to get back to work, and I went back to the St. Francis, and tried to sort out the noninformation.

Cunningham intrigued me. So did Friedman's black address book. There was something in it he didn't want me to see, which had to be his client or something that would lead to his client.

I rang Dick Mathison and we went up to Vanessi's in North Beach for dinner. I told Mathison about my visit with Friedman and his nervousness about his address book. I said I thought the book had the answer to my problems.

"You've got a gleam in your eye, sport," said Mathison. "You're thinking about breaking and entering? That's against the law, in case you haven't heard."

"It's not against the law to *think* about it," I said. "I've bumped my head on so many brick walls that I've got a headache. My head feels better when I think about what's in that address book."

"There is a guy here in town," said Mathison. "He's an ex-burglar called Eddie the Cat, recently out of the can. I've been talking to a writer about doing his reminiscences. He's very good. You that desperate?"

"I don't know. It wouldn't hurt to *talk* to him."

Mathison went to make a phone call. He came back and said he would know more the next day. "Eddie is staying with a Presbyterian minister who is trying to rehabilitate him. I'll see what he says. Eddie, not the minister."

The next evening Mathison came around to the St. Francis.

"I talked to Eddie and he said it would be a piece of cake," Mathison said. "But he insisted on discussing it with the minister, because Eddie is getting religion. The minister stomped on the idea. He said he could hardly rehabilitate Eddie by okaying burglary, no matter how noble the motive."

Afterward I was glad to have been spared the decision on whether to suborn someone to perform a burglary. It firmed up a principle that I've tried to observe, that you don't break the law because someone else may be breaking the law. One feels better getting a story by legitimate means. As Hemingway once said, that thing is moral that you feel good about *after* you have done it.

A couple of weeks in San Francisco produced nothing more except a sheaf of hotel and restaurant bills. Hank Ridder came back from his vacation and flew up for a few days, and I gave him a nonprogress report. He hired a team of San Francisco detectives to pursue the thin leads I had. They charged him a bundle and produced a lot of irrelevant information. He said he was going down to San Jose to talk to Assemblyman Allen and later, in Long Beach, gave me a report on his encounter.

He said that Allen had told him he, too, didn't know who was financing the California Tidelands Protective Association, and that he wasn't interested. "I told him he ought to find out for his own self-interest, because I intended to find out. He said he had a good piece of legislation and it didn't matter who was trying to help him pass it. I suggested that would depend on who it was, and their motives," added Ridder.

I drew another chunk of his money and made a second swing

around California, talking to directors of the Protective Association. The word was out that the *Press-Telegram* had a major project going to uncover the Association's backers, and nobody wanted to talk to me. I wound up in San Diego, trying for an interview with Charles Forward, chairman of the CTPA. He was out of town, but I finally got him on the telephone.

He said the Tidelands Association, to the best of his knowledge, had been organized by Tom Dammann, the southern California public relations representative for the CTPA. He said he had no idea who was financing the organization he headed, and expressed surprise when I told him it was spending a lot of money. He said he wasn't being paid anything and conceded that the expenditures "raised an interesting question" about who was footing the bills.

I interviewed Tom Dammann. Unlike Friedman, who looked upon the CTPA as just another account, Dammann apparently viewed it as a holy cause. He denounced Long Beach's ethics, financial integrity, and their "mishandling of the tidelands trusteeship." He also took off my hide for associating with such scoundrels. I told him that at least I was out in the open and working for an employer I was not ashamed to acknowledge, and gigged him about who was paying him. "There's no secret about who is paying me," he said, indignantly. "I'm being paid by John Fleming, a Los Angeles attorney." I asked him who Fleming was representing, and he said that was Mr. Fleming's affair.

The next day I made an appointment with Fleming at his office on Wilshire Boulevard, and found that I had inched ahead from an old stone wall to a new one. Fleming, a beefy, good-natured man with a firm handshake, greeted me almost effusively. "I've been getting reports about your travels from all over the state," he said. "And I've been waiting for you to show up. I think I know what you want to ask me, but go ahead."

I asked him who was bankrolling the CTPA. I was sure he wouldn't tell me, but I had to put the question to him. He said he had some clients who did not wish to disclose their identity, and that he was bound by the lawyer-client relationship not to reveal who they were. I asked why they were purporting to act in the public interest while hiding under a rock, and he said they were afraid of "retaliation" by "powerful forces in Long Beach." I told him Long Beach thought that it was itself being retaliated against by some powerful forces. He laughed and said I was entitled to my opinion.

At any rate, he had a situation of lawyer-client confidentiality that he was bound to honor, so he couldn't help me. We sparred around a while, good-naturedly, and I went out empty-handed.

I checked out his previous clients in Martingdale's legal directory, talked to some friendly law firms in Los Angeles, and found nothing that seemed to have any connection with the oil industry.

The assignment I had thought might take me away from the magazines for a month had now stretched out to four months, and there was no light in the tunnel. I had spent more than $20,000 of Ridder's money, and it had all gone down the drain. Some of my ex-colleagues began to stick pins in me with questions about how "the big assignment" was progressing. I began to develop insomnia, and wake up at three in the morning from dreams of wandering in a maze or sinking in quicksand.

I called Hank Ridder and went out to see him at his house overlooking the golf course. I told him how much money I had spent, and how little I had accomplished. He genially chewed me out, not for wasting his money, but for worrying about it.

"You think too *small,*" he told me. "The money doesn't bother me, so stop worrying about it. If you've spent twenty thousand dollars and found out nothing, spend fifty thousand and find out. Or seventy-five thousand, or even a hundred thousand. For example, maybe you can get what we're looking for by buying someone's secretary a mink coat. So buy her a mink coat. Now go on back to work." And he gave me a locker-room whack when I left.

In less than a month, we pried open the CTPA and found the source of its money. It was an article in Max Ascoli's *The Reporter* magazine, not a mink coat, that provided the can opener.

The article, by Robert Bendiner, was entitled "The Engineering of Consent." It dealt with a false-front operation in Pennsylvania conducted by the Carl Byoir public relations firm on behalf of some high-powered trucking interests. The Byoir agency had set up a series of paper organizations to influence legislation on behalf of the truckers while concealing their identity.

I read the article shortly after Ridder had given me his pep talk. Bendiner's account struck me as a blueprint for what the California Tidelands Protective Association had under way. The article focused on the issue of secret *lobbying,* and when I read it I got a sudden prickle of excitement. I had put in months of work, and had had a blind spot in my research. California had a law regulating lobbying and lobbyists, and I hadn't even thought about looking it up.

Most states have such a law. In an old federal case, the U.S. Supreme Court ruled that anyone attempting to influence legislation "should honestly appear in their true characters" and "a hired advocate or agent assuming to act in a different character is practicing deceit on the legislature" and imposing "a direct fraud of the public."

I flew back up to Sacramento and checked with the office of Attorney General Edmund "Pat" Brown to see what California law said about lobbying. It declared that "Any person who shall engage himself for pay or for any consideration for the purpose of attempting to influence the passage or defeat of any legislation by the legislature . . . shall register with the Clerk of the Assembly and the Secretary of the Senate." It required that lobbyists file monthly financial statements listing their expenditures and the *source of their fees*.

Brown's press officer told me that the lobbyist registry was maintained by the secretary of state. I went over to that office, checked the registry, and then rechecked it. None of the three public relations men had registered, or filed any reports.

The secretary of state also kept track of incorporation records, and when I had checked months earlier, the CTPA had not filed. I looked again and found that the association had recently incorporated as a nonprofit organization. Its charter declared that the association would act on behalf of "all the people of the State of California," and named no other client or interest. It would not engage in influencing legislation *"except with respect to any legislation . . . which in any manner concerns or affects public trusts in the tidelands."*

Whistling while I worked, I pulled copies of the CTPA charter and the lobbying law and flew back to Long Beach. I wrote a long memorandum for Ridder, summarizing the lobbying law, the Tidelands Association's activities, the fact that they collected no dues, their admission that an unnamed client picked up their bills, the fact that the publicists were being paid, my conversation with Fleming, and quotes from their publications urging passage of the Allen bill.

Ridder was a man for whom one did not have to draw pictures. "Now we *have* something and now I can be of some use," he said happily. "Take some time off and let me go to work." Once I had charted a new path into the CTPA maze, I enjoyed the luxury of letting someone else do the track-down, a pleasure that rarely befell me.

The Long Beach Bar Association, shortly thereafter, addressed a request to the attorney general, charging the CTPA with violation of the state lobbying law. It asked for a formal investigation.

Pat Brown moved in on the case with admirable speed and ingenuity. I had a visit from one of his investigators, a taciturn one-time deputy sheriff from northern California. He asked me to pinpoint when the CTPA had come into being. When I told him he thanked me and went away.

A few days later I came home from playing golf and found an urgent phone message from Hank Ridder to come and see him. He was relaxing on a chaise alongside his pool, with a bottle of twenty-five-year-old Scotch.

"We've got it," he said happily, "and it's so good you won't believe it."

The attorney general's man had gone to Fleming's bank with a subpoena and looked at his bank account, in a duly authorized inquiry into the charges of lobbying violations. He found that shortly before the Protective Association had come into being, there had been a large transfer of money into the account from the Southern California Gas Company, a major private utility that serviced Los Angeles communities, but not Long Beach.

Long Beach had a municipal gas company that had been a thorn in the side of the big private utility for years. The city utility got natural gas from the tidelands and had a substantially lower rate than Southern California Gas, which recently had been losing customers when bordering communities annexed themselves to Long Beach.

"It wasn't the oil anyone was after, it was the gas," said Ridder. "And Southern California Gas didn't want the gas themselves—they just wanted to take it away from the city and improve their competitive position. The gas is chicken feed compared to the value of the oil, but they were willing to throw the baby out with the bath water."

We discussed how to handle the story. I pointed out that the movement of Southern California Gas money into the Fleming account was circumstantial, and I didn't want to write a speculative story.

"Now that we know where to look," I told Ridder, "we can nail down the corners in a couple of days."

John Fleming and the Southern California Gas Co. did that for us. After six months of stony silence, they suddenly went public with their confidential lawyer-client relationship, in separate press releases. Later I learned that someone at Fleming's bank had tipped him about the attorney general's investigator and his subpoena. The CTPA and the gas company had hurriedly decided that the time had come to speak out with fearless candor.

I wrote a banner-line story for the *Press-Telegram*. It went into somewhat more detail than the gas company's press release.

In the end, the case of The City with Too Much Money was resolved with surprising amiability, once the cards were all on the table and none up anyone's sleeve. After a hearing in Sacramento, Southern California Gas announced it was withdrawing financial support of the CTPA, and the lobbying charges were dropped. The city negotiated a compromise with the state. It left a substantial chunk of oil revenue under city control. That was more than enough to pay for an expensive program to repressure the tidelands oil field with pumped-in sea water, which stopped Long Beach from sinking. The city turned over $130,000,000 in impounded oil money to the state, which used the windfall as seed money for the water project. Even Bruce Allen expressed satisfaction with the eventual compromise.

Pat Brown decided to run for governor and went up against the formidable Republican U.S. senator William Knowland. The Long Beach papers, which had been Republican since the year one, broke ranks and endorsed Brown, who walloped Senator Knowland.

There was one lone pocket of discontent. The newspaper's official bean-counter never reconciled himself to the outrageous price-per-word at which my tidelands oil story costed out. When I left his payroll and went back to the magazines, Hank Ridder made things much worse, cost-wise. He gave me a whopping bonus.

5

Rehearsal
for Watergate

In the final week of the 1960 presidential race, columnist Drew
Pearson, an incurable political boat-rocker, reported that Richard
Nixon's brother, Donald, a restaurant owner in Whittier, Califor-
nia, had received $205,000 from Howard Hughes in a secret transac-
tion disguised as a loan. The loan, Pearson said, had been made back
in 1956, immediately after Richard Nixon had been reelected Vice-
President. The loan had been adroitly concealed by a peculiar series
of transactions in which neither the source of the money, the
Hughes Tool Co., nor the ultimate recipient of the money, Donald
Nixon, had been publicly identified.

Since Hughes had extensive and highly profitable dealings with
the government as a major defense contractor and airline operator,
the clandestine transaction posed questions of political ethics and
possible influence-buying. Because Pearson was a persistent critic of
Nixon, and because the story broke at the eleventh hour in the
campaign, few newspapers picked it up. Those that did reported it
in such a fragmentary and cautious manner that readers could make
little sense of it. Candidate Nixon frostily ignored it, while his
supporters and a number of newspapers dismissed it as a "last-
minute smear" not worthy of comment.

Nixon lost the presidential election by such a razor-thin margin
that a shift of a few thousand votes in key states could have given

him victory. There was no way the impact of the Hughes loan story could be measured, but Robert Kennedy—who had covertly played a key role in breaking the story—claimed later that it may well have won the election for his brother.

One of the few newspapers in the country that soberly addressed itself to the loan story in 1960 was the Long Beach *Press-Telegram*, traditionally a staunchly Republican publication. Publisher "Hank" Ridder wrote the editorial himself, and this raised hackles both in Republican ranks in Long Beach and among his relatives in his family newspaper chain, most of whom were ardent Nixonites. The editorial, entitled "Questions for Mr. Richard Nixon," made no accusations against Nixon, but laid out the ethical issues posed by the Hughes loan. It declared in part:

> The Hughes Tool Co. and its associated corporations are certainly not in the general business of making loans to restaurant proprietors in Whittier. Mr. Hughes is not well known for doing something for nothing. The questions raised . . . which have to be answered not by Mr. Donald Nixon but by other people involved are as follows:
>
> 1. Did Mr. Richard Nixon know of this loan at the time it was made?
>
> 2. If he did know about it, does he generally approve of the theory that corporations which have enormous government contracts should make loans to relatives of prominent members of the administration?
>
> 3. As far as Mr. Hughes and . . . the Hughes Tool Co. are concerned, what was their intent in making the loan?

A major factor that moved Ridder to confront the Republican candidate in the columns of a fairly rock-ribbed Republican newspaper was his insight into billionaire Hughes's misuse of political power. He knew how Hughes could bend the political process to his own personal caprice.

After his defeat by Kennedy, Nixon returned to his native California, went into law practice, and wrote his book *Six Crises*. In that book, he dismissed the Hughes loan with a brief paragraph, long on self-righteousness but short on facts. It addressed none of the ethical issues raised by the loan. In its entirety, it asserted:

> During the last days of the campaign, the opposition had resurrected the financial troubles which had forced [his brother Donald] into bank-

ruptcy two years before and had tried to connect me with a loan he had received from the Hughes Tool Co. during that period. They had, of course, conveniently ignored the fact that my mother had satisfied the loan by transferring to the creditor a piece of property which represented over half her life savings and which had been appraised at an amount greater than the loan.

Simultaneously with his publication of *Six Crises,* Nixon moved back into the political arena in 1962 as a candidate for governor of California against the Democratic incumbent, Edmund "Pat" Brown. When Nixon threw his hat in the California ring, Hank Ridder asked me to undertake a thorough researching of the Hughes-Nixon loan. Ridder was disturbed at the possibility of Hughes becoming an even more dominant power in California. He was also offended by Nixon's persistent refusal to explain, or even discuss, the implications inherent in the clandestine transaction, which Ridder had spelled out in 1960. And finally, Ridder expected the loan to become an issue in the upcoming campaign and wanted to be thoroughly informed on it.

I told Ridder that I would take on the job, but warned him that it would be difficult. Hughes had totally vanished from public sight several years earlier, and the Nixons were notoriously hostile toward inquiring reporters. With both ends—the giver and the receiver of the money—predictably determined to stonewall it, it would be like jackhammering concrete.

He offered an inducement. He would finance all my research and if I could put the story together, I could sell it independently to some national publication. "Think of it this way," he said. "You'll be getting double pay for combat duty."

I started out at the Los Angeles County Hall of Records, and ran the grantee-grantor files on the Whittier lot Nixon said his mother had pledged as collateral for the loan. The files on the lot had two entries. The first was a trust-deed or mortgage recorded against it on January 18, 1957, in favor of "Frank J. Waters, Trustee," in return for a $205,000 loan to Mrs. Hannah Nixon, the Vice-President's mother. The mortgage did not say for whom Waters was acting as trustee. Three days later, on January 21, Waters had transferred the mortgage to a Philip Reiner. Reiner was not designated as a trustee for anyone. Thus, whoever examined the files would conclude that

Waters had merely acted as trustee for Reiner and that Reiner was the source of the $205,000.

On the transfer of the Nixon mortgage from Waters to Reiner, there was an odd eight-month discrepancy in dates. The transfer, while dated January 21, had not been notarized and recorded until eight months later, on September 11. Either Philip Reiner was a very forgetful fellow—or the document had been backdated eight months.

I went from the Hall of Records over to the county assessor's office, to look at the tax appraisal for the Whittier lot. In *Six Crises* Nixon had claimed that the lot had been appraised at more than the value of the $205,000 loan, but he did not say who had made the appraisal. The files showed that it had an assessed value of only $13,000. The Los Angeles assessor uses a rule of thumb of appraising property at one-fourth its market value. This would have put the lot's true value at $52,000—some $150,000 short of what Hughes had come up with.

To make sure that the Whittier lot had not been undervalued by the assessor, I went back to the recorder's office and checked other real estate transactions in the vicinity of the Nixon lot. The records showed that on the open, or non-Nixon, market nearby property had far less value. An adjoining and larger lot had sold in 1955 for $49,000. A year later, a lot of the same size, a half-block away, had brought only $33,000. Hughes had thus lent the Nixons about four times the true worth of the lot.

The next question was how—and why—Philip Reiner had wound up holding the Nixon mortgage. If Hughes Tool Co. had put up the money, why did Reiner get the collateral for the loan?

In his 1960 story, Pearson had identified Philip Reiner as an accountant in the L.A. law firm of James Arditto and Frank Waters, both Hughes attorneys. I had met Waters once. He was an affable former California Republican legislator and occasional Hughes lobbyist. I decided there was no point in talking to him, at least at the outset. As a long-time Hughes functionary, he was an unlikely source of information.

So I went looking for Philip Reiner.

Under the well-known Murphy's Law—"If anything can go wrong, sometime it will"—the people to whom reporters are eager to talk are never available. They are dead, on vacation, suffering from laryngitis, or have just moved to Timbuktu. Reiner proved to be a classic example of this axiom.

He was no longer listed in the Los Angeles phone directory. I had to drop back to the 1959 book before I picked up an old phone number and address for him. I dialed the number and, predictably, the operator told me it was no longer in service. I drove around to the address, a very modest apartment for a man lending anyone $205,000 on a $52,000 lot. The landlord said Reiner had moved out, more than a year earlier, and that he had left no forwarding address. The landlord was one of those rare and delightful people reporters encounter every couple of years: he wanted to be helpful. He told me that Reiner used to hang out a lot at Tang's, a popular restaurant and bar in Chinatown. I went down to Tang's and talked to Mr. Tang. He had the same story—that Reiner had dropped out of sight more than a year earlier. He told me to try Nikola's, a watering spot on Sunset Boulevard frequented by Civic Center politicians and L. A. *Times* newspapermen and reputedly the place from which Los Angeles County is *really* governed. At Nikola's the bartender, Walter, reran Tang's story, and recommended that I try the Cock 'n' Bull, out where the Sunset Strip ends and Beverly Hills begins.

At the Cock 'n' Bull, the barman said, "Sure, I know Phil Reiner."

"But you haven't seen him in more than a year," I said.

"That's right," said the barman. "Whatever happened to Phil?"

At each place, I left a note for Reiner, with my name and phone number, and "Please call. Urgent." Over the years, I have left scores of notes like that for missing people, and they hardly ever worked. This time, they worked.

A few days later, the phone rang and a man said, "I'm a friend of Phil Reiner. You left a note for him at the Cock 'n' Bull. He wants to know what you want." I told him I was a reporter and wanted to talk to Reiner about the Hughes-Nixon loan. The man said he didn't think that was possible, and I would have to talk to him first. He said he was Reiner's attorney, but would not give me his name or phone number. We sparred a while and then arranged to meet on a street corner over on Crenshaw Boulevard. I described my car, and he described himself as a short, fat man who would be wearing light-blue slacks. I drove over to the corner, and there he was. He took me into a coffee shop and we talked for a couple of hours. He was as cautious as a WCTU member touring Skid Row. He told me nothing, and I told him everything I knew. He said he knew something about the Ridder newspapers and had doubts about putting his client in touch with them.

"My client has been burned by everybody he has dealt with—the Hughes people, the Nixons, the Kennedys, the press—everybody except Drew Pearson. He's a basket case, and I don't want anyone scorching him again." When he mentioned the Kennedys, his face flushed and I thought for a moment that he was going to have a stroke.

I told him that Hank Ridder was an unusual kind of Ridder and that he wasn't in the pocket of Howard Hughes or Richard Nixon. I briefed him on the 1960 editorial Ridder had written. The little fat man brightened up at that, and said he would check around and maybe get back to me.

Three days later, he phoned me again. He had made some inquiries about Hank Ridder and had satisfied himself. "What confused me," he said, "is that he has a brother who is a Stone-Age Republican." He gave me his address, a few blocks off Crenshaw. He met me at the door and took me in and introduced me to Reiner.

Reiner was a thin, dark-haired man with sad eyes and a Brooklyn accent. He was wearing a Dodgers cap and watching a baseball game on TV. He had an air of having suffered a lot, which turned out to be true. He also had, as I came to learn, an extraordinarily accurate memory, and the ability to say "I don't know" when he didn't—traits that endear anyone to a reporter.

For the next two weeks we talked every day, and I filled a thick notebook with what he poured out. He told a tangled tale of intrigue and high comedy, of loyalty, betrayal, and deceit, of the way politics works on the upper levels of both the Republican and Democratic parties. When he was through, I closed up my notebook and went forth to check on everything he had told me. And whether it was a name, a date, or an event, it stood up.

In 1956 Reiner had been a free-lance certified accountant, he told me, working out of the law office of Jim Arditto and Frank Waters, Hughes attorneys, for whom he did considerable accounting work. He was a friend and drinking companion of Arditto, who was an assertive and aggressive Italian. Arditto was a deal-maker and political fixer, who later became involved in a widespread tax-assessor scandal in California, in which he had carried envelopes of cash from a brewery owner to a San Francisco assessor. Arditto was a fellow who got things done, one way or another. He was also a man of whom Reiner said, "When he says something once, it becomes the truth, at least to him."

Reiner had learned of the Hughes loan shortly after it was made. He did not know who had originated it, but it had been handled by Frank Waters, and Richard Nixon had been closely informed about it from the beginning. The Hughes group had devised a code name for the Vice-President, which they used in phone calls and memoranda. To conceal his identity, he was referred to as "the Eastern division."

Reiner was brought into the operation in an effort to prop up Donald Nixon's faltering Whittier restaurant. Despite the infusion of the Hughes money, it had continued to slide downhill. Reiner had examined its books and found that it was still losing over $5,000 a week, headed for bankruptcy.

An emergency summit meeting had then assembled at the Hughes headquarters and message center on Romaine Street, presided over by Noah Dietrich. The Hughes organization—which devised satellites for the Pentagon, ran TWA, and eventually put a camera on the moon for NASA—took on another project. It set up a task force to salvage the Nixon restaurant. The group included Reiner, and was headed by Pat DiCicco, the food executive for the Hughes enterprises.

"There was a clash of personalities," Reiner said. "On his first trip to Whittier, DiCicco spotted a big sign at the restaurant advertising NIXONBURGERS. Pat said, 'That sign ought to come down. Democrats eat, too.' " The task force made a number of recommendations, but Don Nixon resented being supervised. The task force then executed a 180-degree turn and dissolved itself with the concurrence of "the Eastern division," and the restaurant shortly went bankrupt. Although his creditors took substantial losses, Donald Nixon survived admirably. He swiftly obtained a well-paid job with Carnation Milk Co., where he went about his duties in a new Lincoln Continental.

In the beginning, Frank Waters had served as the stand-in for Hughes Tool on the Nixon loan, to conceal the source of the money, but in the summer of 1957, Waters, Arditto, and Dietrich got involved in a controversial Los Angeles harbor oil lease. There was a lawsuit filed, and rumbles of an investigation. "Arditto got nervous about Waters serving as dummy for Hughes on the Nixon loan,"

Reiner said, "and one day he called me in and said they were going to assign the trust-deed to me. They backdated it eight months, so it would look as if Waters had immediately turned it over to me when the loan was made."

The Hughes stand-in now had a stand-in for himself, putting two layers of dummies between Hughes and the loan. Reiner thus became the recorded owner of a $205,000 trust-deed, without putting up a penny. In reality, he owned nothing. Arditto had him execute a document acknowledging that he was merely a trustee for Hughes Tool, and agreeing to relinquish his "ownership" of the Nixon mortgage to Hughes whenever he was so instructed. This document was put in a safe, and was never recorded.

There was another unrecorded document in the clandestine transaction. It provided that if the loan was not repaid, the debt could be wiped out by surrender of the Whittier lot, and no one would have any personal liability. So when the restaurant failed, the lot was deeded over—not to Hughes Tool, not to Frank Waters, but to Dummy No. 2, Philip Reiner.

This tangled web then acquired some new strands. A Union Oil station had been built on the vacant lot, under a lease that yielded $800 a month in rent. In 1958, the first Union Oil check came fluttering to Phillip Reiner. Like a dutiful trustee, he turned it over to the Hughes attorney, Arditto. Arditto relayed it to the Hughes executive secretary, Nadine Henley, at the Romaine Street headquarters. It came whistling back like a ball off the racquet of Pancho Gonzalez. "Hughes was not about to take a check that would provide a documented link to the Nixon loan," said Reiner. "I was instructed to bank it myself."

At this point, there occurred a fatal breakdown in communications that brought down the entire Rube Goldberg-designed structure—and, if one accepted Bobby Kennedy's judgment, resulted in the 1960 defeat of Richard Nixon by John Kennedy.

Reiner assumed that the Hughes officials were letting him keep the $800 monthly checks as payment for his services as the billionaire's stand-in. So he banked the checks every month and spent them. At the end of the year, he reported them as income, and paid taxes on them—and showed me his tax return to verify this.

"Everyone knew what I was doing," said Reiner. "Arditto and Waters used to joke that I was the only one making any money out of the Hughes loan. And when I was instructed to keep the checks,

Arditto got up and did a little jig. He said, 'Man, we've got a fifteen-year lease on life.' "

Unfortunately, the Hughes organization was rigidly compartmentalized. In March, 1960, down in the Hughes Houston headquarters, some money-counter ran onto a record of the $205,000 advanced to Frank Waters. Meanwhile, Arditto and Waters had fallen out, and Noah Dietrich had been fired by Hughes. When Houston—where no one knew about the Nixon loan—demanded an accounting for the money, Arditto called in Reiner and asked him what had happened to the Union Oil checks—then totaling $16,000. "Hell, you know what I did with them," Reiner said. "I spent them."

"Arditto told me that was a terrible thing to have done, and that I was in big trouble. Since he had known about it all along, I figured that Arditto was making me the fall guy. We had a shouting match, and that ended our friendship. From then on, it was everybody for himself."

Reiner, a lifelong Democrat, went off and acquired himself a Los Angeles attorney, also a lifelong Democrat, the little fat man who had introduced us. The attorney, with a presidential election coming up, recognized that the defection of Reiner represented a valuable asset to his party. With Reiner's approval, he got in touch with Bobby Kennedy in Washington, who, delighted, referred him to a former U. S. Justice Department official named James McInerney. McInerney was a high-level Kennedy political operator who handled matters that the Kennedys considered incompatible with their public image.

McInerney decided that Reiner should be rendered spotless before he was used. He gave Reiner's attorney the money to settle the dubious $16,000 debt to Arditto, who was pressuring Reiner for repayment. The lawyer went back to L. A. and got a receipt from Arditto "in full settlement of any and all claims of Hughes Tool Co. against Philip Reiner." This strategic move by the Kennedy operator injected an ironic touch into the complex affair. At the time—1962—the only cash Hughes got back from the loan to the Nixons actually came from the Kennedys.

McInerney then gathered together the public records on the $205,000 transaction, all of Reiner's private documents, and an affidavit from Reiner, and put together a long résumé of the loan's history, for the purpose of tipping it to the press.

The story was leaked first to the St. Louis *Post-Dispatch*, which sent its reporter, Richard Dudman, to Los Angeles to check it out. Because it was so late in the campaign, the *Post-Dispatch* opted against the story. *Time* magazine's L. A. bureau chief, Frank McCulloch, put five *Time* staffers on the story and worked it for ten days. McCulloch thought it was a hot story, but the New York editors side-tracked it. The last McInerney leak went to Drew Pearson, who put it together swiftly, but then decided to hold it until after the election. As Pearson told me later, "I thought it was a valid story, but I didn't want anyone charging me with a last-minute political smear."

At this point, the people at the Nixon campaign headquarters got wind of the press activities. Unaware that the McInerney project had been aborted, and the story had been shelved, Nixon decided to beat the Kennedys to the punch. His campaign manager, Robert Finch, sought out a sympathetic national columnist, Peter Edson, and gave him a self-serving and wildly inaccurate account of Donald Nixon's financial affairs. Unaware that the Hughes cover-up had lost its linchpin in Reiner, the Nixons gave Finch a prim account that left out Hughes entirely. Edson then rushed it into print.

In his column, headed "VP BARES STORY OF KIN'S 'DEALS'," Edson wrote that Richard Nixon had learned that the Democrats were researching his brother's finances. "In an attempt to offset any such move, the Nixon headquarters . . . has made available to this reporter a full explanation of all relevant facts in the record, to get the story out in the open and end the gossip." Edson then reported that Frank Waters had lent Donald Nixon the $205,000 because Mrs. Waters and Mrs. Donald Nixon had gone to high school together. "So it was natural that Mr. Walters should have assisted in financing Don's business ventures." He described "Frank [sic] Reiner" as a Nixon creditor "who had threatened foreclosure." When Donald Nixon's restaurant failed, Mrs. Hannah Nixon had deeded over her Whittier lot to Waters, Edson reported, and Waters had then, with remarkable generosity, given the lot to Reiner to satisfy his claims. There was no mention of Hughes Tool anywhere in the column. "All this is a matter of court record in Whittier," Edson concluded.

The Edson column, published October 24, provoked a swift reaction from Drew Pearson. Reversing his decision to hold the story until after the election, he went to print with his own version of "the relevant facts."

"They boil down to this," he wrote. "Four years after Nixon had given his famous TV explanation of the $18,000 expense fund"—the so-called Checkers speech—"his family received a much bigger financial benefit from the Hughes Tool Co., wholly owned by Howard Hughes."

At Nixon headquarters, Robert Finch promptly told the Associated Press that Pearson's story was "an obvious political smear in the last two weeks of the campaign," and reaffirmed that Frank Waters, not Hughes Tool Co., was the source of the $205,000. But in the next few days, the awful truth was relayed from Los Angeles to "the Eastern division" that the stand-in, Reiner, for the stand-in, Waters, had pulled his finger from the dike and the dike had collapsed. Whereupon Donald Nixon finally admitted publicly what he and Richard Nixon had known all along, that the $205,000 had come from Hughes Tool.

In untangling this web and verifying Reiner's account, I interviewed everyone involved who would talk. In Washington, columnist Peter Edson was still smarting from the misinformation that had been laid on him. He said he had picked up a rumor that the money had come from Hughes Tool before he wrote his skewed account, and had asked both Finch and the Nixon family lawyer, Thomas Bewley, about it. "They said they didn't know anything about it," Edson said, "and I didn't check further. I guess they made a sucker out of me."

In Los Angeles, Robert Finch conceded that when he gave Edson all the facts, he hadn't known all the facts. He said his misinformation came from attorney Bewley. In Whittier, Bewley angrily blamed "those high-powered L. A. lawyers" for mucking up the story.

I made a call on Arditto. He complained that the Nixons had "lost their heads" and "put out a cock-and-bull story." He went into a tirade about Philip Reiner, accusing him of stealing the Arditto files and "selling them to Drew Pearson for fifty thousand dollars." I told Arditto I gravely doubted that Pearson would pay $50,000 for an exclusive account of the Second Coming, and that Reiner was flat broke. "I'm delighted to hear that," said James Arditto.

Frank Waters invoked the lawyer-client privilege, and told me nothing.

Hughes, as always, was bunkered *in absentia*, and unreachable.

Donald and Richard Nixon did not respond to my requests for interviews. I telephoned Richard Nixon's office three times, and sent him a registered letter. All I got was a return receipt, autographed by his secretary, Rose Mary Woods, the lady who later—in the Watergate scandal—was involved in the famous 18 1/2-minute tape gap.

On the other side, the Kennedy functionary who had put the story together, James McInerney, confirmed Reiner's account, but stopped short with that. He said that all his documents on the matter, and his personal research, were locked in his safe and would stay there. Later, an emissary from Governor Pat Brown tried to get them, and got stiff-armed. "Apparently the Kennedys consider Richard Nixon a national problem, not a California one," the emissary told me.

(When I told this to the little fat lawyer who had delivered Reiner and his story to the Kennedys, he almost had another stroke. "When the Kennedys had used Reiner and were through with him," he raged, "they dumped him back on me. They might well have found some kind of job for him in their family enterprises or with some of their well-to-do friends. I never asked them for anything and didn't expect anything. But given what I had delivered to them, I was the last guy in the United States they should have dumped Reiner on.")

I spent a week in Washington, tracking rumors of various favors Hughes had received as a *quid pro quo* for his $205,000. They were impossible to verify, other than by speculative "linking." Hughes received a whole stack of favorable federal agency rulings, airline routes and contracts, and other federal largesse, both when Nixon was Vice-President, and later in his two presidential terms. But there was no verifiable evidence that Nixon personally intervened at the request of Hughes. Politics rarely works that way, except in such atrocities as the Teapot Dome scandal. The exercise of political influence is more subtle; one uses one's money to make friends and then waits hopefully for the functioning of gratitude.

When I emerged from the mole tunnel of the Hughes loan, I wrote a 6,000-word account of my subterranean travels. It was not cast as a heavy-breathing exposé, but rather as a political farce on the perils inherent in striking righteous poses while engaged in dubious sleight-of-hand maneuvers. It made no accusations of corruption against either Nixon or Hughes, but recounted the unusual series of pratfalls that they had suffered playing cloak-and-dagger with money.

I wrote the story for the *Press-Telegram*, and also sold it to Max Ascoli's *The Reporter*, a well-respected national magazine with a modest circulation of 200,000 but a prestigious readership that included Supreme Court Justices, the President and Vice-President, Cabinet officers and a large percentage of the U. S. Congress. My account was published as the lead story in the August 16, 1962, issue simultaneously with publication in the *Press-Telegram*. Since the article contained no explosive sensations, I was not prepared for the wild brannigan it set off. And once again, as with the original Pearson column, it was the Nixonites who provoked and escalated the brannigan.

With an unerring instinct for self-destruction, they tried to suppress distribution of *The Reporter* magazine.

The magazine was due to go on the stands August 13, and I received my own copy in the mail on schedule. A number of my friends knew the article was upcoming, and began to call me the following week, and asked what had happened to it. They complained that it was not on the newsstands anywhere in Long Beach or the vicinity. After about twenty calls, I toured the newsstands that regularly stocked *The Reporter* and none of them had received it. They told me there had been an unusual number of requests for the magazine after my *Press-Telegram* story, which they had relayed to the wholesale distributor.

The distributor for the southern Los Angeles and Orange County area was the Drown Agency, and the owner of the agency was Jack Drown, an intimate friend of Richard Nixon, an ardent Republican, and Nixon's Los Angeles County campaign manager.

When ten days had passed and still no magazines had been distributed, I called *The Reporter*'s executive editor in New York, Philip Horton, and asked him to check on the West Coast shipment of the magazine. He called back and said it had gone out from the Ohio printing plant on August 6 via Railway Express, and gave me the waybill number, 14233. I went to the Long Beach Railway Express agency, only to find that they forwarded their shipment records to their headquarters in San Francisco. I called the office there, gave them the waybill number, and they looked up their delivery receipt. It showed that *The Reporter* shipment had been received by

Drown on August 13, and signed for by a man named Paul Jiminez. I asked for a copy of the receipt, and they said they would send it back to the Long Beach office, where I could pick it up.

By this time, two weeks had passed and the next issue of *The Reporter* was due out. The Nixon loan issue had not shown up anywhere in Drown's area. But in downtown Los Angeles, which had a different distributor, the magazine had been put on the stands and had sold out everywhere.

I went to Hank Ridder and told him what I had learned. "That is absolutely outrageous," he said, and told me to confront Drown and demand an explanation. "Then write it for the paper."

Before I saw Drown, I called Bill Stout, a Los Angeles television reporter, and told him what I had found. "That's quite a story," Stout said. "I'll get a crew and come down and put Drown on camera."

At his agency, Drown told me that *The Reporter* shipment "had just arrived by parcel post the day before"—August 31. He said he had distributed it, but when I asked him where, he said, "That's none of your business." I then told him he had received the shipment more than two weeks earlier. He called me a liar, denounced the magazine article, and asked me, "Who financed you to write that piece?" When I was leaving the office, Stout was rolling up with a mobile television unit. The next day, the *Press-Telegram* and TV station KTLA disclosed the suppression of the magazine with the loan story.

Drown came charging into the *Press-Telegram* office, complained about me, and demanded equal space to reply to my story. Meanwhile, I had gone to the local Railway Express agency to pick up the receipt documenting the August 13 delivery date—and had hit a rock. The Railway Express agent told me the Los Angeles manager had instructed him not to give me a copy. I called the L. A. manager, who said he would not give me the receipt. "We now understand what this receipt involves—it is a very controversial matter, involving important people, and we will deal only with the principals in the affair—the consignor and the consignee."

I called *The Reporter* in New York and told Horton what was going on. He said he couldn't believe it, and I said, "Believe it. You guys will have to get the Railway Express receipt, because they won't give it to anyone but you or Jack Drown." Horton said he would get on the matter at once.

I went down to the newspaper, and its editor, a staunch Republican and friend of Drown's, told me about Drown's angry visit. Meanwhile, he had sent another reporter to interview Drown and back-check me. Drown had shown the reporter his entry ledger, where he listed the arrival dates of all magazines. "It showed *The Reporter* arriving August 31, exactly as Drown claimed," the editor said. "We have a picture of the ledger, and I want to know what evidence you have of any August 13 date." I told the editor I wasn't working for him, but for Ridder, and I would deal only with the publisher.

The photo he had of Drown's ledger showed that the entry of August 31 was on a full page of entries, and was written below the last line. I pointed this out to the editor, and told him the entry was faked, and he was being flimflammed. When I went out to Ridder's home, with steam blowing out of my ears, I told him about the problem I was having getting the Railway Express receipt, and *he* went into a flap.

"The Nixon people have the connections and the clout to have that receipt destroyed," Ridder said. "And then where are we if we have to prove the magazine's suppression?"

I reassured him that the truth was mighty and would prevail, and that meanwhile he should whistle his editor off my back, because he was making me angry. "I'll get the receipt," I said, "and when I do, pay me off, because I won't be sniped at by the people who ought to be backing me up."

In New York, Horton was manfully supporting me. He had *The Reporter*'s law firm serve notice on Railway Express that they demanded evidence of delivery of the magazine shipment. The nervous Railway Express manager dutifully sent the receipt to New York, and Horton sent it speeding to me via special delivery. It arrived at my home at 7:30 A.M. and I got Ridder out of bed to turn it over to him. He was jubilant, I had cooled down, and we resumed our friendship. He ordered a follow-up story documenting the suppression of *The Reporter,* and we heard no more from Jack Drown.

The story of *The Reporter*'s suppression by Drown was picked up by other California publications and escalated the Nixon-Hughes loan into a major campaign issue. In his recent *Memoirs,* Nixon complained that "The media loved the story and played it up big —both because it made such tantalizing copy and because it was so damaging to me . . . Despite my efforts to campaign on the issues, every press conference brought questions about the personal attacks being made against me."

He dealt with the Hughes loan only once, in a joint appearance with Pat Brown before a group of editors and publishers in San Francisco. Instead of confronting the ethical questions the loan posed, he accused Brown of exploiting Donald Nixon's personal financial troubles, and charged Brown with raising an issue "which President Kennedy refused to use" in 1960. That was an absolution that must have surprised both the Kennedys and their political provocateur, Jim McInerney. Pat Brown, who made no references to the Hughes loan in the campaign, responded by saying "All I know about that loan was what I read in *The Reporter*."

The loan, however, was seized upon exuberantly by Dick Tuck, the Democratic political prankster. When Nixon was campaigning in San Francisco's Chinatown, he was greeted by a line of smiling residents holding aloft placards with a message in Chinese characters. Nixon, thinking they were supporters, went down the line, shaking their hands. Belatedly, when a Chinese friend translated the message for him, he seized several of the placards and angrily shredded them. They had been prepared and passed out by Dick Tuck, and bore the question: "WHAT ABOUT THAT HUGHES LOAN?" Later, at a Chinatown luncheon rally, guests opened their Chinese fortune cookies and found the same question tucked inside.

Although he expressed outrage at Tuck's "dirty tricks," in the 1972 Presidential campaign Nixon had Bob Haldeman seek out his own trickster "with a Dick Tuck capability." Haldeman came, up, instead, with Donald Segretti, whose notion of political fun-and-games consisted of faking letters accusing Nixon's opponents of homosexuality and fathering illegitimate offspring. Mr. Segretti wound up with a prison term, which deepened Nixon's conviction that there were two sets of rules in politics, one for his opponents and a harsher one for Nixon.

What lost Nixon both the Kennedy and Brown elections, in my opinion, was the same mind-set that did him in later in the Watergate scandal. It consisted of a stubborn hostility to candor and an insistence upon impugning the motives of anyone who questioned his rectitude. He had a compulsion to be seen as flawless, a total lack of humor, and an almost manic rage at whoever dared intimate that his imperial trousers were slipping kneeward. He is by no means the only politician who lusted after approval, but Nixon's fierce reaction to criticism tilted him out of touch with reality. Most Americans are well aware that their leaders are human, and they have a good-natured ability to forgive and accept politicians who occasionally can say "I made a mistake there." In one of his early biographies, he is quoted as saying that his worst nightmare was to be caught "with egg on my face," a fear that eventually warped his responses monstrously.

When the Watergate scandal began to unfold, I watched it from the sidelines with an intense sense of *déjà vu*. His handling of Watergate paralleled his mishandling of the Hughes loan with such exactitude that it appeared that the loan fiasco was a rehearsal of his final disaster. In both instances there was the initial denial that anything was amiss. Watergate was only a "third-rate burglary," just as the convoluted and concealed Hughes loan had been characterized as a legitimate business transaction. There was the same behind-the-scenes cover-up, the demeaning of the motives of his critics, the misuse of his own colleagues, the self-pitying portrayal of himself as victim, not offender. His release of the expurgated transcript of the Oval Office tapes, and his expectation that they would exculpate him, matched the wildly innacurate account of the loan that was fed to columnist Edson "to get the story out in the open." There was even a reemergence of covert money from Howard Hughes—this time the secret passage of $100,000 in cash to a new stand-in, Bebe Rebozo.

There was, once again, the question of "What did the President know, and when did he know it?" and the final "smoking gun" that answered that question. In the case of the $205,000 loan, although it was apparent that Richard Nixon had known about it a month after it had been made, his prior knowledge of it was not established. That time, the "smoking gun" came from Noah Dietrich, sixteen years after the transaction. Dietrich had been in on the loan from the outset, but remained buttoned up until 1972, when he published his memoirs. He then disclosed that when the loan had been proposed, via Frank Waters, he had objected to it as improper and potentially disastrous—both to Hughes and to Richard Nixon. But Hughes, Dietrich said, had overruled him and said, "I want the Nixons to have the money." Dietrich had liked Nixon and didn't want to see him hurt himself, so he had flown to Washington, met with Nixon privately, and strongly advised him to scuttle the transaction. Dietrich warned him that it was almost certain to come out, and might destroy him. But Nixon told him, "I have to put my family first." If the loan had been a legitimate business transaction, as Nixon later maintained, the Nixons could have obtained the money through an above-board loan from any bank, instead of getting it in an under-the-table transaction with a wealthy federal contractor.

"So I went back and processed the $205,000," Dietrich told me. "He got what he wanted for his brother, and he got the fallout I predicted."

6

The Case of
the Duplicate Murder
Confessions

Mountain Home, Idaho, some years back, was a raw little bedroom community for the huge Strategic Air Command base ten miles out of town. Like such towns everywhere, it had many trailers and small frame cottages for enlisted men and the families who follow them from base to base. A central fact in their life-style is the periodic and unpredictable absence of the husband and the resultant vulnerability of his wife and children.

When someone murdered Nancy Johnson, the wife of Airman Alec Johnson, and their two-year-old son, Danny, on the night of April 9, 1962, the crime sent a shock wave through Mountain Home and the air base, terrorizing service families, abrading anxieties of the base personnel, and spurring on the civilian and military authorities to find the killer. The sense of panic was deepened by the fact that the double killing seemed mindlessly vicious and without any motive.

The airman's wife and son were alone in their small frame house and preparing for bed when they were attacked by someone with a knife who slashed the boy's throat and repeatedly stabbed Nancy Johnson with such force that one of her ribs was broken. The intruder made off with a handful of objects—a hammer, a hatchet, the base of an old lamp, and a couple of Nancy's purses with only two dollars in them. This pitiful haul was glaringly inconsistent with the brutality of the killings. The murderer left no clues; what proved to be the most important piece of evidence was not a clue but the absence of one. There was no murder weapon. Whatever instrument the killer had used, he had apparently taken it with him when he fled.

Nancy's body, clad only in a housecoat and lying in the kitchen, was discovered by her husband when he returned home from the air base at 1:00 A.M. His son's body was partially concealed by a nearby washing machine, and Airman Johnson did not see it when he bolted out for help. He ran to the home of his nearest neighbor, a fellow SAC airman named Gerald Anderson, roused Anderson and his wife, Jane, and shouted, "Nancy's over there all cut up and dead and I can't find Danny. Get the police." The Johnsons and Andersons were not only neighbors but close friends. The Andersons had three children of their own, frequently picnicked and went fishing with the Johnsons, and baby-sat for each other.

Airman Anderson threw on some clothes, drove to the police station, and told the woman dispatcher that there had been a murder. She summoned a squad car, and Anderson rode back to the Johnson home with two police officers. As they pulled up to the little house, there occurred the first of a series of events that were to weave a web of suspicion around Gerald Anderson.

He knew that the front door to the Johnson house was nailed shut and that the kitchen door was the only usable entrance. Later, he claimed that he told the police, "Go around to the back." But the officers, reconstructing the conversation two days later, declared that he had said, "The bodies are around in back."

When Alec Johnson had aroused Anderson, he had not known that Danny had been killed. Anderson could not have known that there were two victims, or where in the house their bodies were lying.

The next day Anderson wove a few more strands of suspicion around himself. He stayed home from the air base and, late in the morning, went into town to the Cozy Bar and got drunk. As he told me later, he was a beer-drinker with a limited capacity, and his wife disapproved of his drinking. At the Cozy Bar he had a few bottles of beer and began to talk compulsively about the murders.

"The murders were big news," he said. "Since I was the guy who called the police and all, I figured I'd be the center of attention."

Among the people he talked to was a married couple. Later they told the police that they had driven Airman Anderson home from the bar and had overheard a peculiar conversation between him and his wife. They said that Anderson looked over at the Johnson house, broke down and sobbed, "I didn't want to do it, but I had to," and that Jane had replied, "Shhhh, don't say another word."

"Heck, I was just talking about going into town and getting beered up," Anderson said. "I went under false pretenses, telling her I was going to get some Pepsi. And I bawled because when we drove up I looked over at the Johnson home and got thinking about those terrible murders. I felt sorry about Nancy and Danny, and I thought how it might easily have been Jane and my kids."

On his return to the base, the second day after the murders, the military police called Anderson in for questioning. At the outset, they treated him as a potentially useful witness; by Anderson's account, he had been the last person known to have seen Nancy and Danny alive. He told the police that around 8:00 P.M. on the night of the killings, he had left his house to get a gallon of milk at a nearby dairy. He said he had stopped at the Johnson house and offered to bring some milk back for Nancy, went on to the dairy, dropped the milk off at the Johnson house, chatted briefly with Nancy and gone on home. He put his return home at around 8:25 and explained how he arrived at the timing. He and his wife had wanted to watch the Motion Picture Academy Awards on television and he had arrived home, Anderson said, during the last few minutes of *M Squad*, which preceded the Oscar awards. When the show was over, Anderson said, he and Jane had gone to bed and he had not left the house until Johnson came pounding at his door at 1:00 A.M.

While Anderson was recounting his movements to the base police, it became known later, other information about him was being relayed to the base from the police in Mountain Home. This consisted of four pieces of circumstantial evidence that, taken together, tilted Airman Anderson almost imperceptibly from witness to potential suspect.

1. The police dispatcher said that when she called for a squad car, she had said that there was a "murder or suicide" at the Johnson home, and that Anderson had corrected her and said, "It wasn't a suicide."

2. The police who had taken Anderson to the Johnson home related their version: that he had said, "The *bodies* are around in back."

3. The couple at the Cozy Bar told the police about Anderson's breaking down and sobbing to his wife, "I didn't mean to do it, but I had to."

4. Several witnesses said that they had observed Anderson, on the afternoon after the murder, walking around the Johnson yard "as if he were looking for something."

On the receipt of this information, the base police called in two plainclothes members of the Office of Special Investigations. The OSI is the military counterpart of the FBI, and charged with investigating serious crimes. Their first action was to take Anderson to his car, where they shook it down, sweeping the dirt from the floor into envelopes and turning an ultraviolet light on the upholstery. The light showed a spot, which, without testing, the agent guessed correctly was blood, and put a question to Anderson.

"There's blood on the upholstery," he said. "How did it get there?"

"It's an old spot," Anderson said.

"How did it get there?" the agent persisted.

On the spur of the moment, Anderson told a small lie that was to swell to monstrous proportions. Months before, he had been out with his wife, had got into an argument and slapped her, starting a nosebleed. He was ashamed of what he had done, he told me later, and reluctant to go into a private family quarrel with the OSI agent.

"The spot was there when I got the car," he told the agent.

"Come with us," the agents said. They took him to the OSI headquarters and into a crude, bare-looking interrogation room. It was a deceptive little room, well equipped for its purpose. Hidden in the wall was a microphone, which was attached to a tape-recorder in an adjoining room. On the wall was what appeared to be a mirror. It was a one-way window, from which a hidden OSI agent in the tape-recording room could look out unseen on the interrogation room.

The OSI interrogation of Anderson, who had risen early that morning, began at 9:15 P.M. and continued until after dawn the next morning. At 6:00 A.M. the agents took Anderson to the base detention facility and let him go to bed. Anderson, a slight, gaunt-faced young Californian with a deep-seated respect for authority, offered no objections, although he was charged with no crime and was under no restraining order.

In the next six days, he was kept on the base and questioned daily by four OSI agents, working in relays. On April 18, Anderson signed a confession that he had killed Nancy Johnson. As to the murder of Danny Johnson, the confession did not specifically admit guilt, but was worded ambiguously, asserting that Anderson did not "recall doing any harm to Johnson's son, Danny." Nine days after the double murder, Anderson was turned over to the civilian authorities at Mountain Home and charged with the first-degree murder of his neighbor's wife.

Shortly after he was moved from OSI to civilian jurisdiction, Anderson repudiated his confession and underwent a hysterical breakdown in which he sobbed that he had been coerced into signing it. He obtained a civilian attorney and from that point on continued to insist that he was innocent. "Nobody would believe me because I had signed the confession," he told me later. "I don't think my own attorney believed me."

For the next seven months, Airman Anderson sat in a Mountain Home cell while the legal processes inched along toward his trial. Then, in November, the Johnson murder case took a series of sudden, bizarre turns.

Over in Boise, some forty miles from Mountain Home, a blond young drifter named Theodore Dickie was arrested and charged with the rape-murder of a ten-year-old girl. While sitting in his cell, he called in a Boise television reporter and told him he wanted to give him a good story. "They've got the wrong guy out in Mountain Home," he told the reporter. "I'm the one who killed that woman and her little boy."

The civilian authorities at Mountain Home went over to Boise and questioned Dickie at length. They were aware, as most experienced law-enforcement officers are, that there are certain criminals who will snarl up law enforcement with the game-playing of false confessions. Some do it for sociopathic enjoyment, some out of deep-seated malice, and some because of an overweening sense of guilt that compels them to seek additional punishment. Under their questioning, Dickie related an account of the murders that was a peculiar mixture of accurate descriptions of the murder scene and either errors or deliberate misstatements. As he subsequently made clear, Dickie was a skillful game-player with considerable insight and inventiveness. But in an admirable exercise in the art of criminology, the civilian authorities focused on testing Dickie's story against certain undisclosed hard evidence.

When they were through with Dickie, they took swift action. The prosecuting attorney went into court at Mountain Home and moved to dismiss the murder charge against Airman Anderson. The county prosecutor went into court at Mountain Home and moved to dismiss the murder charge against Anderson. He informed the court that "evidence has now been discovered that completely exonerates the defendant" and that "an investigation of the facts has revealed physical evidence in full corroboration of the confession . . . of Theodore Thomas Dickie."

The court dismissed the murder charge and took an unusual legal action. It entered an order that Anderson was "adjudged and decreed . . . not guilty" and ordered that the airman be freed immediately.

"It's wonderful, just wonderful," Anderson told newsmen when he was released. "I knew I didn't commit this crime, and I just waited, hoped and prayed for some break."

Reunited with his wife and children, Airman Anderson celebrated what seemed to be a story-book resolution of a long ordeal. His celebration lasted less than forty-eight hours. Although he had been decreed not guilty by a civilian court, technically, when the court freed him, he dropped into the net of military jurisdiction, where the OSI was holding a murder confession signed by the airman. If the Air Force absolved Anderson, it faced an ordeal of its own—explaining how its investigators had obtained a murder confession from an innocent man. To resolve this dilemma, the Air Force announced that an impartial Air Force legal officer would be flown in from March Air Force Base to review the entire charge and recommend a course of action. This action was executed with a swift efficiency that confounded those cynics who maintain that military red tape unwinds with the pace of an Alaskan glacier. The legal officer flew in, scanned the voluminous file of the evidence and legal proceedings in a single working day, and made an instant, on-the-spot judgment.

He recommended that the Air Force proceed with its case against Airman Anderson, and that he be held for a military hearing. Anderson was taken back into custody, and this time was charged with the murders of both Nancy and Danny Johnson.

With that action, the Air Force set off a fire-storm that elevated the seven-months'-old Mountain Home murders from an Idaho news story to a national one. Idaho newspapers raised the cry that the Air Force was flouting the state's judicial process. Senator Thomas Kuchel of California requested a congressional inquiry into the case. And at my home in Long Beach, I had a telephone call from the *Saturday Evening Post,* with the assignment to fly to Idaho and see what could be made of the Case of the Duplicate Murder Confessions.

The military hearing at the Air Force base ran twelve days. Anderson was represented by his civilian attorney, Robert McLaughlin, and by an Air Force attorney, Major Peter McKinney. There normally is a convention of mutual respect between military officers, but Major McKinney soon made it clear that he had no stomach for niceties and protocol. He was a defense attorney first and a military officer thereafter. From the outset he turned the hearing into a trial of the OSI rather than a hearing on whether Anderson should be court-martialed for murder. He had a strong, well-researched case, and he brought it all out with his aggressive cross-examination of the men who had made the case against Airman Anderson. As he hammered away at the OSI officers, the hostility toward Major McKinney became open and glacial. During the hearing breaks, the military men would turn their backs on McKinney and huddle together at one end of the hall, while the maverick major was left to pore over his files or make small talk with the press. A month or so after the hearing ended, I learned that McKinney had retired from the Air Force and gone into private practice.

The only real evidence against Anderson was his signed confession, which upon examination proved to be a peculiar document. Although it was handwritten, it had not been written by Anderson, but only initialed by him where there were alterations and signed by him at the end. It had been written for him by one of the OSI agents, a young rookie named David Mangold, who had never before worked a homicide. The confession had been "reconstructed" by Mangold and another OSI agent, Joe Townsend, on the final night of Anderson's marathon interrogation from scattered admissions they said Anderson had made during his questioning. There were a number of bare patches that left key aspects of the murders unaccounted for. The confession left the murder of Danny Johnson totally unexplained. The key passage set forth that when Anderson brought the milk back from the dairy, he had made a verbal pass at Nancy, and that she rebuffed him with a slighting reference to his manhood.

"This remark of Nancy's enraged me," the confession read. "I immediately became violent . . . We scuffled shortly, and I possibly knocked her down; however, I am not certain. I recall seeing some blood on the floor and know that I did stab her, but I do not know what knife or instrument I used to stab her, and I have no idea where the instrument is now. During this short period it seemed to me that I blacked out, and I do not recall seeing or doing any harm to Johnson's son Danny."

In the earlier accounts of his actions, Anderson had insisted that he had returned to his home at 8:25 P.M. and he had been able to describe the closing minutes of *M Squad*, which concluded at 8:30.P.M. But in his confession, the time of his return home was altered to 8:35 P.M. Independent testimony put Anderson at the dairy shortly after 8:00 P.M., corroborating his own account. The murder scene was liberally splashed with blood. With Anderson leaving the dairy after 8:00 P.M., it would have been virtually impossible for him to have driven to the Johnson home, delivered the milk, talked to Nancy, become enraged, killed her and the boy, washed up the blood on him, looted the house, and then hidden the loot and disposed of the murder weapon in time to get home and sit down to a television program by 8:25. The confession written for him by the OSI gave him an extra ten minutes to get all this done.

After he had signed the confession, the hearing developed, new evidence had been discovered that ripped a hole in this tight timetable. An autopsy showed that Nancy Johnson had been sexually violated, and that what was believed to be the murder weapon, a hunting knife with a piece freshly broken from the blade, was found on the roadside more than a mile from the Johnson home. Further evidence exculpated Anderson. Laboratory tests of the material "shaken down" from his car had shown no connection to the crime. And finally, skin and hair samples scraped from Nancy Johnson's fingernails had been determined by laboratory analysis not to be Anderson's.

In contrast, there was an impressive array of corroboration for Dickie's account of the killings. He named the articles he had stolen from the Johnson home, described the two purses and their contents, and told where he had thrown them. He described the Johnson home in detail, down to the location of a shotgun shell on the top of the television set, and the position of a baseball bat on the rear porch. He described how Nancy Johnson was dressed and admitted that he had sexually assaulted her. He accounted for the murders by asserting that Nancy had rushed into the kitchen and picked up a knife, and that he had knocked her down and stabbed her and then killed Danny when the child came in and began crying. He put himself at the scene of the crime on the night of the murders with two witnesses. He said that shortly before going to the Johnson house his car had stalled and he had got a push from a Mountain Home resident. The man and his wife verified this.

But what riveted Dickie to the murders was the murder weapon. He accurately described where he had discarded it, and added a chilling touch that the authorities knew but had not publicly revealed—that when he stabbed Nancy a moon-shaped piece of the blade had broken off. The segment of the blade had been recovered from her body in the autopsy, and had fitted precisely into the gap in the hunting knife found shortly after Anderson had signed his confession. Dickie also told the authorities something they hadn't known—where he had obtained the murder weapon. He said he had stolen it from a trading post in Mountain Home. The trading-post owner confirmed this and identified the retrieved weapon.

All in all, Theodore Dickie eventually signed six confessions to the Johnson murders and liberally sprinkled them with minor inaccuracies and one major contradiction. After his first confession, the dismayed OSI reentered the case and grilled him at length in his Boise prison cell. He obligingly accommodated the OSI by repudiating his first confession and coming up with a fresh one in which he implicated Airman Anderson. In this version, he said that he had entered the Johnson home, found Anderson there with the bloody victims, and that Anderson admitted to him that he had killed the mother and son. Having tangled up the OSI with this new account, he had shortly repudiated it and gone back to his original version. "I just gave the OSI a big old spiel," he boasted. "I knew what they wanted—to tie Anderson into that crime—so I told them what they wanted to hear."

During a recess in the hearing, I drove to Boise and talked to Dickie for several hours in his maximum security cell. He reiterated his story of killing Nancy and Danny and, interspersed with occasional giggles, told me how much fun he had had with the OSI.

By the time the hearing reached its last few days, the only unresolved question was how the OSI had induced an innocent man to confess a murder he had not committed. In their cross-examination of the OSI agents, Anderson's attorneys had worked from a thick document that they used as a central guide for their questioning. One evening I was given a copy of it and I spent most of the night filling a notebook with quotations from it.

It consisted of a full transcript of the covert OSI tape-recording of the interrogation of Airman Anderson, from the time he had entered the little bugged room at 9:15 the night of April 11 until that moment, seven days later, when he had signed the confession the OSI wrote for him.

The OSI had preserved the tapes and they had been taken over, when the case became a scandal with the emergence of Theodore Dickie, by the inspector general's office. They had been transcribed and made available to Anderson's attorneys by that office in one of the more admirable instances of legal rectitude in the sorry case.

Why the OSI had preserved the tapes for seven months went to the heart of what had happened to Airman Anderson. "Until Dickie showed up," Major McKinney told me, "the OSI thought that breaking Gerry Anderson was one of the great feats in criminal investigation. They *believed* in the case they had made and they probably thought the record of how they had made it would be studied as a classic by future generations of OSI agents."

The interrogation of a crime suspect, when done with proper responsibility and restraint, is a delicate art. Few subjects sit down with an officer and say, "All right, I did it, and here's the story." They are brought to that point by a variety of psychological pressures that have been tested over the years and can be taught in a classroom, like weaving Panama hats underwater or any other special skill. For an interrogation to produce a false confession does not require that the interrogators set out to railroad an innocent man. They can become convinced that a subject is guilty and set about breaking his defenses by a variety of techniques. In the belief that they are cracking a strong-willed person who is guilty, they may unwittingly crumble the inadequate defenses of a weaker person who is innocent.

The tapes were a chilling record of how to break a man "by the book"

The first inquisitor was William Welsch, head of the Mountain Home OSI detachment. He began the questioning in a friendly, relaxed manner. He read Anderson Article 31 of the Military Code, dealing with his Fifth Amendment rights.

"This is the routine we go through," he told the airman. "Generally what it means is that you don't have to make any statement, and any statement made by you can be used in evidence against you."

Anderson's response showed that he had not understood what Welsch had said. "Anything I would say wouldn't hurt me?" he asked.

Welsch avoided answering the question and moved easily into his interrogation. With the hidden tape machine recording every word, he told Anderson, "You understand that everything we say here is between you and me. In other words, the only thing, I just want to shoot the bull and get a little background from you . . . "

They talked about Anderson's early life, his parents, his schooling, his religion, how he joined the service, his marriage.

In this easygoing little chat, the OSI picked up four pieces of information that it used to break Anderson. Anderson told Welsch the truth about the blood spot in his car, that it was from his wife's nosebleed when he slapped her. He admitted that he had been in trouble as a juvenile and had been sent to a reform school. He told the agent that he had once got into a fight with his wife's stepfather, who had moved in on them without paying his way. And he volunteered that when he was a boy he had fallen at a roller-skating rink, struck his head, and blacked out from the blow. He remembered this mishap vividly, and it had made quite an impression on him. He had "come to" at home several hours later, he told the agent, and couldn't remember how he had got there.

When he mentioned the juvenile trouble that had sent him to the reform school, he told Welsch that he would rather not talk about it because "it's all past and done with and I'd just as soon not bring it up."

"Sure," said Welsch and let the matter drop. But it was relayed to the next agent for his use.

Welsch led Anderson around to the day of the murders. Anderson had already told his story to the Air Police, but ran through it again. When he finished, he made his first mild complaint. "Whew! When are we going to call it quits there, podner? Boy, I tell you, I'm getting sleepy."

Legally, he could have got up and walked out. But up to this point, the transcript showed, he had taken a cooperative attitude and had repeatedly assured the agent that he wanted "to help you fellows."

Welsch ignored his complaint of fatigue and ran him back again over his account of what he had done after leaving the Johnson home. Then, without warning, Welsch threw an accusatory question at Anderson.

"Why did you get rid of those two people?" the agent demanded.

"I beg your pardon?" Anderson said.

"I said," Welsch repeated, "Why did you get rid of those two people?"

"Get rid of what two people?" Anderson asked.

"Nancy and Danny."

"You're out of your mind!" Anderson replied.

Welsch withdrew from the questioning and was replaced by another agent, Robert Jent. He picked up where Welsch left off, with the unexplained assumption that Anderson had killed his neighbor and her son.

One of the basic techniques of procuring confessions is to give the suspect a way to admit guilt and save some remnant of human dignity. The agent began opening a path for Anderson to confess the knifings, using the scraps of information the first agent had picked up in his relaxed chat about Anderson's "background."

"There are times when, due to environment, due to illness, due to many reasons, people don't follow the straight and narrow path," Jent told Anderson. "Sometimes we can't help what we do. Sometimes we do things in a moment of passion, a moment of anger and maybe because things just aren't clicking off right up here in our heads.

"Normal human beings want to get things straightened out, where we know we have done wrong. Whether there are circumstances that drove you to this, I don't know."

When Anderson insisted that he had done nothing to the Johnsons, the agent swung over to the juvenile incident that Welsch had graciously passed over. He demanded to know what kind of "trouble" Anderson had been in as a boy. Anderson resisted him on the grounds that it had nothing to do with the investigation.

The agent pressed on, demanding to know what the airman was hiding. For the first time since the interrogation had begun, Anderson showed signs of panic.

"Can't I have somebody in here with me?" he asked the agent.

The correct answer to this was "Yes." Under the Military Code, when he shifted from the role of witness to suspect, Anderson was entitled to the advice of a lawyer, either a civilian attorney, if he wanted to pay for one, or free counsel from the air base legal office, which was next door to the OSI interrogation room.

"You've got to stand on your own two feet," the agent told him. "You're a man. Everything is going to come out. Something like this there is no stopping. This investigation can go on for years and years . . . We're going to check out everything, every stinking thing that happened to you . . . We're going to stop nowhere until this matter is solved."

Reluctantly, Anderson told him that he had been involved in a minor sex offense. It had stemmed from his adolescent curiosity and the girl had not been physically harmed. Anderson said the offense had never been repeated, and that he had an enduring sense of guilt and shame about it. In making this admission, Anderson misstated his age and said that the offense had occurred when he was twelve, when in fact he was fifteen. The OSI now had two new weapons to use against him—that he had "a sex problem" and that he "lied" frequently.

The agent told Anderson that some of the people at the base had been saying for a year that he was "mentally off" and had psychological problems.

"Like what?" Anderson challenged the agent.

"Well, I'm not going to sit here and bullshit you and tell you exactly, because I don't know exactly. I just know that it's all putting you in a bad light."

He worked over Anderson on the incident reported by the couple from the Cozy Bar, when he had broken down and cried when he met his wife. Then he went back to Anderson's misstating the origin of the blood in his car.

"I think you're a psychopathic liar," the agent said. "That's what I think you are. I think you're sick. You're sick whether you admit it to yourself or not. You're sick in the head. When are you going to admit that you need help? . . . The only way you are going to get help is by coming clean and asking for forgiveness for what you've done, and you're never going to do it by sitting there telling me little piddly chicken-shit lies . . . You have told lies when the truth would have served the same purpose. Why? What are you trying to hide?"

"I've told you the truth," Anderson said.

"You have lied to me, and now you're sitting there telling me another lie by telling me you told the truth . . . You're a sick man . . . You are a man of violence. You know you are. Will you say it to yourself? Will you admit to yourself that you aren't quite right? Huh?"

"There isn't anything wrong," Anderson insisted.

"There you go again," said the agent. "You're a sick man that took the life of that young mother and little boy. It could happen again. It could happen to your own family . . . Where is it going to lead? Where is the next bit of violence going to be?"

"Sir," said Airman Anderson. "I didn't do it."

"You don't know you didn't do it because you don't know what the truth is. We have already established that you don't know what the truth is . . . Is your conscience something that left you many years ago, huh?"

"Please leave me alone," Anderson pleaded. "I didn't do it, I tell you."

"I'm not going to leave you alone until I get the truth out of you . . . Now we will stay here until tomorrow night at this time, until I get the truth . . . You're a sick man. You're sick. Did you ever think about that? You're sick. You're a twisted up, violent, sick man. That's what you are. Look at yourself. Inspect your heart, inspect your mind, look at your brain . . . Are you proud of what you are, huh?"

Throughout this assault on his personality, Anderson responded with denials of any knowledge about the murders. Early in the morning, the agent gave up. Between the OSI and the Air Police, Anderson had been under interrogation for over fifteen hours. Now they moved in a fresh agent, a boyish fellow, David Mangold, with a soft voice and a sympathetic manner. Mangold was only twenty-three and had been with the OSI for eighteen months. His total training in criminal investigation consisted of a ten-week course at the OSI school in Washington.

One of the established techniques of interrogation is the "good guy, bad guy" ploy. It consists of alternating harsh, hostile agents with a gentle and sympathetic one. The psychology is to build up resentment of the aggressive agents and then give the suspect an understanding audience in the form of an apparently sympathetic agent. Experience has shown that suspects on the verge of confessing are more likely to pour out their story to the "good guy."

"Now I don't know what your trouble has been with Mr. Welsch and Mr. Jent, and I don't care," Mangold said. "All I'm interested in is what you're going to tell me, and I'd like to hear it, hear your story of what happened. Would you like to tell me, Gerry?"

"No more," the exhausted airman mumbled. "No more."

"Just once more, huh?" Mangold wheedled.

In a remarkable display of endurance, Anderson outlasted the fresh young agent. At dawn, he was still stubbornly asserting his innocence. The exasperated Mangold suddenly abandoned his "good guy" role and began to flay Anderson verbally.

"If you're afraid of getting in any deeper, you needn't have any worries," he told Anderson, "because you're at the bottom of the well, man, and they're getting ready to put the plug in over you . . . I want you to get it off your chest, and don't give me any of this bullshit because I've had it. If a man had nothing to hide, he'd come out with these answers . . .

"You're the type of man that hits his own wife. I don't hold with any man who hits a woman at all. Frankly, I think he's the lowest son of a bitch on the face of the earth."

With that, the OSI terminated their first session and took Anderson to the detention facility and let him go to bed. "Everyone else was just getting up," Anderson told me later. "They were banging around, going in and out, cleaning the place, with the radio going. I didn't get much sleep."

The next day they brought in Joe Townsend and his "lie box" from Denver, the regional OSI headquarters. Townsend was a spare, balding fellow with a small-town, earthy wit and an abiding faith in the potentials of the polygraph machine. The OSI built up Townsend and his lie detector in advance to Anderson, conditioning him toward the notion that Townsend and his box were infallible. "This man's a specialist," Welsch told Anderson. "I have never known him to be wrong, and if a man is lying he can tell it."

Townsend was equally dogmatic. Before he attached Anderson to the machine, he told him, "If a person tells me the truth, I know it. If he doesn't tell me the truth, I know it."

"Well, I'm pretty sure I'll pass it," Anderson said.

"No, there is no pretty sure about it," Townsend told him. "You know right now whether you will or not . . . because you know right now whether you did commit this act. If you didn't, there is no way in the world that I'm going to show that you did."

This was a gross misstatement of the capabilities of the polygraph, and one that no responsible polygraph operator would make. The lie detector is an investigative tool, not an omniscient machine, and because of its limitations lie-detector readings are not admissible evidence in court. Capable operators freely concede that reactions to the "box" require human interpretation, that there are guilty suspects who can "beat the box," and innocent people who will yield readings that indicate guilt under a variety of circumstances.

Townsend initially ran two long series of tests on Anderson, and got some baffling and contradictory readings. When questioned on the murder itself, Anderson showed "blips" on his tapes that were indicative of deception in denying guilt. But when questioned about the murder weapon and how and where he had disposed of it, the polygraph tape showed that he came out "clean." In simplistic terms, Anderson indicated "guilt" about Nancy's murder and "innocence" on the weapon with which she had been hideously stabbed and slashed. When asked where he had obtained the knife, what kind of knife it was, and where he had got rid of it Anderson said "I don't know," and the tape didn't blip. Faced with this anomaly, Townsend reran Anderson three times on the murder weapon and got the same results.

When he was through, Joe Townsend told Anderson that he had failed the lie-detector test. He then took over as the prime interrogator of the airman, and in the next three days grilled Anderson for twenty-seven hours.

The tape-recording transcript showed that the polygraph test had a profound impact on Anderson. When he continued to insist that he was innocent, Townsend simply replied, "We've already crossed that bridge, and there's no going back . . . We both know it happened and you and I are the only two that know for certain it happened."

Joe Townsend now began to press Anderson for his motive. Anderson was no help; he continued monotonously to affirm his innocence. Using the skating-rink incident, the OSI agent suggested that he had blacked out and killed the Johnsons without knowing it. "You can say that you were completely off your rocker," Townsend told him. "Neither myself nor anybody could prove that you weren't momentarily insane for a period of ten minutes."

"I swear to God I didn't do it," Anderson replied.

But his protestations became more uncertain. He began to discuss with Townsend, on a "just-suppose" basis, that maybe he *had* blacked out in the Johnson home. Under the long hammering, his memory of the night of April 9 began to fade. On the fourth day of interrogation, for the first time, he told his inquisitor that now he could not clearly recall his actions after delivering the milk to Nancy. "I can't remember leaving her house," he said.

The agents seized on this as confirming their blackout explanation, and Anderson began to entertain this frightful possibility.

"The first couple of days there was no doubt in my mind," he told the agents. "And then I started talking to you people, and your questioning me, and I began to wonder myself, because nothing is impossible. I could have blacked out, and I can't remember doing it . . ."

During one of the breaks, Joe Townsend went off and ran a polygraph test on Jane Anderson and trapped her in a small deception. On the day after the murders, she told a police officer that she had spotted a prowler over in the Johnson yard the day before. Now she retracted this and said she had told the story to steer suspicion away from her husband. Whatever else she told Townsend is a matter of dispute. The lie-box expert asserted that Jane Anderson, while insisting that her husband had not admitted any guilt in the murders, had declared that she personally believed that he had committed them. Jane Anderson bitterly denied having made this statement. "There couldn't have been anything of the sort," she said. "I don't know what Townsend was talking about."

Back to the OSI interrogation room went Townsend, with his version of the interview. He told Anderson that his wife had now incriminated him in the murders. Anderson pleaded frantically with the OSI men to let him talk to his wife, but got nowhere. Shaken by the lie-detector tests, the suggestions that he had killed while in a blackout, his belief in his innocence cracked with the claim that his wife thought him guilty.

The shove over the brink, Anderson told me, came when Townsend threatened to name the airman's wife as an accessory after the fact.

"And when I do that," Townsend said, "I put those three young kids in a reformatory or an orphanage."

When his will shattered, Anderson asked the OSI agents to tell him what his motive could have been in the murders. Townsend began reconstructing the crime for him, and it was Townsend's scenario that was set forth in Anderson's confession. After explaining to Anderson how he might have killed Nancy and why, Townsend summoned young Mangold and began dictating the confession as if it were being made by Anderson.

"Townsend did all the talking, Mangold did all the writing, and I did all the listening," Anderson said. The tape recordings show that Townsend spoke to Anderson only sporadically throughout the dictation, to check a few specifics. Near the end of the dictation, there was the following exchange:

> TOWNSEND: My wife and I remained awake [early in the morning after the murders] and discussed the—what?—incident, or?
> ANDERSON: Whatever you want to call it.
> TOWNSEND: The murder or stabbing?
> MANGOLD: Call it the murder or stabbing.
> TOWNSEND: Happenings at Johnson's home. We'll just let them draw their own cotton-picking conclusions.

When Mangold finished his writing, the agents swore in Anderson and presented him with the document. In a final upsurge of resistance, he threw down the pen and refused to sign.

"I want to know one thing, Joe," he appealed to Townsend. "Did my wife really say I did it? . . . I'm so mixed up I don't know what I want to do . . . My wife really said I did it, huh?"

Townsend assured him that this was true. They swore him in again, and this time he signed his name to the OSI's scenario for the death of Nancy Johnson.

They had him initial each page and each of Mangold's corrections in the manuscript. When the tape-recording was timed, from the moment he began initialing the six pages until he signed the last one, only forty-five seconds elapsed.

"Well, that's it," said Joe Townsend. "I thank you for your cooperation."

They were not quite finished. When the civil authorities in Mountain Home examined the confession, they pointed out a gaping inadequacy. There was nothing about Nancy Johnson's sexual violation. The OSI agents went back to Anderson and tried to plug this gap. But Airman Anderson was through cooperating and he fought off their suggestions that in addition to murdering his neighbor's wife, he had also raped her.

During this last interrogation, one of the four OSI agents, Jent, broke ranks and asked to be taken off the case. "I felt in my mind," he said later, "that he wasn't the man."

Airman Anderson also had a final flash of prescience. Awash with fresh guilt at what he had done when he signed the confession, he asked the OSI agents:

"What happens to a guy when he confesses to something he didn't do —and then they find out that someone else did it?"

What happens, all too often, is what happened to Airman Gerald Anderson. Structured bureaucracies—governmental or private— are ill-equipped to utter those most human of words, "We screwed up on this, and we're sorry." Individuals can say this to one another, but the words clog in the bureaucratic or corporate throat. Ford produces an Edsel, or Chevrolet a Corvair, and the team's duty is to sell it, not search out its flaws. When a Nader documents the flaws, the organization turns on Nader, not on its erring engineers. The classic example is the Air Force cost analyst Fitzgerald, who blew the whistle on the enormous overruns on the C-5 plane and was fired for trying to save the taxpayers' money. In the Anderson affair, the OSI agents got carried away with zeal and incompetence, and if they had reversed themselves they would have damaged the image of the Organization. The Organization, in turn, protects the loyal and dutiful members of the ant heap. Such is the nature of ant heaps. The whole is far more important than any of its parts, and what is perceived as the well-being of the Organization takes automatic precedence over the ordeal of a single ant.

When the Mountain Home hearings concluded, the OSI case against Anderson had reduced itself to rubble and everyone knew what the finding would be. But meanwhile there were procedures to be followed, records to be studied, judgments to be arrived at, and mistakes to be justified before Anderson could be turned loose. I asked the hearing officer, a fair-minded and unhappy major, how long this would take and he estimated five or six weeks. He would return to his home base, go through the routines, and file his report with the commanding officer of the 15th Air Force, for his "review and decision."

It had taken the Air Force only a single day to put Anderson behind bars after the civilian court had cleared him, but getting him back out would take a total of more than two months. That was not exactly fair, the officer conceded, but that was how things were done. We went out to dinner on his last night and discussed the Anderson affair cautiously. In a burst of candor the officer told me, "If I were God, I would wad up the whole case now and throw it in the wastebasket."

The next day I phoned New York and told my *Saturday Evening Post* editor, Don McKinney, that Anderson would be cleared but that it would take five or six weeks.

"Write it now," he told me, "and we'll put it in the first open issue."

I wrote a 6,000-word account, and the *Post* published it under the title "Innocent's Grim Ordeal." Later I was told by his daughter that Secretary of the Air Force Eugene Zuckert read the article the day the *Post* came out, picked up the telephone and ordered the immediate release of Airman Anderson. The next day, at Anderson's request, the airman was given an honorable discharge. I flew up to Mountain Home and congratulated him on surviving.

We had a long talk about lie detectors, and I explained some of the quirks and oddities that Joe Townsend hadn't told him about them. He came up with a theory about why he had blipped so markedly whenever Townsend questioned him about Nancy Johnson. He said that when he went to the Johnson house with the police on the night of the murders, Nancy's body was lying naked, with her housecoat open, on the kitchen floor. He said that he had looked at her "a couple of times," and thought that was a terrible thing for him to do, and that he felt guilty about it. Apparently it was that guilt that recorded itself on Townsend's lie-box.

A few months after Anderson was freed, the OSI quietly dispensed with the polygraph services of Joe Townsend. He went off to Florida, where he tangled up two murder cases with his lie-box by obtaining confessions from black suspects who were eventually cleared. In one case, it took a dogged reporter for the Miami *Herald*, Gene Miller, four years to undo the work of Joe Townsend and the lie detector he so passionately believed in. Miller's work won him a Pulitzer prize and he wrote a fascinating book, *Invitation to a Lynching,* about the case and Townsend's role in it.

I wanted to send a copy of it to Gerald Anderson, but I didn't know where to reach him. After he left Mountain Home, I never heard from him again.

7

Big Pearl

Think of Pasadena and what comes to mind is the Rose Parade, its fresh-faced beauty queens, endless sunshine, and those legendary little old ladies who never abuse their automobiles. It is not a likely locale for a modern Gothic horror story, and when I heard, in the summer of 1966, about what had happened to a ninety-five-year-old Pasadena millionaire named Otis Birch, I didn't believe it.

Don McKinney, chief articles editor for the *Saturday Evening Post*, got onto the story first and relayed it to me by telephone. National magazines, like metropolitan newspapers, get a stream of tips on sensational stories, most of which go nowhere. Many of them come from cranks, but this one baffled and intrigued McKinney.

"We got an odd letter from a subscriber out in Des Moines, Iowa," he said. "He tells a far-out tale, but he doesn't sound like a nut. If the story is true, we ought to look into it.

"He writes that he has a rich old aunt and uncle in Pasadena. Their names are Estelle and Otis Birch. They're both in their nineties. He says they've lived at—let me see—431 Oaklawn Avenue for about sixty years.

"The relative complains that a nurse named Pearl Choate spirited the old couple away months ago. Shortly after she disappeared with the Birches, their house was stripped of a fortune in furnishings and antiques. The relative complains that the disappearance was reported to the police, the district attorney, and the FBI but nobody will do anything about it. So he wrote to the *Post* and asked for help."

I told McKinney I hadn't read anything about this in the newspapers.

"The relative says the papers haven't carried anything about it," McKinney said.

"That doesn't make sense, Don. How could a millionaire and his wife vanish without the newspapers reporting it?"

"Don't know," said McKinney. "That's why I'm calling you. Maybe there isn't any Estelle or Otis Birch or any 431 Oaklawn Avenue. But it's out in your area, so how about going up and looking around?"

There was a 431 Oaklawn Avenue. It was a big, eerie old two-story house called Bridgecrest. It stood on spacious grounds in a good neighborhood and looked like a set from that Gloria Swanson movie, *Sunset Boulevard.* An aura of sad neglect, of long-gone splendor lay over it. The lawn was burned out and the shrubbery was untrimmed and dying. I went up the curving, graceful walk and pushed the doorbell. No one answered. Peering through a leaded-glass window, I could see a spacious, empty living room. On the floor were tufts of padding where the carpets had been ripped up. Behind the house was a five-car garage with no cars. There was an aviary with a door swinging on rusty hinges, and a fish pond with no water in it.

Down at the South Pasadena police station, a clerk confirmed that a missing persons report had been filed on the Birches six weeks earlier. There was no follow-up report in the files. The clerk couldn't explain why; the officer who handled missing-person cases was on vacation. The complaint had been filed by a distant relative of the Birches, a local aerospace worker named Harlan Moehn.

I looked him up and talked to him for several hours. He was a mild-mannered, earnest man full of quiet indignation. He confirmed the details that had been reported to the *Post,* and added a lot more.

He had put a private investigator on the old couple's disappearance. The eye had charged $200 a day and expenses, and Moehn could afford him for only three days, but he had developed one good lead.

What Moehn told me sent me into Los Angeles the next day. I ran the grantee-grantor file on the property at 431 Oaklawn, talked to the D.A.'s office, and made twenty or thirty phone calls. Then I went out to West Hollywood and talked to the lead the private eye had dug up. She was a gravel-voiced nurse named Marie Rickman who had worked with Pearl Choate at Bridgecrest for about a month. Marie was uneasy and nervous and wouldn't talk to me until she had inspected my credentials. By midnight I was back home in Long Beach, with thirty pages of notes that read like the outline for a John D. MacDonald mystery.

Old Otis Birch had been ninety-five and his wife ninety-three when Pearl Choate came into their lives. Otis was stone-deaf and half blind, and his wife was a terminal cancer case. Otis Birch had made millions in years past; he had brought in a major California oil field long ago, when you could make millions and keep them. They were devout Baptists, and had given more than $20 million to church charities.

They had once had five maids, a butler, and a gardener, and on one well-remembered day, Harlan Moehn had told me, they had given a lawn party for evangelist Billy Graham and fifteen hundred guests. But they had outlived all their servants, and Bridgecrest had gradually deteriorated into a geriatric disaster area. Old Otis was a peppery little eccentric, an odd combination of open-handed generosity and skinflint parsimony. By 1966, he had given away most of his fortune by a carefully thought-out life plan, and was down to his last million. Since he had no children or close heirs, he had arranged to dispose of the last of his estate while he was still alive. He had invested his final million in irrevocable grant loans to a series of Baptist charities. These loans, plus three oil wells he owned up near Bakersfield, yielded him an annual income of about $70,000 a year. He owned Bridgecrest outright, and when he died, everything would go to the church charities.

But when he got up into his nineties, his parsimony overtook him. He was devoted to his dying wife, but he wouldn't hire a doctor, and tried to take care of her himself. Finally Harlan Moehn and some of Otis's Baptist friends insisted that he get some help. They picked two nurses out of a commercial nurse registry at nearby Altadena. One was Marie Rickman; the other was Big Pearl.

Pearl was a raw-boned woman, Moehn told me, six feet tall, over two-hundred pounds, strong as a draft horse and a hard worker. "We were well pleased with Pearl," said a Baptist pastor. "She seemed a real take-charge type." She tidied up Bridgecrest, made the old couple eat regularly, and was shortly running the establishment like a marine sergeant. After a few weeks, by appealing to Otis' penny-pinching, Pearl prevailed on him to dismiss Marie Rickman.

She brought in a doctor of her own choice. He was a Beverly Hills medic named Dr. Bernard Pearson. He had helped Big Pearl get listed on the nurses' registry by providing her with a glowing recommendation, and she now returned the favor.

She then set out to take old Otis Birch for everything he had. The first thing she got was his three oil wells. She borrowed $5,000 from a bank and acquired title with impeccable legality and a fine eye for a good business deal. The royalties from the wells brought in enough money for Pearl to recoup her investment in a little more than four months.

Nine months after she had descended on Bridgecrest, she removed her two charges from their spacious home and took them down to a tiny, two-bedroom duplex that she owned in Compton, California. When Baptist friends of the Birches objected, she explained that Bridgecrest was too big and that the move was intended to enable her to give Mr. and Mrs. Birch better care. She closed up the Pasadena house and installed one of her brothers as "caretaker."

Then, after a few weeks, she disappeared with the aged pair. Before she left, she threw everyone off the trail by telephoning some of the Birches' friends with the message that she was taking the pair to Palm Springs "to get out of the terrible smog." Instead, she had loaded them into a black Cadillac and taken them over the Mexican line and down to Ensenada, a garish oceanside resort south of Tijuana.

Back in Pasadena her "caretaker" brother showed up one day with three old trucks and some helpers and carted off everything movable in the old mansion—antiques, statuary, Oriental rugs, silverware, every stick of furniture, and even the lawn mowers. Some neighbors, observing the house being stripped, called the police. Pearl's brother produced a bill of sale, neatly typed, listing everything at Bridgecrest and signed with the wavering signature of old Otis Birch. The Birch relatives estimated the furnishings to be worth $80,000.

At the Hall of Records, I discovered an interesting document. On June 2, a deed had been recorded in which Otis Birch conveyed Bridgecrest and its grounds to Pearl Choate and Dr. Bernard Pearson "as tenants in common." Such deeds carry revenue stamps based on the sale price of the property. There were no revenue stamps on this deed, indicating that no money had changed hands.

But it was nurse Marie Rickman's story that had put everything into chilling perspective. After easing Marie out, Pearl had tried to stay on a friendly basis with her, and telephoned her frequently. Pearl was a compulsive talker.

"She was furious over the fact that old Otis had given most of his fortune to the Baptist charities," Marie told me. "She called them 'those vultures.'

"She bragged that she was going to take everything the Birches had left. She said that if the vultures could get it, she'd get it too.

"I told her, 'Pearl, you're going too far,'" Marie Rickman said. "But she just laughed and said she had two lawyers in Los Angeles advising her. She said she'd have everything so legalized that no one could touch her."

"Why on earth would she tell you all this?" I asked Marie.

"She was trying to play me along," Marie said. "She told me when she had everything in her name, she was going to open her own nursing home and take me on as a partner."

I asked why Pearl had taken a dying cancer patient down to Ensenada, a border resort town with only minimal medical facilities.

"Pearl told me," Marie said, "that when Mrs. Birch died nobody was going to know it, and she was going to go ahead and bury her and then take Mr. Birch and marry him. That poor Mrs. Birch has been dying for months now, and hasn't long to go. She may be dead already."

Marie said that Big Pearl had "pumped Mr. Birch full of lies" about his relatives and friends. "She told him that they intended to separate Estelle and him, and put him in a mental institution and Estelle in a hospital," Marie said. "It's just *pitiful* the way that poor old man trusts that woman. He thinks she's the only friend he's got left in the world. Can you imagine that? Here she is, just looting that old boy, and he thinks she's some sort of guardian angel."

Marie's story explained what I'd found out at the district attorney's office. It turned out that they *had* taken a quick look at Otis Birch's plight after the relatives had lodged a complaint about his disappearance. They had telephoned Dr. Bernard Pearson and he had reluctantly disclosed that Nurse Choate had taken the pair to Ensenada. Two D.A.'s men, with an FBI agent along as an observer, had gone to Ensenada and briefly questioned old Otis. Communicating with him was difficult: one had to print a question in big block letters on a piece of paper, then Otis would study it, letter by letter, with a magnifying glass until he comprehended it.

Otis Birch had told the D.A.'s men he had gone to Mexico with Big Pearl of his own free will. Asked why he had chosen Ensenada, of all places—in view of Mrs. Birch's terminal condition—Otis replied, "Because Mrs. Choate told me that was a good place to go." With that, the D.A.'s men decided there was nothing to be done, and returned to L.A. They passed on their report to the Birch relatives, who immediately raced to Ensenada and found that Big Pearl had gone on the run again with the aged pair. And this time there was no trail.

Because of Marie Rickman's macabre story, I decided to check into Pearl Choate's background. The D.A.'s office already had run a make on her, their investigator told me, with the criminal identification bureau in Sacramento.

"All she has is two old misdemeanors down in San Diego," the D.A.'s man told me. "One is for loitering and another for disturbing the peace."

I asked if I could take a look at her record, and he handed me the printout from Sacramento.

Over the years I've learned to *read* documents. Sometimes there is some little thing in them, seemingly unimportant, that may turn out to be significant.

In this case, the D.A.'s office had retrieved the wrong rap sheet, and no one had read it carefully. The record described Pearl as being five feet, seven inches tall, weighing 138 pounds, and being twelve years younger than the woman Harlan Moehn had described to me. I cleared my throat apologetically and pointed out these discrepancies to the D.A.'s man.

"Well—hmmm," he said. "But this is an old record, from some years back. Maybe she has put on weight."

"But she could hardly have grown five inches and got twelve years younger," I said.

He conceded that that was unlikely and said he guessed someone had goofed. How much they had erred emerged weeks later when a wise old country sheriff down in West Texas ran a make on the real Big Pearl.

•   •   •

McKinney was pleased that he had spotted a real live mystery amid all the dubious tips the *Post* got. But what we had wasn't a magazine article. It was just a starting point for one.

He asked if I thought I could find Big Pearl and her two aged charges. I said I didn't know, but I'd like to try.

"Why don't you spend some time on it?" Don said. "It would be great if the *Post* could run them down, when no one else has done anything. You got any leads?"

I told him that the property records showed that Pearl owned a couple of duplexes down in Compton where she had taken the Birches before blowing out to Ensenada. If she had tenants, she'd have to have some way of collecting the rent.

"Draw some expense money and give it a try," McKinney said.

Don McKinney was the ideal editor for this kind of story, where all you can do is give a writer some money and turn him loose. McKinney and I had worked together off and on for more than ten years, first at *True* magazine and later at the *Saturday Evening Post*. I had put together thirty or forty stories under McKinney at *True*, back in its prosperous days in the 1950's, when it did considerable initiative reporting and was willing to underwrite the expenses of developing a story. McKinney was demanding but fair-minded. Above all, he understood a writer's problems. Once he had approved a project, he didn't pluck at one's sleeve or try to shape a story from the airy remove of a Manhattan office. He was the opposite of those *Time* magazine functionaries Paul O'Neil once described in a memorable passage as:

> brigades of editors . . . who are popularly believed to be helping the writer, [but] are actually just riding around on his back, shooting at parakeets, waving to their friends, and plucking fruit from overhanging branches while he churns unsteadily through the swamps of fact and rumor with his big dirty feet sinking in to the knee at every step.

So I drove down to Compton, a scruffy suburb attached to the southern side of Los Angeles. Pearl's property consisted of two of those standard little California stucco duplexes that some giant production liner must stamp out like Nabiscos. Her own unit was locked up, but through the windows you could see that it was stacked to the ceiling with the furnishings taken from Bridgecrest.

At one of the other units a lady opened the door a crack and told me, "Miz Pearl ain't here no more."

I told her I was anxious to get in touch with her on an important *legal* matter, which bent the truth slightly without fracturing it. Could she tell me where she mailed her rent to Pearl?

"Don't mail it," she said. "I just give it to Pearl's husband."

"Her *husband?*" I asked. "I thought Mrs. Choate was a widow."

The lady said that Pearl had married a Compton black named Houston Perry about six months earlier down in Tijuana. She volunteered, with a small smile, that Mr. Perry was somewhat younger than Miz Pearl. Then she ran out of information. She didn't know where Houston Perry lived; he just showed up once a month and collected the rent. I thanked her kindly and went off to a phone booth and dialed information. There was no Houston Perry listed in Compton, Watts, or anywhere in Los Angeles County.

There was one more possible lead I hadn't told McKinney about. Harlan Moehn had mentioned that years ago Otis Birch had purchased two crypts at an Inglewood mausoleum—out near L.A. International Airport—where he and Estelle could be entombed side by side. And he had paid cash for them.

Meanwhile, shortly after I had talked to him, Moehn had quit his California job and moved to Iowa. But before he left, he had a Pasadena bank named conservator for the missing Otis Birch. So I went back up to Pasadena and talked to the bank officials. They arranged with the Inglewood mausoleum to be notified if any bodies showed up for entombment in the Birch crypts, and they agreed to let me know.

"We'll be glad to give you a call," the banker said. "This case doesn't seem to have a very high priority with the police or anyone else."

A few days later, back down to Compton. I'd overlooked a thread-thin chance. I asked the lady who rented from Pearl to give my name and phone number to Houston Perry the next time he showed up to collect the rent. She wanted to know what she should tell him.

"Just tell him I want to talk to him," I said.

"Houston's not a very talky fellow," the lady said. "He's gonna want to know what you want."

"I'll tell him when he calls," I told the lady.

After that, there wasn't anything to do except wait. I went over to L.A. and prodded the D.A.'s office once again. Would they mind rechecking Pearl Choate's background, in view of the fact that they had pulled the wrong rap sheet? The D.A.'s investigator said he didn't think there was any point in this, since there wasn't any case pending against Big Pearl.

I told him that, if Marie Rickman was to be believed, Big Pearl had set out cold-bloodedly to loot a ninety-five-year-old man of everything he had. He promptly pointed out that they had checked with Mr. Birch and he had said he had gone with Pearl of his own free will.

"But he's senile, totally deaf, and almost blind," I said. "I think she's got him programmed like a computer. Why on earth would he let Pearl take his dying wife to Ensenada? That's hardly one of the great cancer-treatment centers of the Western world."

The D.A.'s man shrugged. "I think," he said, "that you're getting overcommitted to this case."

I told him he was right.

Ten days later I came in late in the evening and the phone was ringing. It was Harlan Moehn, calling from Iowa. He said that Estelle Birch's body had shown up at the Inglewood mausoleum, and that she was to be entombed the next day at 11:00 A.M.

The Inglewood mausoleum stood on a green hill and resembled a branch library in some prosperous suburb. The interior was like a giant marble filing cabinet. The crypts, one above the other in neat rows, held one body each, indexed with the occupant's name. Identical vases of bright-hued plastic flowers adorned each crypt face.

There was no one to mourn Marguerite Estelle Conoway Birch, resident of Pasadena for more than half a century and patroness of dozens of charities. No friends, relatives, clergyman—just a sealed casket. Promptly at 11, the entombment crew put the casket on a rubber-tired carriage, rolled it silently down the dim-lit marble hall, and slid it into the assigned niche. I remembered what Marie Rickman said Pearl had told her. *"When Mrs. Birch died nobody was going to know it, and she was going to go ahead and bury her and then take Mr. Birch and marry him."*

A jetliner whined down through the thin smog toward L.A. airport. I thought of the title of one of Ray Bradbury's books, *Something Wicked This Way Comes,* and went over to the mausoleum office. They said that Mrs. Birch's body had been delivered for entombment by a downtown L.A. mortuary. I went down the green hill and drove into L.A.

The mortician said the body had been flown in, unattended, by American Airlines out of Dallas. It had been consigned by a funeral home in Breckenridge, Texas, for delivery to the Inglewood mausoleum.

Why was there no minister or burial service?

The undertaker pulled a form out of Mrs. Birch's file. Under "Burial Instructions" was a bold scrawl, "No service or view, no newspaper notices," over the signature of Dr. Bernard Pearson.

The reason—as Pearl had planned—that no one had come to mourn Estelle Birch was that none of her friends knew she had died.

I went home and looked up Breckenridge in the atlas. It was a town of 6,300 about 120 miles west of Dallas. There was a late-afternoon flight, so I packed a few clothes, stuffed all my notes into a flight bag, flew to Dallas and got a rental car, and headed west to Breckenridge.

Breckenridge strings out on both sides of Highway 180, which runs straight as a ruler through the flat plains of west Texas. I checked into the Ridge Motel at the edge of town and went around the next morning to the offices of the Breckenridge *American,* a three-times-a-week newspaper. It had carried a two-inch story about the death of Mrs. Birch, who was described as a resident of Breckenridge and the wife of Otis Birch. It gave her address as 1213 West First Street, and no background whatever. The telephone book listed that as the home of an S. H. Choate, who turned out to be another of Pearl's brothers, a Breckenridge tavern operator.

The house was a modest frame building near the edge of town, out where the sidewalks end and the empty fields begin. A truck and two cars were parked in front. One of the cars was a white Ford with California license RVA-068. I drove back into town, called the attorney general's office in California, and asked a friend to check the ownership. It was registered to Pearl Choate.

I went back to my motel and called Harlan Moehn in Iowa and told him I'd found Pearl Choate. He said he'd come down to Texas at once with another of Estelle's relatives, named Dean Gaines. He said he was going to inform the Pasadena bank conservator, and have them hire a Breckenridge attorney.

The bank hired the attorney by telephone, and the next day we got together. He was a blunt-spoken native Texan named Ben Dean, Jr., and we hit it off well from the start. He knew everyone in Breckenridge, and once he was briefed on Pearl's bizarre project, he pulled together an astonishing amount of information in twenty-four hours.

Pearl had slipped quietly into town two months earlier, Dean learned, convoying her two aged charges in an ambulance. Somewhere along the way, between Ensenada and Breckenridge, old Otis had broken his hip. Pearl had put Otis and Estelle in a Breckenridge nursing home and kept them there for three weeks, feeding and tending them herself.

"Talked to the nurses there," Dean said. "They said Mrs. Birch had occasional spells of lucidity. She kept moaning, '*Why must we travel so much? Why are we at the mercy of this woman?*' As you know, the old boy is stone-deaf, and he couldn't hear his wife's complaints.

"After three weeks Pearl moved both the Birches to her brother's house," Dean continued.

"She had the old boy hire a local attorney. He's Jack Eden, and he's county attorney for Stephens County.

"I checked the courthouse. Big Pearl has been quite active. She's acquired a comprehensive power of attorney for herself, so she can act legally in Otis Birch's behalf—if that's the proper word. Then she filed a petition to be named Birch's guardian, on the ground that he's of unsound mind. Had a hearing in court on October 7, and she brought old Otis into court in a wheelchair. The judge turned her down as his guardian because Estelle wasn't represented before the court.

"She took Otis back to the house around noon," Dean said. "And you know what? At 4:45 that afternoon, Pearl Choate reported that Mrs. Birch had died. I talked to the doctor who had handled Mrs. Birch at the nursing home. He said that in her final four weeks, Pearl never called him once. The old woman died without medical care. The cause of death was listed as cardiovascular failure, which in little words means her heart stopped beating.

"Five days after her death," Dean went on, "a petition was filed in court for Otis to adopt Pearl Choate *as his daughter*. The purpose, according to the petition, is to enable Pearl legally to inherit his estate. That's where things stand now."

He looked at me and raised an eyebrow. "You seem to have taken the lid off a can of worms," said Ben Dean.

When Moehn and Dean Gaines arrived from Iowa, they put in at the Ridge Motel and the three of us had a strategy session with Ben Dean. Both Moehn and Gaines were blood relatives of Estelle Birch, not Otis, and they were outraged at the way she had been abused in the final months of a long, gentle life. They wanted something done about Pearl Choate. They asserted earnestly that they had no interest in Otis's fortune. "We're not in his will," they said, "and we do not expect to inherit anything. We never have."

But they felt that old Otis ought to know how his wife had been mistreated—if he was capable of understanding. "Then he can make up his own mind," Moehn said. "If he wants to keep that big old gal on, that's all right with us. But none of his friends or relatives have talked to him in months. We don't know if he's even aware of what's happening."

The next day, the two Iowans arranged through Attorney Jack Eden to go out to the little frame house and see Otis Birch. They went alone; I'd arranged to have lunch with Stephens County Sheriff Chase Booth. Because of the malfunction by the Los Angeles D.A.'s office, we still didn't know who Big Pearl really was.

Chase Booth was a lean, leathery, taciturn old lawman. He listened to a capsule account of what Pearl Choate had done and said, "Think I'd better check this lady out down in Austin." He finished his coffee, and shoved his chair back.

"Be talking to you," he said, and stalked off.

I went back to the Ridge Motel and about ten minutes later all hell broke loose.

Moehn and Gaines came bursting into my room, white-faced and stuttering in terror.

They'd gone out to the house at the edge of town and found old Otis Birch propped up in bed in a back bedroom. Big Pearl, attended by Attorney Eden, looked on at the reunion. The Iowans said that it was a tense scene.

The Iowans got a pad and began block-printing questions for old Otis to decipher. They went swiftly to the point.

Moehn printed: DID YOU KNOW ESTELLE HAD CANCER WHEN YOU WERE TRAVELING AROUND THE COUNTRY?

Otis had peered at the question with his magnifying glass for several minutes. Then he said, "No, not at first."

Moehn started to print another question, when suddenly Big Pearl bolted out of the room.

"She came running back a few seconds later waving a big butcher knife," Moehn said. "Her face was all twisted and she lunged toward us, screaming, 'I'll cut your heart out, you————! I'll kill you!'"

Eden seized Big Pearl and wrestled her to a sofa, Moehn said. The Iowans ran for their lives. "During all the commotion," Moehn said, "Old Otis just lay there calmly, unaware of what was going on. He can barely see and can't hear."

While the Iowans were spilling out their story, a car slid to a halt outside the motel room. In came Eden, full of apologies and eager to calm the two relatives. He kept saying that Big Pearl was just "distraught" and "upset" and hadn't meant what she said.

The Iowans wanted her arrested for attempted murder. The county attorney tried to explain that in west Texas rushing at someone with a knife and promising to cut his heart out did not constitute "a legal offense."

While this exchange was going on, the telephone rang. It was Sheriff Chase Booth, and he sounded as if someone was after *him* with a butcher knife.

"Hooo-eeee, mister," said Chase. "Been on the phone to Austin. This big old gal's got a record long as Dillinger's, and it's got murder one on it. Get your tail down to my office fast."

I elbowed the county attorney out of the room and told the Iowans what the sheriff had said. They had just got their normal color back and they went white again. I told them to lock themselves in their room and not talk to anyone except Ben Dean, then sprinted for my car.

Pearl's police record was so long that the sheriff had a secretary taking it down in shorthand. Her rap sheet went back to 1926, on charges ranging from vagrancy to first-degree murder. She had been convicted of murder, drunk driving, shoplifting, malicious mischief, and felony theft, and there was a long list of other arrests on which the disposition was not listed. In 1949 she had been sentenced to the Goree unit of Huntsville Prison for twenty-two years for putting four fatal shots in the back of a carpenter named Alfred Allison. Mr. Allison had offended Big Pearl by dunning her for a little overdue carpenter's bill.

She had been paroled in 1954 on the carpenter's murder, but two years later was tucked away again for parole violation. What had sent her back to prison had a blood-chilling familiarity. Pearl claimed that she had been employed as "a companion to a semiretired lady" and had been "traveling around the state" with her in a house trailer, when the lady's daughter "made trouble for her" because she thought that Big Pearl was going to get the ailing woman to name Pearl in her will.

Over the years, she had married six elderly gentlemen. All six were dead.

The prison record called Pearl a "companion to the elderly," and rated her rehabilitation prospects as "poor."

Texas had kept her behind bars for seven years the second time around. She had been turned loose in 1963, and the following year had migrated to California where she resumed "nursing" elderly patients. Despite the glowing recommendation that Dr. Pearson gave her, she had never completed any training for any kind of nursing license.

While I was transferring all this from the prison record to my notebook, Attorney Ben Dean came striding into the sheriff's office with Harlan Moehn in tow. I showed him Pearl's lengthy record.

"I'm going to make it a little longer," Dean snapped. "Mr. Moehn is going to sign an assault complaint against her."

An hour later the sheriff brought her in on the butcher-knife charge. She was riding in the front seat of the squad car, and I got my first look at the lady I'd been hunting for weeks.

She was a huge, slope-shouldered woman with gray hair streaked with yellow dye and pulled back in a tight bun. She had a mean-looking mouth pulled down at the corners. When she got out of the car she took off her coat and draped it over her head like a mobster, to foil the photographers. After the sheriff booked and fingerprinted her, she posted $200 bail in cash from a cavernous leather bag. Then she draped the coat over her head, groped her way out of the building and was driven away by Jack Eden.

When the Iowa relatives learned that Big Pearl had been freed on bail, they refused to stay on at the Ridge Motel. "No way," Harlan Moehn said. "No sirree, no way! Not with that killer on the loose."

Ben Dean arranged for a wealthy local rancher to put up the Iowans at his house, and we all assembled there late in the evening. Dean brought along the Breckenridge state legislator, Representative Burke Musgrove. I'd gone three days with little sleep, and my mind was groggy with fatigue. About 10:00 P.M. the Alfred Hitchcockian horror of the situation suddenly hit me. Old Otis Birch was out at that little house at the edge of town with a convicted murderess and he didn't know who was taking care of him, unless County Attorney Eden had told him.

Representative Musgrove and I got on a phone and an extension and roused Eden. Had he told Otis Birch about Pearl Choate's murder record? He said he hadn't. Didn't he think his client ought to be told who was taking care of him? Eden allowed that he would bring old Otis up to date the next day. We urged him to go out to the house, but he wouldn't budge.

When we hung up, Musgrove said, "Hell, we've got to do something about this." He called the sheriff and told him to stake out the house, and then called the Texas Rangers and had them move two teams to Breckenridge to take over the stakeout.

The Rangers parked in a copse of trees near the house and watched it all night. The next morning they learned that Big Pearl had again outguessed and outmaneuvered everyone. Shortly before the stakeout had been set up, she had loaded old Otis into a brand-new Dodge Charger she had recently bought and, with a nephew at the wheel, had gone roaring out of Breckenridge.

Ben Dean went trekking back to the courthouse with Harlan Moehn, and Moehn signed a kidnap complaint against Pearl. The news was flashed to the Texas Highway Patrol and all the Mexican border-crossing points were alerted.

The kidnap warrant and the border alert turned the story of Otis and Pearl into a media happening. The TV networks, the Texas stations, the wire services, radio reporters, and about a dozen major newspapers, including the Los Angeles *Times*, sent representatives racing to the tiny west Texas town.

The next day they all had the kind of story that news editors find irresistible. Big Pearl came back to town in her red Charger with a new husband. Instead of heading for Mexico, she had run north, over the border to Altus, Oklahoma, and married Otis Birch. When she returned to Breckenridge, she carried her ninety-five-year-old bridegroom over the threshold and replaced him and his broken hip in his bed of pain. Then she went down to the courthouse, posted $5,000 bail on the kidnapping charge, and began giving interviews to one and all—except the representative of the *Saturday Evening Post*.

She said that "my only bond with Mr. Birch is love," because she already had all his money and possessions. "He gave everything to me seven months ago," Pearl said. She insisted that the whole point of the wild, cruel flight from California was to "protect him from those devil ministers who were trying to get his money." She even claimed that Estelle Birch, before she died in agony, had approved Pearl's taking over the remnants of the Birch fortune. "She was a wonderful person," said Big Pearl. "I loved her and she loved me."

The editor of the Breckenridge *American*, Virgil Moore, was more interested in Otis Birch's view of the kidnapping-that-turned-into-a-wedding. It turned out that old Otis hadn't realized he was marrying Pearl Choate up in Altus, Oklahoma. They had been married in the red Charger by an Oklahoma minister who conveniently provided curb service for incapacitated bridegrooms. "I didn't go inside," Otis told the Breckenridge newsman. "I just sat in the car. I didn't know the man was a preacher."

This got Big Pearl all upset again, but instead of taking a butcher knife to Moore, she printed a message to Otis. He read it slowly and painfully, and then said, "We were married."

That Saturday the central figures—Pearl, Otis, Moehn, and Ben Dean—all assembled in the Stephens County Courthouse for a habeas corpus action filed by Dean. Its purpose: to determine legally whether Otis was being held against his will. The courtroom was jammed to the walls by reporters and curious residents. "I've seen all this," said one courthouse loiterer, "and I still don't believe it."

Throughout the hearing, Otis sat in his wheelchair like a small waxen statue. He could see the outlines of people only dimly and could hear nothing. His world had been like this for a long time. From the day Pearl had taken him and his dying wife out of Bridge-crest, all he knew about the silent outside world was what Big Pearl chose to tell him.

Pearl wheeled him to the witness stand, where he was able to croak the few sentences that took her off the legal hook. He said he had gone with her willingly and that he had left California because the "authorities wanted to take me and make a test for insanity." He didn't identify the "authorities" and said this information had come from Pearl Choate. That was what Marie Rickman had told me, weeks earlier, and it was remarkable to hear old Otis, like a dutiful computer, read back Big Pearl's programming from a Texas witness stand.

The judge said that the single issue was whether Otis was being held against his will, and he ruled that he was not. You couldn't quarrel with his verdict; the law is the law, and he went by the only evidence before the court.

Pearl was jubilant. "He was a good judge," she told reporters, "and he done what was right." Then she wheeled her old bride-groom out to her new red car. She looked like a maternal Amazon trundling a small, withdrawn child in an oversized perambulator.

The next day I drove back to Dallas, took a plane into New York, and wrote "The Case of the Missing Millionaire" for the *Post.* It drew many indignant letters that asked what the hell had happened to justice.

I went back to the guardians of law and order in L.A. and suggested that, if nothing more, they had a bigamy case against Big Pearl. Under considerable prodding, they dug out a Tijuana marriage license issued a year earlier to Pearl and Houston Perry. They brought Houston in for questioning, but he proved evasive on whether he had engaged in matrimony with the much-married Pearl Choate. "I won't say I did," said Houston, "and I won't say I didn't."

The guardians of the law gravely studied the case and focused on its legal inadequacies. Tijuana licenses are notoriously frail as evidence of valid marriage. Besides, they argued, how did they know that Houston and Miz Pearl hadn't got a Mexican divorce? They finally decided that an interstate bigamy charge involving California, Oklahoma, and Texas, and resting on a Mexican border-town marriage license, was too complex to pursue. Then old Otis died in Texas and rendered the whole matter moot.

Free as a bird, Big Pearl came winging back to California. I had continued keeping tabs on her through Ben Dean because she stirred anxieties in me. She had told a reporter in Breckenridge that I was the cause of all her troubles and she didn't like me very much. Being Irish and fatalistic, I'd never really worried about the hazards inherent in my line of work. But Pearl had a hair-trigger temper and a lamentable lack of restraint. I kept remembering that she'd killed one man because he'd dunned her for a little debt, and that she had rushed at Moehn with a butcher knife—in the presence of the county attorney.

Maybe there is some big karma wheel up in the sky that turned against Big Pearl, or maybe the old Greeks were right in believing that we fashion our own fates. But after outsmarting, outthinking, and outrunning the law in two states and Mexico, she tripped herself up and went back to jail. And no thanks to the D.A., the FBI, the Pasadena police, and no thanks to me.

She went back to her Compton rentals and got into an argument with a tenant. The tenant called the Compton cops and two of them went out to her duplex. When they set foot on her property, Pearl was waiting at the door with a rifle. She screamed some obscenities at them and told them to bug off.

"We're police officers, lady," one of them said, and they kept coming toward the house. Then Big Pearl lost control again. She leveled the rifle and winged two fast shots at the officers. She missed twice and they disarmed her at gunpoint, handcuffed the compulsive old killer, and hauled her away.

She rallied her lawyers and fought the case. Inefficient though law enforcement may be now and then, it takes a dim view of people who try to shoot law enforcers. They gave her a speedy trial and a judge tucked her away at Chino for assault with intent to kill.

There were two little sequels. The attorney general's office called in Dr. Pearson for questioning about his peculiar relationship with the nurse-who-was-not-a-nurse. He came in with his lawyer and took the Fifth Amendment. The attorney general referred the case to the California Board of Medical Examiners. They decided not to do anything about Dr. Pearson.

But the state of California did something about the D.A.'s man who blew the case at the outset by pulling the wrong rap sheet on Big Pearl. He was elevated to a judgeship.

8

Jim Garrison v. Clay Shaw

"This could be one of the biggest stories of our times," said Don McKinney, handing me a sheaf of newspaper clippings. "If Garrison has what he says he has, he is going to rewrite history. People will be reading about him and what he did a hundred years from now.

"And you've got the inside track with him."

It was late February 1967, in the New York offices of the *Saturday Evening Post.* A few days earlier, the name of New Orleans District Attorney Jim Garrison had erupted on front pages across the country. He had announced that for months he had been quietly reinvestigating the 1963 assassination of John F. Kennedy. The Warren Commission had been dead wrong in its central finding that Kennedy had been killed by an alienated loner, Lee Harvey Oswald. The President had been assassinated instead by a band of conspirators in a plot hatched in New Orleans. Garrison and his staff had uncovered the details, and they would arrest the conspirators and take them to trial.

"My staff and I solved the case weeks ago," Garrison told newsmen on February 24. "I wouldn't say this if I didn't have evidence beyond the shadow of a doubt. We know the key individuals, the cities involved, and how it was done. We are going to be able to arrest every person involved—at least every person who is still living. The only way they are going to get away from us is to kill themselves."

One key conspirator, Garrison said, was a New Orleans pilot named David Ferrie, whose dead body had been found in his apartment two days prior to Garrison's sensational announcement. "The apparent suicide of David Ferrie ends the life of a man who, in my judgment, was one of history's most important individuals. Evidence developed by our office has long since confirmed that he was involved in events culminating in the assassination of President Kennedy." Garrison had had Ferrie under surveillance and had planned to arrest him. "Apparently we waited too long," Garrison said, but the arrest of the other conspirators would be forthcoming.

"We saved the assignment for you because Garrison knows you and likes you," said McKinney. "Draw some money and get down there. All we want is what he has uncovered and how he put it together. Exclusive for the *Saturday Evening Post.*"

Four years earlier I had written a *Post* article, "The Vice Man Cometh," about the newly elected New Orleans district attorney and his maverick cleanup of sinful old Bourbon Street in the French Quarter. Garrison and I got along well together, he had liked the article, and we had stayed casually in touch.

"Before we start blocking out a cover story on this, Don, we've got one little problem," I complained. "Every television network, wire service, major newspaper, and magazine is already down there trying to lock up the same story."

"Of course they are," McKinney grinned. "So get going."

I caught a night plane south. The next morning I found the corridor outside Garrison's office a media madhouse. It was clogged with milling reporters, television cameras, lights, and cables. Everyone was in town except Norman Mailer. There was a team in from *Paris Match*, the French version of *Life*. They were cultivating Garrison with the Gallic device of sending daily bouquets to his attractive blond wife. Oriana Fallaci, the internationally known Italian woman reporter, and two colleagues were in from Rome. The British Broadcasting Company had a team in town, and so did Canadian Broadcasting. Plus *Life, Newsweek, Time,* AP, UPI. There were even two reporters from the Soviet Union, and a radio correspondent from Anna, Illinois, population 4,000.

You had to queue up to request Garrison's receptionist for an appointment to talk to Garrison's secretary about an appointment with Garrison. You couldn't get the secretary on the phone; the switchboard was clogged with stacked-up calls from all over the United States and from abroad. I finally collared an assistant I knew and gave him a note for his boss. I told Garrison that I had joined the thundering herd and asked him to call me at the Royal Orleans Hotel whenever he had time to breathe. Then I went around to the *Times-Picayune* and the *States-Item* picked up all their local clips, and holed up in my hotel.

I had expected a heavy press turnout, but the massive international response stunned me. It reflected, in part, the European rejection of the Warren Commission's findings from the outset—in Europe the assassination of a political leader was automatically equated with political conspiracy. Erosion of the Report in the United States had taken longer, but by 1967 there was widespread public belief that the Warren Commission, as Garrison charged, had indeed failed to uncover the ultimate truth about the Kennedy assassination. Public opinion polls indicated that two thirds of the population rejected the Report's central finding, that Oswald alone had fired the fatal shots in Dallas. In its Humpty-Dumpty fall from public favor, the Report had been vigorously pushed by a new brand of specialists, the so-called Warren critics. Led by Mark Lane, a lawyer-author whose *Rush to Judgment* had become a sensational international best seller, criticizing the Warren Report had become a new U. S. cottage industry, and the Commission had been subjected to increasingly savage attacks on its evidence, competence, methodology, and integrity.

In 1967 there was an impressive national consensus that Kennedy had been killed by an orchestrated conspiracy, rather than by a scruffy little misfit with nothing but a cheap mail-order rifle. And if there had been a conspiracy, there had to be conspirators.

Garrison had appeared on the scene at this point like a *deus ex machina*, promising the crucial missing piece—the identity of the conspirators. He was a duly elected prosecutor with subpoena power in the jurisdiction where he had uncovered the conspiracy. But above all, his bold pronouncements were those of a prosecutor who had copper-riveted his case. In promising arrests in a conspiracy the Warren Commission said it couldn't find, he was putting his career on the line in a showdown of his own making. And no experienced district attorney—the reasoning went—would do that unless he held a pat royal flush.

I got out a fresh notebook and began playing catch-up. The only conspirator Garrison had named was the dead David Ferrie, and according to the clips, he was an exotic fellow indeed, even for colorful old New Orleans. He was a former airline pilot, a self-proclaimed psychologist, an ex-seminary student, an amateur hypnotist, an inventor, a private investigator, and an adventurer with a penchant for cloak-and-dagger projects, some of which trailed rumors of CIA involvement. Physically, Garrison could not have picked a more ominous-looking suspect if he had ordered him up from Central Casting. Ferrie was totally hairless from an obscure medical ailment, and remedied this by pasting on false eyebrows that he often got askew, and by donning a homemade red wig that bore little resemblance to human hair. "You had to see Ferrie to disbelieve him," a New Orleans newsman told me, adding that, along with everything else, Ferrie was an active homosexual, a violent anti-Communist, and a friend of Carlos Marcello, the reputed Mafia capo in the New Orleans area.

According to the clips, it was Ferrie and not Garrison who had made the initial disclosure that the bewigged eccentric was a target of Garrison's investigation. On February 19 Ferrie had told reporters that he was a Garrison suspect, and that the D.A. "apparently had me pegged as get-away pilot for the assassins" in Dallas. He denied any complicity and said he had never known Lee Harvey Oswald.

Three days later, Ferrie was found dead in his cluttered New Orleans apartment. Because of the sequence of events, his death generated wide speculation that he had either killed himself to escape Garrison's closing net, or darker still, had been murdered by forces intent upon silencing him. Conspiracy adherents had pointed to the obvious parallel between the deaths of Ferrie and Oswald. Oswald had been arrested and then swiftly murdered by Jack Ruby before he could talk. Ferrie had been targeted by Garrison as an assassination conspirator and promptly turned up dead. The deaths seemed too exquisitely timed for happenstance.

Garrison had tabbed the death as "apparent suicide," but in the clippings was a sidebar story that hooked my attention. In the autopsy performed on Ferrie by the New Orleans coroner, the cause of death was found to be a "berry aneurysm." I recalled a sensational murder case years earlier that involved a berry aneurysm, which is medicalese for the failure of a blood vessel inside the skull. In this case, the victim had died during a fight and his assailant had been charged with murder. The autopsy had disclosed the cause of death to be a berry aneurysm, and the assailant had been acquitted.

I picked up the hotel phone and called a friend of mine in California, Dr. Eugene Blumberg, who was a sort of walking National Archives on brain damage. I told him I was working on a story where a man had died of a berry aneurysm, and there were rumors that he had either committed suicide or been murdered.

"Not if the autopsy showed berry aneurysm as the cause of death," said Blumberg.

"That's what I remember, Gene," I told him. "Could you locate any medical findings on this?"

A couple of hours later he called back with two citations.

"This is from 'The Relationship of Brain Injury to Other Organic Diseases of the Brain,' by Dr. I. W. Wechsler," he said. "It's short and I'll read it."

> The rupture of these berry aneurysms is not due to external injury, since these aneurysms are almost always too deep-seated and too well-cushioned by surrounding brain to be so affected.

The second citation was from the murder case I remembered.

"Two men got into a fight," Dr. Blumberg said. "One knocked the other down and he struck his head on the sidewalk and died. The fellow who hit him was charged with murder. But the autopsy showed that the victim died of a berry aneurysm. The New York forensic medical authority, Dr. Milton Halpern, testified for the defense and the man was acquitted. The key portion of Halpern's testimony reads: " *'The rupture of an aneurysm of this nature due to direct physical trauma does not occur. The aneurysm ruptures spontaneously from within.'* "

So much for "The Strange Death of David Ferrie," as some of the papers were calling it. According to Blumberg, a berry aneurysm is a congenital defect. David Ferrie had been born with a weak artery wall in his hairless head, and it had picked a dreadful time to give way.

That he had died of natural causes did not, of course, mean that he had nothing to do with the Kennedy assassination. But he hadn't killed himself to escape Garrison and no one had murdered him to shut him up.

The New Orleans clippings had one other piece of information

or money." He was a well-read man, and an avid fan of Ayn Rand, the author of *The Fountainhead* and *Atlas Shrugged* and leader of a cult of unrestricted individualism. When I had first met Garrison, I had been impressed by the maverick strain in him; he would hold forth at length about the powers of the federal establishment and the threat it posed to the individual.

We did not discuss his Kennedy investigation at lunch. He was continually interrupted by club members who came over to his table and complimented him for his new undertaking, and by messengers from his office, bringing him messages and holding whispered consultations.

When we finished, we took a cab to the Criminal Court Building. He said that he was exhausted from all he had gone through and was going out to Las Vegas for a long weekend to get away from his staff, witnesses, the press and everyone else.

"I'd like for you to meet me there," he said. "We'll have plenty of time and quiet and I'll tell you how I put this whole thing together, from the beginning to the end. You can have it for the *Post*—the whole fantastic story."

He suggested that we go out separately, to throw the press corps off, that I fly out that night and pick him up at the Las Vegas airport the next day. We both grinned when I said I thought I could work that into my busy schedule. I dropped him at his office and took the cab to the hotel to check out.

And just how did you get this incredible exclusive story for your magazine, sir? I asked myself as the cab swung into the French Quarter.

On a silver platter, I replied.

I flew to Vegas, put in at the Dunes, and picked up Garrison the next day. He came off the plane slump-shouldered and exhausted, and told me to drive him to the Sands, where he registered under the name of W. O. Robertson. He said he was going to fall into bed and told me to meet him for lunch the following morning at the Sands Garden Room.

He was rested and eager to talk the next day. When they had cleared the table, I opened my pad and we began the debriefing.

"First off," Garrison said, "the Warren Commission missed the whole story. What they did on the Commission, in effect, was to send a hundred squirrels out to pick up leaves, acorns, and sticks.

Each squirrel brought in something and dumped it into a box. Then the head squirrels looked at this collection of junk and tried to reconstruct the terrain from where it had been picked up.

"What it took to learn what really happened at Dallas was imagination and evaluation. It was like a complex chess game—and I once played a chess expert eight hours to a draw.

"We went back in time, tracked people down, examined old street directories, old telephone books, and uncovered a whole series of odd connections. They fell into place, one piece after another. To understand the overall picture, you have to keep firmly in mind that the Kennedy assassination was like Alice in Wonderland: *Nothing was what it seemed to be. Black was white, and white was black.*"

The idea of reinvestigating the assassination originated, Garrison said, on a plane trip the year before with Senator Russell Long of Louisiana. The senator had expressed doubt that the Warren Report had got to the real truth and since "the senator was a knowledgeable man with inside sources in Washington," Garrison decided to take a harder look at the Kennedy murder. He had read some of the Warren critics' books, "an excellent article in *Esquire*," and began to study the volumes of evidence published by the Warren Commission. The more he read, the more he became convinced that "there was no way Oswald could have staged the killing single-handed." He decided to look into Oswald's activities in New Orleans during the months before the assassination, and he started off with David Ferrie.

"The thing that led me to the truth," Garrison said, "was the trip Dave Ferrie made to Texas right after Kennedy was killed. You know how you pluck at a loose thread and unravel a whole garment? Ferrie's trip was that loose thread. I started pulling on it and unraveled the whole conspiracy. You know Ferrie's background?"

"Some of it," I said. "He was a far-out fellow."

"And brilliant," Garrison said. "Twisted and incredibly brilliant, a criminal mastermind. Take a look at these documents. They'll fill you in."

He handed me two confidential reports from a private investigative agency. They were a rundown on Ferrie procured by an airline where Ferrie had worked as a pilot. The line had fired him for homosexual activity. The reports were a bizarre dossier on a strange man, but there wasn't anything in them remotely touching on the

Kennedy assassination. I asked Garrison what he had got out of the reports.

"Nothing directly," he said, "but the reports gave us a lot of leads to his associations."

I suggested that Garrison tell me about Ferrie's trip to Texas, since that had unravelled the Dallas conspiracy.

"All right," he said, "but first, you're aware that I had Ferrie picked up a few days after the assassination in 1963, on a tip that tied him to Oswald. We questioned him and then turned him over to the federal authorities. That was our big mistake. We had our hands on a key figure right at the beginning but didn't know it. The FBI made a cursory check and turned Ferrie loose. The FBI blew the investigation right there, only I didn't know it at the time."

"But Ferrie was in New Orleans when Kennedy was killed," I said.

"That's right," Garrison said. "But that night he left by car for Texas, with two other men. It was a curious trip, a most curious trip, by a curious man to a curious place at a curious time. With the whole nation sitting glued to their television sets for news about the assassination, Ferrie headed for Texas and drove all night through a severe rainstorm. When I picked him up on his return, he claimed he had gone to Houston to go ice-skating at a rink there. Can you imagine, driving all night through a rainstorm to go ice-skating?

"That story didn't track, so I turned him over to the FBI," Garrison went on. "They checked and verified that he had showed up at the Winterland skating rink in Houston, and they dropped the matter there. That's where they blew it.

"When we came back into the case, a few months ago, we went into it deeper. We interviewed the rink manager and we picked up what the FBI had missed."

He paused dramatically.

"*Ferrie never put on his ice skates,*" Garrison said. "He was at the rink all afternoon and *never put on his ice skates.*"

I looked at Garrison in bewilderment. He had a satisfied smile, like that of Sherlock Holmes explaining to Watson the significance of the dog that didn't bark.

"I'm sorry, but I don't follow you," I told him. "Ferrie went to Houston to go ice-skating but didn't go ice-skating. How does that put him into a conspiracy to kill Kennedy?"

"It broke down his story about why he went to Houston," Garrison said. "It showed he had lied to us and to the FBI."

"Okay," I said. "Why did he go to Houston?"

"Let me tell you the rest of it," Garrison said. "The rink manager told us that Ferrie made a great point of impressing his name on him. Ferrie said 'I'm Dave Ferrie' four or five times, as if he wanted everyone to remember that he had been there.

"Now we come to the important part. The manager told us that the rink had a pay telephone, and Ferrie stuck by the telephone instead of going ice-skating. The manager remembered that distinctly. So it was obvious."

I asked him what was obvious.

"The skating rink was the message center," Garrison explained.

"I see," I told Garrison. "After the assassination, Ferrie drove from New Orleans over to Houston to get a phone message at the skating rink. Who was the message from?"

"We don't know that yet," Garrison said. "But the skating rink had to be the message center."

"But you don't know who called him or what they said?"

"No, but let me tell you about the phone call Jack Ruby made down to Galveston. Then you'll see the pattern."

Ruby had a friend in show business in Dallas, Garrison said, named Breck Wall. Wall was a young comedian and song-and-dance man with his own show, *Bottoms Up.* The day after Kennedy was killed, Breck Wall drove down from Dallas to Galveston. Late Saturday, the day before Jack Ruby shot and killed Oswald in the Dallas police station, Jack Ruby had made a phone call from Dallas to Wall in Galveston.

"And where do you think Dave Ferrie went when he left the skating rink in Houston?" Garrison asked. "To *Galveston.*"

"He met Breck Wall there?" I asked.

"We haven't established that," Garrison said. "But look at the pattern. Ferrie leaves New Orleans and drives all night in a heavy rainstorm to go ice-skating. Breck Wall, close friend of Jack Ruby, takes off from Dallas after Kennedy is killed, drives *through Houston* to Galveston and gets a phone call from Ruby. Ferrie's on stand-by at the message center—the rink in Houston—and he takes off and drives down to Galveston, too. And the Warren Commission would have you believe that all this was just coincidence."

I was about to ask another question when Garrison held up a

warning hand. "We better put this off," he said. "I just spotted something. We're under FBI surveillance. Three agents over in that side booth."

Out in the lobby he told me that the FBI "was all over him" since his Kennedy investigation had surfaced. He said his phones in New Orleans were tapped, and that he and his staff had been using code words for Ferrie, Shaw, Oswald, and other key figures in the conspiracy.

We arranged to meet again early in the evening in his room at the Sands. When I came in, he had his jacket off, and had a holster strapped on him, with a gun in it. He pulled it out and came over to me. "Let me show you something," he said, and broke the gun open. He examined the bullets and handed one of them to me. "That's a magnum load," he said, "and my gun can't handle it. If I used it, the gun would blow up on me. I can't figure out who inserted that one shell into my gun." Then he put all six shells back into his gun.

We resumed his account of his investigation with what he called "the background details." They centered on a group of anti-Castro Cubans, who were intent upon overthrowing Castro and had a training camp near New Orleans. David Ferrie, he said, had joined their movement, which had the support and blessing of the Central Intelligence Agency and Oswald also had a covert connection with this group.

I pointed out that Oswald had a long record as a confirmed Marxist, and had been arrested in New Orleans while distributing pro-Castro pamphlets. Garrison shook his head and told me I had forgotten the Alice-in-Wonderland nature of what he had found out, that "black is white, and white is black." He said that Oswald's pro-Castro stance was a charade, that he had "put on a billboard" as a pro-Castro as a part of the conspiracy. The key figures in the plot were anti-Castroites, and Oswald had merely posed as a pro-Castroite to muddy the waters.

I asked him what Oswald's role had been in the assassination.

"He had three roles," Garrison replied, "as participant, decoy, and patsy. Would it surprise you," he said, "if I told you that Lee Harvey Oswald didn't fire a shot at anyone the day Kennedy was killed?"

As evidence, he cited a paraffin test that had been run on Oswald after he was arrested. The test purports to show whether a person has recently fired a gun by picking up powder-burn marks from his hands or cheeks. The test run in Dallas had showed negative on Oswald's cheeks, and therefore, Garrison concluded, Oswald hadn't even fired his mail-order rifle. Actually, the paraffin test is so unreliable that it had been abandoned by competent criminologists. Some years ago, in a seminar on crime detection conducted by Interpol, the paraffin test was ruled out as an indicator in investigation. The fact that the Dallas police were still using it in 1963 was a commentary on their police methods, rather than proof of Oswald's innocence. I let this pass, because I wanted to get down to Garrison's hard evidence, particularly the testimony of his secret informant.

The anti-Castro Cubans Ferrie had worked with, Garrison said, had become embittered at John F. Kennedy after the Bay of Pigs fiasco. Ferrie had then "spun them off" from their intended target, Castro, and organized them into an assassination team to kill the President. I asked him if he had identified any of the Cubans involved, and he gave me two names. Neither man was ever arrested or charged, and ultimately sank out of sight in the investigation.

In an effort to get Garrison's story into focus, I asked him the motive of the Kennedy conspirators. He told me that the murder at Dallas had been a homosexual plot.

"They had the same motive as Loeb and Leopold, when they murdered Bobbie Franks in Chicago back in the twenties," Garrison said. "It was a homosexual thrill-killing, plus the excitement of getting away with a perfect crime. John Kennedy was everything that Dave Ferrie was not—a successful, handsome, popular, wealthy, virile man. You can just picture the charge Ferrie got out of plotting his death."

I asked how he had learned that the murder was a homosexual plot.

"Look at the people involved," Garrison said. "Dave Ferrie, homosexual. Clay Shaw, homosexual. Jack Ruby, homosexual."

"Ruby was a homosexual?"

"Sure, we dug that out," Garrison said. "His homosexual nickname was Pinkie. That's three. Then there was Lee Harvey Oswald."

But Oswald was married and had two children, I pointed out.

"A switch-hitter who couldn't satisfy his wife," Garrison said. "That's all in the Warren Report." He named two more "key figures" whom he labeled homosexual.

"That's *six* homosexuals in the plot," Garrison said. "One or maybe two, okay. But all six homosexual? How far can you stretch the arm of coincidence?"

I told him that was an intriguing theory, but it wasn't evidence he could present to a court.

"Maybe I'm dense, Jim," I said, "but nothing you have told me adds up to evidence. You seem to have done a lot of work, and dug up a lot of odd things, but it comes across as just circumstances, speculation, theory."

He gave me a patient and tolerant smile. "What I've told you isn't theory. This case isn't even close. If you want to lose money, bet against me."

"I don't want to bet against you," I said. "I want the story of how you uncovered a conspiracy, for the *Saturday Evening Post*. And there is no way I can write what you've told me. It doesn't hang together."

"It all comes together," Garrison replied. He got up and walked over to the dresser in his hotel room. He picked up a thick manila envelope, plastered with air-mail and special-delivery stamps, and ripped it open. He scanned the contents and picked out two documents.

"I'm going to give you something no one knows about but my top people," he said. "I've got the witness who ties this whole case together. He's my case against Shaw. Here's the evidence my witness is going to present in the Shaw hearing next week."

He handed me the documents. "Take them with you and read them tonight. You'll understand everything I've been telling you. We'll get together in the morning, and then we'll see if you think I have a case."

He was friendly and unruffled. "You've got a tough head and you're hard to convince," he said. "That's why I like you."

I folded the papers, put them in my jacket, and said good night. I drove back to the Dunes, my head spinning with the sudden turn of events. Across the country, millions of people had been speculating for weeks about what Garrison had uncovered, and whatever it was I had it in my pocket. It occurred to me that Garrison had been playing a game with me, leading me around the preliminary phases of his investigation while withholding the key. And then, at the last minute, flipping over his evidentiary hole card.

When I got to the Dunes, I spread out the documents and read them. Garrison's secret witness was a young insurance clerk named Perry Raymond Russo, currently living in Baton Rouge. He had come forward as a witness after the death of David Ferrie, when Garrison had labeled Ferrie one of the key figures in the Kennedy assassination. Russo had known Ferrie in New Orleans between 1962 and 1964, when Russo was a college student in New Orleans, and offered to relate what he knew about the bewigged eccentric.

Russo had been interviewed by a Garrison assistant, Anthony ("Moo-Moo") Sciambra, in Baton Rouge on February 25. Two days later Russo had gone down to New Orleans and had been interrogated again, this time under hypnosis. The two documents consisted of a 3,500-word memorandum by Sciambra, on his initial interview with Russo, and a long stenographic report of what Russo had related subsequently under hypnosis.

I read the documents with a deepening sense of horror and disbelief. Russo had told two different stories a few days apart. On the essential issue—the Ferrie, Shaw, Oswald plot to kill Kennedy— they contradicted each other.

According to the Sciambra memorandum, in his initial account on February 25, Russo had said nothing whatever about the three-man plot to kill the President, much less his later claim that he had been present when the plot was laid.

Sciambra had taken a batch of photographs with him to Baton Rouge, *including one of Clay Shaw.* This indicated that Garrison had tagged Shaw as a suspect before Russo had come forward as a witness, which was something Garrison had not told me. When shown Shaw's picture, the memo said:

> [Russo] said that he saw this man twice. The first time was when he pulled into Ferrie's service station to get his car fixed. Shaw was the person who was sitting in the compact car talking with Ferrie. He remembers seeing him again at the Nashville Street Wharf [in New Orleans] when he went to see J.F.K. speak.

That, in its entirety, was Russo's only reference to having seen Clay Shaw.

When shown a picture of Lee Harvey Oswald, Russo had hesitantly identified him as a roommate of David Ferrie's whom he had seen a few times at Ferrie's apartment in 1963. "He said the only thing that doesn't make him stand up and say that he is sure beyond the shadow of any doubt is the fact that the roommate was so cruddy and had a bushy beard," the memo said. "He then drew a beard on the picture of Oswald and said this was Ferrie's roommate."

The story of the "let's kill Kennedy" plot was elicited from Russo on March 1, when he was hypnotized by a New Orleans general practitioner, Dr. Esmond Fatter. The doctor used the device of having Russo picture a television screen in his mind and then view past events on it. The idea of refreshing his memory by hypnosis was Russo's. He had told Sciambra in Baton Rouge that he had been hypnotized before and that it had helped his recall.

But when Dr. Fatter put him in a trance, he proved a reluctant witness. He said that he had attended a party at Ferrie's apartment on September 16, 1963, accompanied by a girl named Sandra. There were about ten people present, drinking beer, including a man Russo identified as "Clem Bertrand." But in setting the scene for Russo, the doctor himself had injected "a white-haired man" into the party.

The transcript read:

> DR. FATTER: Picture that television screen again, Perry, and it is a picture of Ferry's [Ferrie's] apartment and there are several people there and there is a white-haired man. Tell me about it.

On the key testimony, implicating Shaw in the plot to kill Kennedy, the hypnotist again set the scene for Russo.

> Let your mind go completely blank, Perry . . . See that television screen again, it is very vivid . . . Now notice the picture on the screen. There will be Bertrand, Ferrie, and Oswald and they are going to discuss a very important matter and there is another man and girl there and *they are talking about assassinating somebody.* Look at it and describe it to me.

Up to that point, Russo had said nothing about any plan to kill anyone. But now he responded to the hypnotist, and said, "They planned to assassinate President Kennedy." He said that Ferrie took the lead, with "Clem (not Clay) Bertrand." and "Leon Oswald" largely silent. Ferrie said that "if they were to get the President, they would fly to Mexico or Cuba or to Brazil." For the killing itself, Ferrie "said there would be a crossfire with a mob in between and if everybody was looking at the guy who was the diversionary and made the diversionary shot, the other guy could make the good shot. One would make the diversionary shot and the other would do the job."

There was one final little anomaly in the transcript. The doctor asked Russo about "Brett Wall," an obvious reference to the comedian, Breck Wall, whose trip to Galveston had inflamed Garrison's suspicions. Russo dutifully mispronounced Wall's name, and identified him as a friend of "Leon" Oswald and an acquaintance of Dave Ferrie.

The use of hypnosis in eliciting reliable testimony is a dubious technique, and at best requires a very special skill. Twice in the past I had researched the subject, once on a murder story in Copenhagen, and again on a story involving the Bridey Murphy fad in hypnotic regression to alleged previous incarnations. For information to have any possible validity requires the hypnotist to ask scrupulously neutral questions and to avoid prompting the witness, who eagerly responds to the slightest suggestion of the hypnotist.

Later I had a long interview with Dr. Fatter, a genial old family doctor with no background whatever in the technique of using hypnosis to elicit criminal testimony. He told me that before the hypnosis, Russo had been injected with sodium pentothal, the badly misnamed "truth serum," and had related a briefer version of the assassination plot. Fatter used this as a guide in questioning Russo under hypnosis. Sodium pentothal is not a truth serum; it merely relaxes a subject's inhibitions. If the subject is inclined to fantasize, he may do so even more readily under sodium pentothal. When I reviewed his questioning of Russo, Dr. Fatter volunteered that he "certainly would hate to see anyone taken to trial on what Russo had said in a trance."

At the Dunes I reread the two bizarre documents twice. The hypnosis transcript, with its flawed techniques and scene-setting by the hypnotist, discredited Russo as a witness, but the Sciambra memorandum directly impeached him.

Why had Garrison given them to me? I thought back to the scene in his room. The manila envelope from which he had taken them had been unopened and apparently he had received it during the day from New Orleans. Improbable as it seemed, he had given me the memo and transcript without having read them.

I left an early call, and in the morning went to the executive offices of the Desert Inn, where I knew the manager, and Xeroxed copies of Garrison's papers. Then I went to a pay phone and called Don McKinney at the *Saturday Evening Post.* I had not told him about my secret trip to meet Garrison in Las Vegas. When I told him where I was and who I was with, he said, "Wow! That's terrific!"

"Well, we've got ourselves a story," I told him, "but it isn't what we were hoping for." I briefed him on what had happened and summarized the two documents. I told him my head was still spinning, and I didn't know what to do with what Garrison had unwittingly given me. McKinney said he wanted to confer with the *Post*'s managing editor, Otto Friedrich, and I should call him back in a half hour.

When I called, McKinney told me to hang onto the copies and lie back until Shaw's preliminary hearing, in order to see what Russo would testify to under oath. Given his state of confusion, there was no certainty that he would recount the "conspiracy" story from the witness stand. "If he does," said McKinney, "we'll take it from there."

I went over to the Sands and returned Garrison's copies. I told him that was "quite some witness" he had and that Russo was carrying a hell of a case for a solitary witness.

Garrison told me that some of his assistants had opposed the arrest of Shaw, that he ordered it "as a command decision" and that "this is not the first time I've charged a person before I've made the case."

"People think I'm in the sweatbox on the Shaw arrest," he went on. "It's the other way around. Shaw is in the sweatbox. I'm going to start calling in people that he didn't think I knew about. The pressure will grow on him, and at some point I expect him to break down and tell me everything. If I hadn't attacked the case this way, everything would have been buried in concrete and I'd never have dug it out."

This was a Garrison I had never seen before, arrogant, prejudicial, blindly confident that whatever he suspected had happened had to have happened. I thanked him for the time he had given me and told him I would see him at the Shaw hearing.

"I've got one question, Jim," I said. "You've portrayed Ferrie and Shaw as cunning and cautious men. Russo says that he just happened on the beer party at Ferrie's apartment, and that he hung around when the others left because he wanted Ferrie to give him a ride home. Why did these criminal masterminds discuss killing

Kennedy in front of a casual bystander like Russo? How did Shaw and Ferrie and Oswald know that Russo wouldn't turn them in to the FBI?"

Garrison pondered that in silence, and then shook his head.

"Say, that's a *good* question," said District Attorney Jim Garrison.

On March 14, Clay Shaw's preliminary hearing opened before a three-judge panel in New Orleans. The purpose: to determine if there was "probable cause" to hold him for trial for conspiring to kill President Kennedy. The hearing ran four days under tight security; admission to the courtroom was by pass and all members of the audience were frisked for concealed weapons. The huge press contingent took almost all the seats in the courtroom, and several thousand would-be onlookers were turned away.

Garrison himself presented the case against Shaw. The star witness was Russo, a dark-haired, neat, somber young man who told his sensational story in the flat unemotional terms of a man describing a graduation ceremony or a Rotary convention. The story he told was his version No. 2, with one significant embellishment.

In the middle of September 1963, Russo testified, he had dropped into Ferrie's apartment, found a party in progress with about ten people sitting around drinking. The others drifted away until there were only Ferrie, his roommate "Leon Oswald," "Clem Bertrand," and Russo. He identified "Leon" as Lee Harvey Oswald, and "Clem" as Clay Shaw. Ferrie had opened the conversation and did most of the talking. He outlined an assassination attempt that would use "diversionary tactics" and "diversification." Russo quoted Ferrie as saying "There would have to be a minimum of three people involved. Two of the persons would shoot diversionary shots and the third . . . the good shot." There would be "triangulation of crossfire" and one of the three men would be "the scapegoat." Ferrie then had lectured the others on "availability of exit" and said that the scapegoat would provide enough time for the other two to escape. Ferrie stressed that he was a skilled pilot and "said they could either go to Mexico or fly directly to Cuba. He talked about the risks of flying to Cuba."

Then Russo dropped a new piece of testimony into the case. It was decided, he said, that Mr. Ferrie, Mr. Oswald and Mr. Bertrand would be in the "public eye" when the killing took place. Bertrand then spoke up and said "If this is the alternative," he would go on a business trip for his company and he would go "to the West Coast."

Just the week before, on our return from Las Vegas, the press had carried a story that Garrison had discovered that Clay Shaw had been in San Francisco when Kennedy was shot.

At the conclusion of his direct testimony, at Garrison's request, Russo walked across the courtroom and identified Shaw the second time as "Clem Bertrand" by holding his hand over Shaw's head.

Shaw's trial lawyer, Irving Diamond, had almost nothing to work with except Russo's testimony. He knew nothing about the Sciambra memorandum, and the great, wrenching twist in Russo's story when drugged and hypnotized. He concentrated on the obvious question Russo's testimony posed: Why hadn't Russo come forward with his story of the plot when Kennedy had been killed? Why had he waited until the "key conspirator" Ferrie had died, more than three years after the assassination? Russo gave a variety of answers —that "I never push myself on anybody," that the FBI said Oswald was acting alone, and that he was deeply involved in his school work. He also conceded that he had seen Ferrie "four, five, or six" times after the Kennedy assassination and that neither mentioned the "let's-kill-Kennedy" plot in Ferrie's apartment.

Garrison put a second witness on the stand against Shaw, a witness he had not told me about in Las Vegas. He had not known about him then. He was a black heroin addict, in jail for parole violation, who had offered himself after the Shaw hearing had begun. He testified that in 1963 he had been on the lake front, shooting up drugs, and had seen Shaw meet Oswald there and give him some money. Like Russo, he had told no one about this until four years later.

With only a half-hour of deliberation, the three judges ruled that Shaw should be held for trial, that "sufficient evidence has been presented to justify bringing into play the further steps of the criminal process." Under Louisiana law, a conspiracy must result in some overt act to further the conspiracy. The hearing had produced nothing that Shaw had done to kill Kennedy except—if one believed Russo—to talk about it with Ferrie and Oswald in the presence of Russo. Nor was there any overt act attributed to Ferrie, who was hundreds of miles from Dallas when Kennedy was killed. As for the third conspirator, Oswald, it was Garrison's private contention that —as he told me—Oswald had not fired a shot at anyone on November 22, 1963. But as one of the judges told a newsman later, "This wasn't a question of guilty or not guilty; it was a question of probable cause ... Just think for one minute about the alternative, if we cut him loose ... the nation and the world would have charged a fix."

Before I wrote the *Post* article, I wanted to give Garrison an opportunity to explain the gaping disparity between Russo-in-Baton-Rouge, who had said nothing about an assassination plot, and Russo-under-hypnosis, who recalled the plot in such detail that he remembered what everyone had said. The day after Shaw was held to trial, I telephoned Garrison and told him there was a big hole in Russo's testimony. He asked me to meet him at his home, and that evening I took a cab there. Present was a professional private investigator, William Gurvich, who had been serving as a consultant to Garrison in his Kennedy investigation.

I told Garrison I couldn't understand why Russo had said nothing about an assassination plot when he first came forward as a witness. Garrison seemed upset, and said "He *didn't?*" It was apparent that he still hadn't read the original report on his star witness. He said, "I better get Sciambra out here to explain that." He made a phone call and said Sciambra would be right out.

When I posed the question to Sciambra, a dark-haired, trim Italian who had been a boxer, he told me "You don't know what the shit you're talking about." Garrison obviously had not told him that he had given me his report on Russo, so I broke the news to him. I told him I had a copy of his memo in a safety box at my hotel, that I had read it eight or ten times and had practically memorized it. Not only was there nothing about a Ferrie-Shaw-Oswald plot, I said, there was nothing whatever about Shaw ever having met Oswald.

Sciambra then came up with a new explanation. He said he had reported verbally to Garrison on his return from Baton Rouge, and wrote his memo later. "I was busy with a lot of other things," he said, "and maybe I forgot about the meeting at Ferrie's apartment." I suggested that he produce his original handwritten notes on the interview, but he said he had burned them. Then I pointed out that his memo said Russo had seen Shaw *twice,* and that if Russo had told him about the conspiracy meeting, he would have said he met Shaw *three* times. He had no explanation for this, and the meeting broke up in tense hostility. I said I'd take a cab to my hotel, but William Gurvich offered me a ride.

He told me he had taken the job with Garrison because he

thought he had a case, but he had increasing doubts. "All he's got against Shaw is Perry Russo," Gurvich said, "and the Sciambra memo blows Russo out of the water." He disputed Sciambra's story that he had written the memo in a hurry, and might have "forgotten" the assassination plot. He said that Sciambra had worked on the memo for days, rewriting and polishing it, and that it was the most important report he had written in the investigation. We agreed that if Sciambra had written only two paragraphs about his Russo interview, he would have devoted them to the conspiracy meeting—the only substantive information involving Shaw—and that to write 3,500 words and leave this out was beyond belief. A few weeks later, Gurvich defected from the Garrison staff and stated publicly that there was "no basis in fact and no material evidence . . . for an assassination plot."

There was one last base to cover. I drove up to Baton Rouge and interviewed Perry Raymond Russo. I told him that I was writing an article for the *Saturday Evening Post*, and planned to use the Sciambra memo. I gave him my copy—without any comment—and asked him if it was accurate. He made four minor corrections, and did not complain that Sciambra had omitted the heart of his story. I asked him, "Then you first related the assassination plot when?" Russo said, "Down in New Orleans."

The *Post* put the article, "Rush to Judgment in New Orleans" on its cover, and Shaw and his lawyers learned for the first time why Shaw had wound up in the dock. They went back to court and asked for a court order to take my testimony at once for Shaw's forthcoming trial, to forestall the possibility that I might die or leave the country. The court refused. Shaw's personal attorney, Edward Wegmann, flew to New York and asked me if I would accept a subpoena to testify, since I was beyond the jurisdiction of the court.

There are two schools of thought about journalists and the judicial process. Some newsmen believe that they should have nothing to do with the process, that they have a duty to resist it, and should go to jail rather than testify. It is a complex issue. There are circumstances, particularly when a court is pressuring a newsman to disclose confidential sources, where I think a reporter should go proudly to jail rather than break his word to an informant. There was no such breach of confidentiality involved in the Shaw case. When protecting one's sources is not involved, I believe that a reporter has the same obligation of any citizen to testify when he has evidence that affects the course of justice. It is, in my opinion, an odd reporter indeed who refuses to testify under oath to the accuracy of what he has published under his by-line. I told Wegmann I would repeat in court what I had written in the *Post*.

In New Orleans, Sciambra went on television and challenged me to go before the local grand jury and repeat the story about Russo's 180-degree turn in his account of the "plot." I heard nothing further, from either the district attorney's office or the grand jury.

But I heard from Perry Russo. He sent word to New York that he wanted to talk to me. I telephoned him and he said he couldn't understand why people were so upset about my article. He was friendly and said he'd like to see me the next time I was in New Orleans.

A day or so later, I was contacted by NBC's *White Paper* documentary producer, Fred Freed, who wanted to do a network show on the Shaw case. He hired me to assist in the research, and with the district attorney's office threatening to take me before the grand jury and my friendship with Garrison in tatters, I went back to the City that Care Forgot. I spent four weeks there, and learned that the Affair of the Hypnotized Witness was just one part of a tangled tale of justice gone wrong.

The *Post* article sealed off my access to the district attorney, but it opened new sources of information—including some people on his staff who were dismayed by his arrest of Clay Shaw. I set out to try to reconstruct the anatomy of his Kennedy investigation. In the two-year interval between Shaw's arrest and his trial, I interviewed more than thirty people and put together, one piece at a time, the following account of how an innocent man was accused of the crime of the century.

Jim Garrison's "solution" to the Kennedy assassination had its origin in the imagination of a roly-poly little jive-talking New Orleans attorney named Dean Andrews. Andrews had had some brief, peripheral dealings with Lee Harvey Oswald in May 1963, when Oswald showed up in his office seeking legal help with his less-than-honorable discharge from the Marine Corps. Accompanying Oswald, according to Andrews, were some Mexicano "gay" kids. Andrews saw Oswald a few times but did nothing for him when he discovered Oswald had no money.

When Kennedy was killed, Andrews was hospitalized with pneumonia in New Orleans. He called the FBI office and said he had had some dealings with Oswald, and two "fee-bees"—Andrewese for federal agents—dropped around to interview him. He told them about his passing contact with Oswald—and then manufactured an incident and a character that did not exist. It was an exercise in fantasy that was to have horrendous consequences for Clay Shaw. Andrews told the "fee-bees" that shortly after Oswald had been arrested in Dallas, he had received a call at the hospital asking him if he would go to Dallas to represent Oswald. The call was from a voice he said he recognized as "Clay Bertrand." He described "Bertrand" as a man he had seen only once or twice, but who sometimes referred homosexuals in trouble to Andrews. He said he didn't know where Bertrand lived, but said he was six feet one or two inches tall, with brown hair. Later, questioned by Wesley Liebeler of the Warren Commission, he revised his description and said "Bertrand was five feet eight, with sandy hair." Taxed about the disparity in these descriptions, Andrews airily replied, "I don't play Boy Scout and measure them."

Eager to know who had tried to procure a lawyer for Oswald, the FBI had scoured New Orleans and found no trace of a Clay Bertrand. They abandoned the lead, but the Warren Commission picked it up again via Wesley Liebeler. Given Andrews's elliptical, contradictory description of "Bertrand" and the FBI's failure to find anyone else who had ever heard of him, the Commission concluded that this was just one more of the thousands of false leads that encrusted the Warren investigation. But they included Andrews' story in their massive twenty-six volumes of testimony and exhibits, and Garrison picked it up from there.

Shortly after he activated his own investigation, Garrison began to pressure Andrews about the identity of Clay Bertrand. Andrews, who was a friend of Garrison and himself a critic of the Warren Commission, was caught in a dilemma. He couldn't help Garrison because he had invented the phone call from "Clay Bertrand" and had pulled the name out of the air on the spur of the moment—using a homosexual nom de plume he had heard years earlier "at a fag wedding." As he conceded much later, he had invented the "Clay Bertrand" phone call to "get on the publicity gravy train and ride it to glory."

"I was just huffin' and puffin'," Andrews said. "I let my mouth run away with my brain."

But Garrison had a peculiar attribute that became clear, with almost pathological enormity, in the two years before Shaw was taken to trial. He had a lively imagination in postulating possible scenarios of what had happened in the Kennedy assassination, using circumstantial evidence and supposition. Such an approach is common among puzzle-solvers, whether prosecutorial or journalistic. In its simplest form, if A knows B and B knows C, it is sensible to examine whether C had any dealings with A, and if so, whether they had any bearing on the matter being explored. Where Garrison departed from the norm was that once he had established an ABC relationship, even by circumstance and without any substantive evidence, it became set in concrete. Instead of testing a postulate against the evidence, and discarding it if it didn't fit, he persisted in trying to hammer the evidence into a shape that would fit his postulate.

Months before Perry Russo appeared as a witness, Garrison had concluded that David Ferrie and the shadowy (and nonexistent) Clay Bertrand were key figures in the Kennedy assassination. During a staff brainstorming session, he outlined what was "known" about Clay Bertrand from Dean Andrews's fictional account. He was well-to-do, homosexual, spoke Spanish, and lived in New Orleans. One of Garrison's staff members jokingly said that Clay Shaw fit that description. There was the added factor of the somewhat unusual first name. Overwhelmed with all these circumstances, Garrison concluded that Shaw was Bertrand, and having made this judgment, set out to prove it true.

He called in Andrews again and told him he had identified Clay Bertrand as Clay Shaw. Andrews disputed him, and Garrison began to get hostile. He had other witnesses, he told Andrews, who could make the identification. Andrews told him again that he didn't know Clay Shaw, but refrained from telling Garrison the much more important fact that he had invented Clay Bertrand. Under pressure from Garrison, Andrews struck a peculiar bargain. He would not identify Shaw as Bertrand, but he would not assert publicly that Shaw was *not* Bertrand. Secure in the knowledge that there was no Clay Bertrand, Andrews expected that the Shaw-Bertrand identification would fail of its own total lack of substance. He underestimated Garrison's will to believe that whatever he suspected had to be true.

When I heard Andrews's full story, my mind went back to my

meeting with Garrison in Las Vegas. He had told me that "a lawyer friend of mine in New Orleans is impeding my investigation and I'm going to break him."

During Shaw's preliminary hearing, the district attorney's office called in Andrews and questioned him at length about Bertrand and Shaw. He refused to say that Shaw was Bertrand, and was then taken before the grand jury and indicted for perjury concerning "a conspiracy to murder John F. Kennedy." After two subsequent perjury indictments, Andrews realized that his pact with Garrison hadn't worked, and he finally came out and flatly declared that Shaw was not Bertrand. "The emphasis on Bertrand's identity is a waste of time because he never existed . . ." He was eventually convicted on two counts of perjury, and accurately predicted that he would be the only person convicted in the entire Garrison affair.

When he had abandoned his "huffin' and puffin'," Andrews sadly acknowledged that what had "put Clay Shaw in the sack" was his choice of "Clay" as the first name for the fictitious "Clay Bertrand." If he had only named Bertrand "Leroy" or "Louie" or "Dooby-Doo" Bertrand, Shaw might have been spared his ordeal.

In his determination that David Ferrie was a "key conspirator," Garrison employed the same technique of constructing a scenario and then trying to fit the facts into his script. After he quit the Garrison investigation, William Gurvich told me that, as Ferrie had told the press, Garrison had indeed tabbed Ferrie as "the getaway pilot for the assassins." Gurvich said Garrison told him that he had information that Ferrie had been sitting in a plane on a runway in Dallas when the President was killed. Gurvich flew to Dallas and tried to establish this, but failed. He then pulled thousands of airport gasoline requisitions, looking for evidence of Ferrie's presence. On his return to New Orleans, he discovered that Ferrie had been in a federal courtroom in New Orleans the day Kennedy was killed.

"Garrison asked me how I knew that," Gurvich said, "and I told him I had picked it up from a couple of federal marshals. He told me, 'You know who *they* work for—the U.S. Justice Department,' and refused to accept my information. Then I verified this independently through some other people." It was also established that Ferrie's plane was inoperative in a New Orleans hangar with flat tires. Nevertheless, Garrison continued to pursue Ferrie relentlessly. If he wasn't the getaway pilot, he had to be something. Garrison had his investigators check out Ferrie's story of the all-night drive to the Houston ice-rink. When that story proved to be true, Garrison still clung to Ferrie as a key conspirator. Ferrie had said he was going ice-skating—and then had not put on his ice skates —and thus was concealing some dark deed.

Finally there was the song-and-dance man, Breck Wall, who had landed on Garrison's flypaper by driving to Galveston after Kennedy was killed and then receiving a phone call from Jack Ruby. This information, like a huge amount of Garrison's "evidence," had been gleaned from the Warren Report. Their investigators had questioned both Ruby and Wall about the phone call, and had got the same explanation. Ruby had closed his Dallas strip joint in deference to the Kennedy tragedy, but a rival joint-owner had kept his place open. Both Wall and Ruby, independently, related that Ruby had called Wall to complain about this impropriety. But to Garrison, who had tracked the song-and-dance man and the nonskating Ferrie to the same city on the night after the assassination, this could not be happenstance, but a red arrow pointing to complicity. It tied Ferrie to Wall, and via Wall, to Jack Ruby.

Having thus "linked" Wall to two of the Kennedy "conspirators," Garrison embarked on a separate investigation of Wall. By 1967, Wall had taken his show to Las Vegas, where it became a popular act in the casino show rooms. Gurvich and a photographer were sent to Las Vegas to gather evidence against Wall.

"You won't believe this," Gurvich told me after his defection, "but Garrison told us to cover Wall's performance at the Thunderbird casino. The photographer was instructed to snap pictures of Wall onstage, and I was told to tape-record his act. The photographer had a minicamera rigged up in a pack of cigarettes and I had a small recorder on my chair, with the mike open. When Wall came bounding onstage, the photographer stood up, put the cigarette pack up to his eye, and started snapping pictures. I expected some bouncer to come over and ask him why he was pointing his cigarettes at Wall, and then he'd spot my tape recorder. I kept thinking about what I could say if he asked what we were doing. I could hardly have told him, 'Well, sir, we're investigating the assassination of President Kennedy.' "

What Gurvich told me, and the eventual trial of Shaw made clear, was that when Garrison announced on February 24, 1967, that he had uncovered a conspiracy, he had no evidence whatever. Contrary to his claim that he had "solved the case" and knew "the key individuals" and "how it was done," all he had on that day was a dead eccentric who had neglected to put on his ice skates, and a personal conviction that Clay Shaw was the nonexistent Clay Bertrand. At this critical juncture he had acquired his lone witness, Russo, a man who claimed under hypnosis that he had heard these two plot with Oswald, but who had neglected to mention this when he first surfaced with his story.

When I returned to New Orleans for NBC, I saw Russo six times. He was friendly and eager to talk, despite the implications of the *Saturday Evening Post* article. Some of his friends had told him he was in deep trouble and ought to hire a lawyer, and he asked me what I thought. I told him the only advice I would ever give him was to tell the truth.

In our first meeting, we went to a neighborhood beer tavern and shot a few games of pool. On our way back to his house—he had moved back to New Orleans—he suddenly blurted out that "If Garrison knew what I told my priest in Baton Rouge after the Shaw hearing, he would go through the ceiling." He said he had told the priest that he wished he could sit down alone with Shaw, "listen to him breathe and talk" and ask him some questions so he could resolve his own doubts about his identification of Shaw. I reminded him that he had positively identified Shaw under oath. He said that his problem was that he had learned that Ferrie knew a former FBI agent—now dead, named Guy Bannister—and that Bannister had a strong resemblance to Shaw. He asked me to arrange a confidential meeting with Shaw, but then changed his mind. He said that if Garrison found out about it, he would "clobber me" and "charge me with perjury or something."

His interrogation under hypnosis bothered him. He volunteered that on coming to New Orleans for the sodium pentothal and hypnosis tests, he "had picked up a lot of information from Garrison's people just from the way they asked questions. I'm a pretty perceptive guy, and besides, when they got through asking me questions, I asked them a lot of questions—like 'Why is this man important,' and so on."

He also said that Shaw's lawyer "could destroy me as a witness with five questions." All the attorney had to do "is study the hypnosis transcript—it's all there right before him." He complained repeatedly about his position as the sole witness against Shaw on the crucial issue of the Ferrie-Shaw-Oswald assassination plotting. He had been led to believe that he was only one piece of a solid case, and was distressed that the only other witness was the black heroin-addict convict. He was going to have "a showdown with Garrison's people," and if they couldn't convince him that they had a good case against Shaw independent of his testimony, he would not repeat his accusation against Shaw at his trial.

During these conversations with me, he repeatedly edged up to the line of explicitly disavowing his testimony and then shied away. In the last session, he told me, "I lied to you about why I decided not to meet Shaw. I was afraid that if I talked to him I'd know he wasn't the man. What could I do then? I could go on the run to Mexico, or to California and become a beatnik, but I couldn't run from myself." I urged him, as I had throughout, just to tell the objective truth. He replied that he no longer knew the difference between reality and fantasy and that he brooded about this a great deal, and often discussed it with his roommate, Steve Derby. "Maybe one of these days," he said, "I'll give you a call and tell you to come down with the television cameras and give you a story."

Throughout the interviews I scrupulously avoided giving him any advice other than to testify honestly. Although I had met him at his request, I wanted no allegations of witness-tampering. I also became aware, on our second meeting, that his living room was bugged, which Russo later confirmed in a tape-recorded interview with William Gurvich.

It was an inept job. When I called on Russo, he would suggest that "we play a little music" and go over and switch on his record player. After a few bars, he would say "I don't care much for that" and cut off the record. But there was a red "On" light in the record player and it always continued to glow. So I would make a little speech and tell him that if he was certain of his story about Shaw, he was obligated to repeat it at the trial. Then we would go down to the pool hall or take a long walk among the magnolia trees and Russo would unburden himself about his problems.

In the public's mind, the judicial ruling in 1967 that there was "probable cause" for a trial of Shaw was a clear-cut victory for Garrison and gave an aura of substance to his conspiracy solution. Other than the late-surfacing heroin addict, the only witness he had produced was Perry Russo, but a prosecutor is not required to reveal his whole case at a preliminary hearing. No one but Garrison and a few of his top aides knew that he had played all of his evidentiary hole cards. He implied that there was much more to come, and then set out to discover what it was. "Jim Garrison has got something" became a conversational cliché, and shortly he began spelling out an astonishing array of "somethings."

The preliminary hearing victory made him a national media celebrity, and while his staff was energetically seeking new evidence, he embarked on a long series of speeches, talk-show appearances, television, radio, and magazine interviews. He had a seemingly endless supply of "new disclosures," all revealed with the granitic confidence of a man who knew exactly what he was doing.

He had quietly abandoned his homosexual thrill-killing solution a month after our meeting in Las Vegas, and did not refer to it again. The conspiracy against Kennedy was now more far-reaching and sinister. It involved military-industrial-intelligence forces—"the warfare state" in Garrison's phrase—who were embittered by Kennedy's decision to pull back on Vietnam and seek a détente with the Communist world. The conspiracy had been heavily financed by unnamed Texas oil millionaires, angry at Kennedy's plan to reduce their beloved oil-depletion tax allowance. The Warren Commission was no longer merely inept; it had perpetrated a deliberate fraud with its lone assassin finding. "The objective was to keep the people of this country thinking that they were still living in the best of all possible worlds; that they were not living in a world in which big business, Texas style, financed the assassination, as it did, in which the paramilitary right-wing elements were financed and encouraged in their training and given weapons by the Central Intelligence Agency . . ."

As the scope of the conspiracy widened, so did the number of figures involved. At various times, he declared that the conspirators included some members of the Dallas police force, elements of the CIA domestic intelligence operation, right-wing extremists, anti-Castro-Cubans, wealthy anti-Communist Russian émigrés, "a precision guerilla team of at least seven men," a California associate of a right-wing fundamentalist preacher, and an unnamed gunman who had hidden in a sewer in Dealey Plaza, fired the fatal shot with a .45 caliber handgun and "then fled through the drainage system to another part of the city."

The list of accessories after the fact was even longer. It included the then U.S. Attorney General Ramsey Clark, who had stated publicly that he had "seen nothing new" in Garrison's case. "Of course they have seen nothing new," said Garrison. "They knew all along that the Central Intelligence Agency was deeply involved in the assassination. That's why most of the men selected for the [Warren] Commisson were CIA oriented . . . Apparently it is felt in Washington that if the truth of President Kennedy's murder can be kept concealed, President Johnson's promotion to the Presidency will appear to be more legitimate."

As to Lyndon Johnson himself, Garrison was ambivalent. "Of course I assume that the President of the United States is not involved, but wouldn't it be nice to know it?" he said in a California speech. He had a long series of questions on this subject—plus an answer:

> Who appointed the Warren Commission? Who was aware that there was a CIA problem and caused the seven-man Commission to be weighted in advance by the defenders of the CIA? . . . Who controls the CIA? Who controls the FBI? Who controls the Archives where this evidence is locked up for so long that it is unlikely that there is anybody in this room that will be alive when it is released? . . . Who has the arrogance and brass to prevent the people of this country from seeing that evidence? Who indeed? The one man who profited most from the assassination—your friendly President, Lyndon Johnson.

Elements of the press who criticized Garrison's polemics were attacked as a part of the subplot of concealing his truths and sabotaging his investigation. He charged "a large part of the news establishment" with "doing everything it can, literally desperately, to try and conceal whatever news comes from New Orleans . . ." He attacked "the brainwashing and the protection of the establishment lie by the Washington *Post, Newsweek,* the New York *Times,* the Los Angeles *Times* and NBC and all these other propaganda machines . . . There's something wrong with this country."

After the NBC documentary, Garrison arrested one of its reporters, Walter Sheridan, and accused him of attempting to bribe one of his witnesses. Sheridan had formerly worked for Attorney General Robert Kennedy, and Kennedy issued a statement supporting him. This prompted what was perhaps the most unusual accusation of Garrison's long litany. He attacked the brother of John Kennedy for making "a positive effort to stop the [Garrison] investigation."

In a New York ABC television interview, a newsman commented, "What you are saying, then, is that Senator Kennedy by not cooperating is, in effect, letting the murderers of his brother walk the streets." Said Garrison, "Well, yes, that's a fair statement."

In the two years between the Shaw hearing and the trial, Garrison's staff interviewed hundreds of would-be witnesses. There are certain sensational cases that have a fascination for unstable people and fetch them forth in droves. A classic example was the "Black Dahlia" mutilation murder of playgirl Elizabeth Short in Los Angeles. Over the years, dozens of people came forward and confessed to this crime, which still remains unsolved. Celebrated cases also attract witnesses who are not psychotic, but who falsely identify key figures out of faulty memory or a desire to lift themselves out of dull anonymity into the spotlight. Chief Justice Frankfurter once commented that eyewitness testimony is the greatest single cause of miscarried justice. In a sensational case, a careful prosecutor often spends more time winnowing out false witnesses than he does working with authentic ones.

The Garrison investigation had a disastrously low threshold, across which trooped a bizarre parade of people eager to bolster his conspiracy scenario. There was a musician named Donald Norton who showed up in Vancouver with the story of two "CIA missions" involving Garrison's suspects. He claimed to have met Shaw in August 1962, in Alabama, and to have received from a man accompanying Shaw an attaché case containing $50,000 which Norton delivered to "Harvey Lee" in Monterrey, Mexico, in exchange for certain "documents." The Harvey Lee had turned out to be Lee Harvey Oswald. In an earlier "CIA operation", he said, his agency contact had been David Ferrie. Although a polygraph test by a newspaper indicated deception on Norton's story, Garrison sent an aide to Vancouver to interview him and brought him to New Orleans for further questioning.

Another witness surfaced in Boston. He wrote a letter to Garrison claiming to have a photograph taken in Jack Ruby's Dallas nightclub a few weeks before the assassination. The photo, he said, showed Ruby, Oswald, Perry Russo, and the informant, a twenty-six-year-old dishwasher. Garrison's office sent him an airline ticket to New Orelans, which the dishwasher cashed and never used. He showed up in his hometown in Maine, confessed that he had written the letter while drunk, and admitted not only that there was no photo but that he had never been in Dallas.

One of the most remarkable volunteers was a backwoods Louisiana preacher, the Reverend "Sliding Clyde" Johnson, who almost made it to the witness stand in the Shaw trial. Johnson had been an eccentric candidate for Louisiana governor in 1963, attracting audiences by playing a banjo and sashaying erratically across his impromptu speaker's stand. He told the district attorney's staff that he had met an "Elton Bernard," whom he identified as Clay Shaw, in a Baton Rouge hotel in September 1963. Shaw was accompanied by three men, Lee Harvey Oswald, Jack Ruby, and a big "Mexican-looking" fellow. He said he heard one of the three say "he would get him" and Shaw declare "others are working on this" and "he's got to come down from Washington." The preacher declared that Shaw gave him a brown envelope containing $5,000 in $100 bills, and gave similar thick brown envelopes to both Ruby and Oswald.

Despite his peculiar public record and manifest instability, the Garrison staff processed Sliding Clyde as a prospective witness. His story bolstered the weakest aspect of the case against Shaw—the necessary overt acts that had to arise out of a conspiracy in order to make it an actionable plot. Pressured by Shaw's attorneys to specify these acts, Garrison filed a reply declaring that Shaw had met with Oswald and Ruby at the Capital House Hotel in Baton Rouge on September 3, 1963, and had there given them money. Later, Johnson fled to a backwoods cabin in Mississippi, ignored a Garrison subpoena and was dropped from the case. So was the Baton Rouge "overt act."

Little of this desperate behind-the-scenes search for witnesses to bolster Perry Russo's story surfaced at the time. Although Garrison was criticized in segments of the national press, others soberly reported his increasingly wild and undocumented claims as legitimate news. Throughout the Shaw affair, neither New Orleans newspaper commented editorially on his behavior or methods. *Playboy* magazine gave him a national forum with its "Playboy Interview," and he received lengthy and favorable treatment by the *New Republic,* the *New York Review of Books,* and *Ramparts* magazine. Although the NBC documentary was highly critical of his methods, the network gave him a half-hour of unedited time to reply, plus a lengthy appearance on the Johnny Carson show.

He retained, until the Shaw trial, a huge national constituency among the United States majority who rejected the Warren Report, were convinced of the existence of a conspiracy, and looked to Garrison to convert what they wished to believe into reality. In maintaining this constituency, he was abetted by the climate of the times. By the late 1960's, offended by governmental deceptions about the Vietnam war, the nation was deep into a convulsive rebellion against established authority and eager to believe that deception had become a national policy. Among millions, especially the young, the Presidential imprint on the Warren Report was sufficient evidence to inspire rejection.

In constructing his ever-widening conspiracy scenarios, Garrison was aided and encouraged by a number of the leading Warren critics. Mark Lane moved to New Orleans and became an unpaid consultant to Garrison, and Garrison publicly acknowledged the "invaluable assistance" of such other critics as Vincent Salandria, Harold Weisberg, and Professor Richard Popkin of the University of California, who preached the theory that there were two Oswalds, the real (and innocent) one and a Doppelgänger who flitted about impersonating and incriminating the real one.

The trial of Clay Shaw opened late in January 1969, and ran five weeks. Despite his many public promises of blockbuster disclosures, Garrison presented substantially the same case he had offered at Shaw's preliminary hearing. His sensational accusations of CIA involvement were abandoned, and he produced no witnesses at all to support the charges he had made for two years against that agency. He had a gaggle of new witnesses, all acquired after the arrest of Shaw. Only one of them directly incriminated Shaw in an assassination plot, and he proved to be a self-destructing disaster.

He was a tense little New York accountant named Charles Spiesel. He testified that he, too, had gone to a party in New Orleans in 1963, several months earlier than the party Russo had told about. David Ferrie and Shaw were present, and near the end of the party they went out in the kitchen with Spiesel and discussed their plans to kill Kennedy. Like Russo, he did not explain why they openly discussed their secret plot to kill the President in the presence of a casual bystander.

Spiesel was intended to be a surprise witness, but a member of Garrison's staff had learned some things about his background. Appalled that the district attorney would use such a witness, he had tipped Shaw's attorneys about Spiesel and they had made a background check on the accountant via a New York investigator. A hastily assembled report on Spiesel was flown to New Orleans and turned over to Shaw's trial lawyer, Irving Dymond, just minutes before he began his cross-examination.

Under Dymond's questioning, Spiesel admitted that he had filed a $16,000,000 law suit, drawn up by himself, against the city of New York, a psychiatrist, the New York police, and the Pinkerton detective agency. Having related, under direct testimony, the details of a Shaw-Ferrie conspiracy, he now poured out details of an anti-Spiesel conspiracy. His New York lawsuit had charged that he had been "tortured mentally" by a "new police technique" and that his enemies had created "hypnotic illusions" in his mind and "chaos" in his business. They had also deprived him of a normal sex life and "gained entry to my house" by disguising themselves as his relatives. He had once fingerprinted his own daughter, he told the jury, in order to make sure she wasn't one of his disguised enemies. He complained that he had been hypnotized by strangers "against my will" some fifty or sixty times; they put him in a trance, he explained, simply "by catching my eye."

For all of the self-doubts he had discussed with me, Russo again took the stand, told the story of the meeting in Ferrie's apartment, and again identified Clay Shaw as "Bertrand." But now he denied ever having characterized Ferrie, Oswald, and Shaw as "conspirators" and conceded that the talk he claimed to have overheard might have been just "shooting the bull." Then, in a brief exchange with Dymond, he virtually took Clay Shaw out of the case.

DYMOND: In your presence, did David Ferrie ever agree to kill the President?
RUSSO: He said, "We will kill him."
DYMOND: He had said that many times before, had he not?
RUSSO: Right.
DYMOND: He had made that direct statement to you alone, had he not?
RUSSO: Right.
DYMOND: Did Leon Oswald ever, in your presence, agree to kill the President?
RUSSO: No.
DYMOND: Did Clem Bertrand ever agree to kill the President?
RUSSO: No.

As a number of New Orleans attorneys pointed out, one "plotter" does not a conspiracy make.

The trial of Shaw turned out to be two separate trials—one of Shaw and the other of the Warren Report. Although no testimony was presented tying Shaw or Ferrie to the fatal shots in Dealey Plaza, the judge permitted Garrison to present five days of testimony attacking the Warren lone-assassin version of the Kennedy killing. During these five days, Clay Shaw became the forgotten man at his own trial.

Under subpoena by Shaw's lawyers, I appeared as a defense witness, identified the Sciambra memorandum as having been given to me by Garrison, and qualified it as evidence. It was passed among the jurors for their examination, to determine that it had no mention whatever of a Shaw-Oswald-Ferrie plot to kill the President.

In his summation to the jury, Attorney Dymond swiftly disposed of the one "overt act" attributed to Shaw—his trip to the West Coast when Kennedy was killed. Since Shaw lived in New Orleans—hundreds of miles from Dallas—why, Dymond asked, would he have to fly to San Francisco to "put himself in the public eye" and establish an alibi?

Late in the evening of March 1, 1967, two years to the day after Shaw's arrest, the jury trooped out to deliberate Garrison's case. Fifty-four minutes later, they trooped back into the courtroom. Their unanimous verdict, on their first ballot, was that Clay Shaw was not guilty.

Shaw barely had time to celebrate his acquittal when Garrison pinioned him back on the legal rack. Less than a week after losing his conspiracy case against Shaw, Garrison filed a new charge against him. This time he accused Shaw of committing perjury at his trial when he denied ever having known Lee Oswald or David Ferrie.

Shaw and his attorneys went wearily back to court. It took them two more years to pry Shaw out of Garrison's grip. On June 7, 1971, U. S. District Court Judge Herbert Christenberry issued a permanent injunction restraining Garrison from prosecuting the perjury case on the grounds that it was brought in bad faith.

Garrison appealed to the U. S. Supreme Court and lost there. He responded by issuing a nine-page press release, reiterating his unproven contention that John Kennedy had been murdered "by the domestic espionage apparatus of the United States government," that Oswald was merely a "scapegoat" and that he, too, had been killed "by a member of the government's espionage apparatus" and that "most of the national news media" had effectively obscured the truth. The Supreme Court's spurning of his appeal, Garrison said, "puts the final nail in John Kennedy's coffin."

Then he wrote a book, *Heritage of Stone,* expanding on this thesis. In the 321-page text, Garrison did not even mention Clay Shaw, and Perry Russo got only a single footnote. Just as he had abandoned his original "solution" of the Kennedy murder as a homosexual thrill-killing, Garrison walked away from the Shaw case without apologies, explanations, justification, and—most incomprehensible of all—no outward show of regret over what he had done to an innocent man.

Garrison's relentless effort to prove in court what he had conceived in his imagination destroyed Clay Shaw financially. After his acquittal, Shaw told me that he had spent his entire life savings— more than $200,000—on his defense. It had cost him more than $4,000 for just the eleventh-hour check on Garrison's surprise witness, Charles Spiesel. He learned later, Shaw told me—and a Garrison aide confirmed this—that Garrison had been aware of Spiesel's unstable background, and had put him on the witness stand over objections from his own staff.

Shaw, in my view, was as near to a true hero as any man I have encountered. He conducted himself with unflinching dignity, leavened by wry humor, and without public complaint or private whimpering throughout his five-year ordeal. When a reporter asked him if he "hated" Garrison for what the district attorney had put him through, he replied, "With the other burdens that I had to carry, hate was a luxury that I could not afford." Some months after his trial, he sent me a form letter he had received, with a brief note that asked, "Would you *believe* this?" It was a request from a political committee, apparently produced by a mindless computer, requesting a contribution for Garrison's reelection campaign.

After his acquittal, he was given a civic appointment as head of a French Quarter restoration project, but he developed a brain tumor and died in 1974. One Warren critic pursued him even into the grave, with an article entitled "The Strange Death of Clay Shaw," which implied that there were dark, covert events—somehow linked to the "assassination cover-up"—connected with his demise. It is possible that there was some connection between his agonizing death and what he had been through. Some of Shaw's friends, citing medical research that correlates psychological factors with cancer, bitterly attributed his terminal ailment to the internal stress he had borne with such external grace for years.

When the federal judge halted Garrison's legal assault on Shaw, a major factor in his decision was Perry Russo. The end of Shaw's ordeal thus circled back to its beginning. Garrison offered Russo as a witness in Judge Christenberry's court in an effort to establish that Shaw had indeed known Ferrie and Oswald, and therefore had perjured himself at his trial. But in the federal court, at long last, Russo refused to repeat his tattered tale of the beer-party "plot" in Ferrie's apartment. Instead, he invoked the Fifth Amendment against self-incrimination.

Later, I learned that after he balked in court, Russo had voluntarily gone to Shaw's attorneys and a private investigator and made a long tape-recorded statement about the role he had played in the case. Four years after Shaw's death, a transcript of the recording came into my possession, and on a trip through New Orleans, I sought out Russo and verified its authenticity.

When I read it, twelve years had passed since the night in Las Vegas when Garrison had handed over to me the documents that impeached Russo. Reading the transcript brought a welling up in me of the same sense of horror and disbelief that the original documents had evoked. I thought of how elusive the truth can be, and how long it sometimes takes to rise from the depths to the open air.

Russo said that after his interrogation by Dr. Fatter under hypnosis, and the day before Shaw's preliminary hearing, he was taken to a hotel room by five of Garrison's assistants. There they ran over what Russo had said under Dr. Fatter's prompting to fix it firmly in his mind for the upcoming hearing.

"They sat in the bedroom there and they were drilling me on the transcript," Russo said. "It was like a script to play. You understand, in other words, you play Hamlet and I'll play Horatio. And you say your lines and I'll say mine. There was Sciambra, reading off [the transcript] like a quiz."

Asked if he could recall, when out of hypnosis, the events he had related while in a trance, Russo said, "No." And asked if he could say that he had "actually been in the presence of Lee Harvey Oswald and actually conversed with him," Russo again said, "No." He also said that prior to Sciambra's first interview with him in Baton Rouge, he had never identified Shaw as either "Clem" or "Clay Bertrand," and that "the name Bertrand was first voiced by Sciambra."

After Shaw had been held to trial, Russo said he told the Garrison staff "ten or fifteen times" that "I sure hope you haven't arrested that man on what I said." Russo said that he was reassured that "We have a closed case against this man" and that Russo "probably won't even be a witness." His distress deepened when he found himself as the crucial witness against Shaw.

To prop him up, Russo said the D.A.'s men offered to show him a movie covertly made of Shaw with a hidden camera from a window overlooking Shaw's walled patio at his home in the French Quarter. The movie, Russo said he was told, showed Shaw engaging in homosexual activity. He had rejected this offer on the obvious grounds that it had nothing whatever to do with any complicity by Shaw in the Kennedy assassination.

When Garrison lost his case in court, Russo said, he was approached by a Garrison aide and told about the plan to charge Shaw anew, this time with perjury. "And once he was convicted on the perjury thing," Russo quoted the aide, "people would just think he was convicted on the conspiracy. You know—it would have the same effect."

When I got this central piece to the Garrison-Shaw jigsaw puzzle, it was no longer news—except by the definition of the late Heywood Broun. "For the truth," Broun often said, "there is no deadline."

I talked to Russo this final time in a rental car on a dark street in front of his shabby New Orleans apartment. He said he was making a living of sorts driving a cab and that things had been going "up and down for me, mainly down." He offered no explanation for what he had done and expressed no regret about what had befallen Clay Shaw. He talked about the whole case as if it happened to some strangers he had read about. After a while I said I had to go and he said, "Yeah, I guess you have to go."

The next morning, I flew out of New Orleans on my way to New York. As the plane climbed, I looked down on the city. Surrounded by steaming bayous and stained by my memories of all that had happened there, it appeared as a strange city on some strange planet. Then the plane banked toward the north and flew on toward the real world.

9

My Life with Howard Hughes

"Life is what happens to you," said an anonymous sage, "while you are making other plans." As testimony to the wisdom of this adage, I did not set out or want to become an authority on Howard Robard Hughes, spook of American capitalism and invisible billionaire. Great wealth has never stirred any lust in me; indeed, no sensible man with such a lust would ever become a reporter. With few exceptions, people who acquire great riches interest me even less than their money. Nevertheless, I became intricately entangled in the life and myths of Hughes more than twenty-five years ago, and eventually acquired the firmly epoxied label of "veteran Hughes-watcher" in journalistic circles. One writer went so far as to assert that I had an "incurable" interest in the billionaire, as if I were a Boswell irresistibly drawn to a latter-day Johnson. The truth is that I found him unattractive, maniacally driven by incomprehensible ambitions, self-centered, coldly manipulative, and finally—when I discovered the ultimate horror of his life-style—a man so hagridden by private demons as to inspire only pity. But it is also indisputable that I spent a great deal of time tracking his secret comings and goings, puzzling over his manifold charades, and manning a one-man intelligence post that produced eight magazine articles, many news reports, and finally a book about his last tragic years.

It was not his money that intrigued me, but the power it gave him, the ways he used that power, and the dismaying ease with which he buckled the framework of our political system with it. He operated from the maxim, which he frequently proclaimed, that "Every man has his price," and he made it come true so often that I kept checking his progress looking for exceptions that would rebut him. In the end, this cynicism did him in, but his undoing was not that of a morality play with virtue triumphant, but the dispiriting reverse.

There was another factor that kept drawing me back to Hughes. He operated out of one of the densest bunkers of security of our security-minded time. Reporters are basically voyeurs, and his window shades were always drawn; to a puzzle addict, he was the ultimate journalistic Rubik Cube. The result of all this was that I became, without intending to, a persistent and unwelcomed chronicler of a man I did not admire, never spoke to, never saw.

Our first encounter was happenstance and peripheral, and had a lasting effect on how I perceived him. It grew out of the Long Beach tidelands oil controversy. When that dispute was resolved, the city and the state began spelling out their compromise in a series of conferences in Sacramento. The negotiations, involving the ultimate disposition of several billion dollars in oil revenue, were complex and time-consuming, and required the approval of the city, the attorney general's office, the State Land Commission, and the legislature. They were proceeding amicably when they suddenly hit a rock, and slowed almost to a standstill.

After uncovering the role of the Southern California Gas Co. in that dispute, I had returned to magazine writing. Some months later Publisher Hank Ridder called me back. He showed me a clipping from the Los Angeles *Mirror*, headlined "Mystery Opposition to Oil Compromise." It reported that two potent lobbyists were working the legislature in opposition to the oil settlement, for unknown reasons. He asked me to fly to Sacramento to find out what was going on.

It took less than a week to locate the trouble and to remove it. This time, unlike the representative of Southern California Gas, the lobbyists had registered and were working openly. They were recorded as representing Hughes Tool Co. and both were veteran members of the "Third House," as Sacramento cynically refers to the lobbyists who swarm the capitol corridors. I looked them up and asked what on earth Hughes Tool Co. had against an oil compromise that satisfied the city, the state, and the Lands Commission. One of them gave me a lofty, nonresponsive answer. "Mr. Hughes is a major California taxpayer," he said, "and he is interested in any matter that affects the state as a whole." The other gave me a clue that sailed right over my head. "You're from Long Beach," he said. "Use your head and you'll figure out Mr. Hughes's interest."

I went off and talked to a friendly legislator who had been lobbied, and got an astonishing answer. He got up and closed his door and told me, "Something weird is going on and Long Beach ought to know about it." He said that Hughes was "sore as a boil" about the city's refusal to extend the lease on the hangar for the billionaire's big wooden plane, the *Spruce Goose,* in the Long Beach harbor. He had sent his lobbyists to Sacramento, the legislator said, "to kick Long Beach in the ass on the tidelands settlement until they gave him a renewal on the plane hangar."

I told the legislator that it was incredible that Hughes would intervene in an oil settlement involving billions in public funds because of a niggardly dispute over a plane hangar. "I agree with you," the lawmaker said, "but he's a man with a lot of clout up here."

I telephoned Ridder. "You're not going to believe this, but there's where the trouble is," I told him. "Hughes is wrangling with the Harbor Commission on the hangar lease for that old wooden plane of his. He's opposing the oil settlement until he whips the city into shape."

"I'll be damned," said Ridder. "I'll be *damned.* That's what I would call shooting a gnat with a cannon." He said he would make some telephone calls, and asked me to stand by in Sacramento.

Within a matter of days, the Harbor Commission did a 180-degree turn and granted a five-year extension of the Hughes lease. The two lobbyists promptly disappeared from Sacramento, and the oil compromise got back on track. It proceeded to a successful conclusion without any further difficulty.

I went back to magazine writing with a new insight into the baleful uses of wealth and a new curiosity regarding Billionaire Howard Hughes. Before I left Sacramento, I asked some of the some of the old pols how one man could wield such potent and capricious influence on the legislative process. They looked at me as if I were not very bright and told me, "Money." For years, they said, Hughes had contributed to every legislator's campaign fund. He was like the golden goose, and when the goose's tail feathers were ruffled, he honked—and the lawmakers listened. It is a process that in more innocent days was called buying influence. In the euphemisms of modern politics, it is referred to as "acquiring access to decision-makers."

The *Spruce Goose* had been hangared in Long Beach since its solitary flight in 1947, when it had lumbered into the air with Hughes at the controls and flown a few feet above the harbor for a glorious mile. It was designed by Hughes to ferry troops across the submarine-plagued Atlantic in World War II, but did not get into the air until two years after the war ended. It was—and remains today—the largest plane ever flown, with a capacity of 750 passengers. It was constructed with federal funds and a horrendous cost overrun that became the subject of a congressional investigation in 1947. When Senator Owen Brewster had disparaged it as a "flying lumberyard that can't fly," Hughes had said that it would fly or he would exile himself from the United States. Having got it off the water, he put it into a closely guarded metal shed in the harbor and enshrouded it with the secrecy that was to become his trademark. The hangar was enclosed inside a high barbed-wire fence and guarded by a gun tower similar to those in maximum security prisons.

Behind the hangar's windowless walls, and amid a fog of rumor and speculation, a tight-lipped crew of workmen continued to labor on the amphibious behemoth. The *Goose* was—or was not—being equipped with more powerful engines for its triumphant reappearance. There were Buck Rogers stories that it was being converted into an atomic-powered plane that would revolutionize air transport. Periodic inquiries from the press were met with an unbroken "No comment" from the Hughes organization. But year in and year out, the work went on.

Several years after the brief Sacramento flurry over the hangar lease, I suggested to *True* magazine that we attempt to learn what was going on with the great hidden plane. I pointed out that the federal funds had long been cut off, and summarized the extraordinary lengths Hughes had gone to in renewing his hangar lease. Whatever Hughes was up to, there was obviously an untold story here—a genre that *True*, then the leading men's magazine, specialized in. I got an enthusiastic go-ahead from *True* and went to work.

I worked for three weeks without approaching the Hughes organization, and what I learned merely deepened the murk around the world's biggest plane. I parked my car out on the pier near the hangar and counted the size of the work crew. There were between thirteen and sixteen men who showed up daily, plus a skeleton crew of guards who maintained twenty-four-hour vigil. I took some license numbers, phoned several of the workers, and they all hung up on me as soon as I identified myself as a writer. I located one hangarworker who had been fired and he reluctantly said he would talk to me. But when I went calling on him, he had had a strange change of heart. He said he had decided that he didn't want to talk to anyone about the Hughes project. And when I phoned him later to try to change his mind, he told me to leave him alone, and hung up.

To check the rumors of new engine installations, or conversion to atomic power, I ran through the electrical consumption at the hangar over a four-year period. The utility company showed only a modest, low-level energy input with no significant variance from month to month. This made any major re-engineering of the old plane unlikely.

Trying to find someone who had seen the *Spruce Goose*—and who would talk—I hit upon what I thought was an ingenious approach —the city fire inspectors. They routinely inspected all major warehouses and industrial installations. But when I interviewed the fire chief, he told me that the Hughes people had barred even his inspectors. He still simmered when he recounted the incident. "I told them that the city charter mandated my department to inspect the hangar, and that we would not respond to a fire call unless our men knew where the water outlets were installed and where any gasoline was stored. They refused to let the inspectors in, although they sent a batch of engineers down and showed us blueprints of the building. If that plane ever catches fire, I'd be inclined to let it burn."

After I had exhausted all other sources of information, I called the Hughes organization and said I would like to tour the hangar. They referred me to "the Hughes spokesman," a representative of the nationally known Carl Byoir public relations firm. He invited me to dinner, and I learned a little more about the Hughes secrecy fetish. The designated Hughes spokesman was a nonspokesman. His name was Richard Hannah, and he was an affable one-time Hearst newspaperman. He took me to a topflight restaurant and spent the evening fending aside every question I put to him, and firmly but politely informed me that there was no way I could even get a foot into the forbidden hangar. I pointed out to him that the *Spruce Goose* was federal property, paid for by taxpayers' money, and that as a taxpayer I intended to get a look at what my taxes had helped pay for.

He said that if I got hard-nosed about things, Mr. Hughes's guards would handle the problem, and we thus began a long, frosty relationship. In the ensuing eighteen years, I never obtained a single quotable piece of information from the Hughes spokesman. Neither, I eventually learned, did any other working newsman. Hughes retained the Byoir agency on a substantial annual fee as a noninformation agency. It was a routine joke among reporters researching a Hughes story to say, before filing, "I've got to call the Hughes spokesman for my official 'No Comment.'"

The next day I telephoned the public information officer in Washington for the General Services Administration, which held title to the *Spruce Goose,* told him I was a magazine writer and wanted to inspect the plane. He said he didn't think that was possible, and I asked him why. He said he would look into that and get back to me, and I never heard from him again.

Shortly thereafter, I had a friendly call from an executive at Twentieth Century-Fox, a man I had never met. He told me he had heard that I was researching an article on the Hughes flying boat, that he would like to help me, and suggested that we have lunch the next day at the studio. We had a pleasant meal, and he pointed out various movie celebrities to me, and then we went up to his office and had a remarkable conversation.

He was a bald, soft-voiced fellow with sad basset-hound eyes. He told me that for years he had been on a retainer from Hughes to "handle unwanted publicity."

"Let me tell you about the flying boat," he said. "There is nothing in that hangar but an obsolete old wooden plane that will never fly again. Mr. Hughes put a lot of work and sweat into that plane and it is a very sensitive subject with him. All the crew does is keep it in topflight shape. Hughes is a man who hates the word 'failure.' If he abandoned the plane and turned it over to the government they would probably chop it up into kindling wood and all the newspapers would run pictures and rehash the story of its one short flight. So he continues to work on it. He has poured more of his own money into it than the original cost. And so, as you can see, there is no story there.

"You've put a lot of work into this, and you're a free-lance writer. I think it would be only fair if we reimburse you for your work—what you would have got from *True*. That would be—what?—about $7,500? Whatever you tell me, I'll write a check and no one will know about this transaction except you and me."

I couldn't believe what I was hearing. I told him that my fee from *True* would be $1,500—not $7,500. I said that what he had told me about Hughes and the *Spruce Goose* was a bizarre story I thought was publishable. But if it wasn't, there was no reason Howard Hughes should pay me for wasting my time on something I couldn't get into print, and there was no way I would take any check.

He pushed on and upped the ante. He told me that, as a busy magazine writer, I ought to be on the TWA "free list." He explained that the Hughes-owned airline "comped" a select group of journalists, and named two of Hollywood's best-known columnists as recipients of this largesse. He said that the free and unrestricted use of the airline would include not only me but members of my family. It then became apparent that he—or someone in the Hughes organization—had done some research on me. "I understand that you recently returned from a year in the south of France," he said. "Maybe you'd like to take your family back there some time for a vacation."

I told him that I didn't believe in journalistic freeloading, and that the magazines I worked for paid for my transportation. Then I thanked him for the lunch and left. It was the first and only time that anyone has ever tried to buy me off a story.

The next day he called me again and said he was flying into New York to confer with "an old friend"—an executive at Fawcett Publications, which owned *True*. He invited me to come along with him, because he liked me and didn't want to do anything behind my back. He said that this was an "unfortunate" time for an article about the *Spruce Goose* because Hughes was having money troubles with the New York banks about financing new jet planes for his airline. We would all meet together and discuss the problem, then we could see some shows over the weekend and fly back to the Coast on Monday. I told him I couldn't afford to fly to New York on the story, and that I would not fly as Hughes's guest.

"I hope you understand, and that there are no hard feelings," he said. "I have a loyalty to Hughes and a job to do."

I told him my only loyalty was to the magazine that gave me the assignment and if they wanted the article I was going to get it for them.

When he hung up, I telephoned Doug Kennedy, editor of *True*, and told him what had happened. He said he knew nothing about the impending conference and would keep me informed.

Monday morning he phoned me and told me the Fawcett executive had lunched with the Hughes emissary and had turned him down cold. The Hughes man had then asked that the story be postponed for a year or so, and had been turned down again.

"You're my kind of magazine," I told Kennedy.

"You're our kind of writer," he said.

Three or four days later, Kennedy called me back. He was angry, dispirited, and apologetic. He said he had just had a memo from the Fawcett executive, killing the *Spruce Goose* story. He explained what had happened.

The Hughes emissary had gone back to Hollywood and got in touch with a leading woman star at his studio—one of the biggest names in the movie business. Sometime earlier she had filed libel suits against six or seven fan magazines in a fit of pique about distorted stories about her private life. Two of the magazines were published by Fawcett, and the Hughes emissary had come up with an offer too good to refuse. As a quid pro quo, the movie star—an old friend of Hughes—would drop the Fawcett publications from the libel suit if *True* would drop the *Spruce Goose* story.

"The memo points out," said Kennedy, "that the flying-boat story does not involve the public interest. It also says that defending the libel suit, even if we win it, will cost a bundle in lawyer's fees. All I can say is that I'm sorry, man. As much for my magazine as for you."

They sent me a semigenerous kill fee. It was less than the article would have paid, but, on the other hand, I didn't have to write it.

This was my first encounter with a deep-seated obsession that possessed Hughes—a desire to control whatever was written about him, and to keep whatever displeased him from making print. I was by no means the only writer subjected to his literary abortionist. Shortly after my *True* piece was killed, New York publisher Lyle

Stuart commissioned a Los Angeles writer, formerly on the staff of *Time,* to do a full-scale biography on Hughes. When the project was well under way, the writer was approached by the same studio executive who had blocked me out. He talked the writer into agreeing to submit the manuscript to the Hughes organization for "approval." In return for surrendering control of the Hughes manuscript, the writer was commissioned to do another biography on a well-known movie producer. For this the Hughes agent paid the writer $40,000—far more than the Lyle Stuart advance for the book on Hughes. When the Hughes manuscript was finished, the Hughes agent refused to approve it. Publisher Stuart never got the Hughes book. The writer retained the $40,000 but never wrote the producer's life story.

Several years later, Hughes set up a corporate book-killing device called Rosemont Enterprises in order to block publication by Random House of a biography of Hughes by John Keats. Hughes sold to Rosemont all rights to "use or publish [Hughes's] name, likeness, personality, life story, or incidents therein." Attorney for Rosemont was a New York lawyer, Chester Davis, who also was chief counsel for Hughes Tool Co, and Rosemont took Random House to court, on the bizarre contention that it owned all the facts about the billionaire, and that publication of the Keats book would trespass on its property rights. A lower court actually issued a temporary injunction against Random House, but Rosemont never prevailed in any suit with its peculiar legal theory, It continued to threaten to sue, however, and now and then to go to court. Just the prospect of litigating with the Hughes-financed Rosemont discouraged many publishers from undertaking Hughes books. Unless the projected book was a built-in best seller, the legal costs of getting it past a Rosemont lawsuit would exceed the book's profits.

Early in the 1960's, Hughes himself became embroiled in a massive legal struggle with a group of Eastern bankers and insurance companies over financial control of his TWA airline. The ensuing struggle resulted in a number of court orders mandating that he appear personally for testimony and depositions. Several years before, Hughes, who had become increasingly reclusive, had disappeared totally from human view, as if he had been whisked off the planet by a flying saucer. He effectively avoided any personal appearance because no one could find him to serve the court orders. Meanwhile, his own attorneys were routinely subpoenaing his opponents for depositions. His intransigence in blocking the legal processes that the banking officials were subjected to set off a great manhunt for Hughes by process servers, private detectives, and ex-FBI agents. This drama, in turn, attracted the national press, and by 1962 there were so many people hunting Hughes that Southern California resembled one of the more lively Feydeau farces. The manhunt also brought me my first assignment from the *Saturday Evening Post*, which drafted me to report on the manhunt and the TWA battle that inspired it. I joined the safari, along with writers for *Life, Newsweek, Time*, and a gaggle of other reporters.

None of us, neither the professional bush-beaters nor the journalistic ones, found Hughes. *Life* wound up with an interview with his former barber, while the nearest I got to Hughes was a telephone message from his wife, asking me to report in the *Post* that her marriage to Hughes was a happy one.

On this occasion, there were simply too many journalists buzzing around for his antiwriter agents to swat. But they actively engaged in a variety of operations, and proved as adroit as the KGB in feeding the press what intelligence agents term "disinformation."

I got drawn into one such operation inadvertently by Dick Mathison, bureau chief for *Newsweek*, who was doing his own story on the Hughes manhunt. His piece was scheduled well before my *Post* article, and when he concluded it, he did what he thought was a favor for me. He told me that he had been approached by a mysterious woman who offered to sell him a contemporary photograph of Howard Hughes. The last known photo of Hughes had been taken eleven years earlier, and acquiring a current photograph was akin to finding a Button Gwinnett autograph or a Brasher doubloon.

"She says that the photo was taken surreptitiously by her brother, a pilot for Hughes, at a cabin up at Lake Tahoe," Mathison said. "She wants fifteen hundred dollars for it. She gave me a fast look at it, in a dim bar, and it certainly looks like Hughes. *Newsweek* is drooling for the picture, but they won't lay out the money unless I guarantee that it is authentic. We closed the Hughes story today, and I don't want to go out on a limb. If you want to make a pass at it, I'll put you in with the lady. She's good-looking and spooky. She won't even give me her name—just a telephone number. And when I met her, she made me stay in the bar when she left, so I couldn't tail her."

Mathison set up a rendezvous, in the same Polynesian bar on La

Cienega Boulevard. In advance, I arranged for a friend, Lynn White, a retired LAPD detective, to stake out the encounter. The mystery lady, an attractive young blonde, showed up on schedule, flashed the picture at me, and made a short sales pitch. "All you fellows are hunting Howard Hughes," she said, "but how can you find him without knowing what he looks like now?"

I told her there was a good chance the *Post* would come up with the money, and she told me to make up my mind soon because she had other prospects. Then she left, warning Mathison and me to "stay put or there won't be any picture." She went out into the night, with Lynn White dropping in behind her. He returned and reported she had gone down the block, around the corner, and got into a waiting Chevrolet. He gave me the license number.

I ran the license with the Motor Vehicle Department and found that it was from a Burbank rental agency, checked the agency and was told that it had been leased by a Mike Conrad at 7000 Romaine Street in Hollywood. I knew both Conrad—by name—and the address. "Romaine," as it was referred to in the Hughes empire, was the intelligence headquarters for the billionaire and the telephone message center from which he ran his organization by remote control, from wherever he was holed up. Mike Conrad was a private eye and an agent for Hughes, specializing in dirty tricks against the billionaire's real—and imagined—enemies. Conrad was a very unlikely man to be helping anyone peddle an authentic picture of his employer.

When I had this in hand, I telephoned Mata Hari and asked what Mike Conrad had to do with the picture she was trying to sell. There was a short silence. Then she instructed me to go do something to myself and hung up.

Later I learned from Robert Maheu what I had got into with the lady and her picture. Maheu was the field marshal of the Hughes intelligence forces during the TWA struggle and later rose to the position of Hughes top executive when the billionaire bought up much of Las Vegas. Maheu had an EBI and CIA background and had been involved in the 1960 CIA plot to assassinate Fidel Castro, and he brought to the Hughes organization the talents of a seasoned spook.

The picture the lady was trying to peddle was not a photo of Hughes and had not been taken covertly, but had been set up by the Hughes forces themselves. The "Hughes" in the picture was a part-time movie actor named Brucks Randall, who had an astonishing resemblance to the billionaire. Maheu used this Hollywood Doppelgänger as a decoy to lure the hordes of Hughes hunters off the trail of his employer. Randall would make appearances in such places as Lake Tahoe or San Francisco and drop enough clues to divert the posses into a series of dead ends. As a result, the Eastern sleuths and process servers spent much of their time chasing sightings of the false Hughes. Throughout the TWA struggle, when Hughes was reported flitting around the landscape like the Scarlet Pimpernel, he was actually securely bunkered in a closely guarded mansion at Rancho Sante Fe, north of San Diego, and later at a French Regency house at 1001 Bel Air Road, overlooking the Bel Air Country Club. The fake picture was just one piece of a much larger charade.

I finished the manuscript for the *Saturday Evening Post,* mailed it to New York, and was assigned to the Airman Anderson story in Mountain Home, Idaho. Within a matter of days, well before the Hughes article was edited and scheduled for publication, I was trailed up to Idaho by two Hughes emissaries. One was the movie executive who had killed my *True* article, and the other an official from the Carl Byoir agency. I was dismayed, but not surprised, to learn that they had acquired a copy of my *Post* manuscript even before the editors of the *Post.* They had obtained the copy from Lawrence Schiller, the photographer assigned by the *Post* to shoot pictures for the article. Although he had been sternly cautioned to show the manuscript to no one, he had handed it over to a Hollywood physician who had promised him a photo session with Hughes in return for a copy of my article.

Hughes was upset, I was told, by a passage in the article where I described how Hughes paid his personal bills. With typical dissembling—I suspect for tax purposes—he paid his bills through a Hollywood Bank of America account set up in the name of the "L.M. Company" which existed only for that purpose. The "L.M." stood for Lee Murrin, an employee of Hughes Productions and one of the denizens of the Romaine Street message center. I had uncovered this oddity from a deposition taken from Murrin himself in an obscure law suit, and the information accordingly had not only been given under oath, but was also libel-proof.

This time no one offered me money or free TWA flights. But as a quid pro quo, they said they would give me the unpublished manuscript of a former Air Force general who had gone to work for Hughes Aircraft Co. after leaving the Pentagon—a manuscript with some intimate anecdotes about his association with the billionaire. If I would remove the two paragraphs about the L. M. bank account, I could take whatever interested me from the general's memoirs. I turned them down, and after a long afternoon of wheedling, they flew unhappily back to Los Angeles.

This time, my article not only made print but also appeared intact. Several years later, however, when the *Post* encountered financial difficulties, there was a period when Hughes tried to buy it. I don't know whether he really wanted the magazine, or wanted to get his hand on a faucet that he had been unable to shut off. During his four-year stay in Las Vegas, he spent considerable time trying to purchase the two daily newspapers there, solely because they periodically published news articles of which he disapproved.

The *Post* article, and a cover story in *The Reporter* magazine on the Hughes-Nixon loan, had the unexpected effect of establishing me as a kind of specialist on Hughes. Thereafter, whenever a new Hughes story developed, my telephone would ring with assignment offers from editors or appeals for background information from other reporters. "Hughes-watching" was not a popular occupation and there was not a great deal of competition. There were no ready sources of information, and much of what had been printed about him in the past was shot through with speculation, rumor, or the kind of contrived "disinformation" that had marked the TWA battle. The problem was compounded by the fact that the Hughes organization itself was compartmentalized much the way the Central Intelligence Agency is made up of sealed-off and self-contained units, inaccessible except on a rigid "need-to-know" basis. Although I was not aware of it at the time, by 1966 Hughes was in such total seclusion that not even his highest executives ever saw him or talked to him, except on the telephone.

His attachment to secrecy surpassed the conventional security measures with which big business tries to cloak sensitive projects in a competitive world. With Hughes, internal security took the form of a pathological compulsion. I have a thick file of his confidential memos that surfaced after his death, and they are replete with such warnings as "You are to tell no one—and by that I mean *no one*—about the contents of this memo." His pathology was of long standing. He once wrote a 2000-word memo complaining about the way Jane Russell's breasts were deployed in a movie his studio was making. Half the memo was devoted to the security procedures under which he wanted the memo itself protected. The memo was to be hand-carried to the head of the wardrobe department by the film director, retrieved when it had been read, and then burned.

As a result of his obsession, the few people with whom he had personal communication operated under a pall of fear. When I became acquainted, and later friendly with Bob Maheu, we had a tacit understanding that he would answer no questions whatever about Hughes himself, and I restrained myself from what I knew would be an exercise in futility. One evening he invited me to dinner at his home, and I was surprised to find that the other guests included four of Hughes' personal aides—the so-called Mormon Mafia who lived with Hughes and attended to his personal affairs. It was a weird dinner, during which the four aides ate in dead silence and Maheu and I did all the talking. As soon as the meal was finished, the four Mormons arose and filed out, like well-schooled zombies.

Given the fact that Hughes was totally inaccessible, even by telephone, and that his associates would not so much as confirm that he had one nose and two ears, and that his official spokesman had a two-word vocabulary—"No comment"—it is understandable that reporters did not vie for Hughes assignments. They would come in, bruise their heads on all the stone walls, go away, and usually not return. Obtaining information about the billionaire was more akin to an archeological project than journalism. If one dug long enough, one would unearth some pottery shards, old bones, and a few scattered artifacts from which one tried to reconstruct an alien existence.

Months after Hughes moved to Las Vegas, a Los Angeles television station finally got into the leased Bel Air mansion where he had lived for three years in impregnable isolation. The station considered this such a coup that they devoted some ten minutes to a camera tour of his abandoned residence. The high point came when they opened his refrigerator and revealed to a waiting world that he had left behind an unopened bottle of Poland water.

When Hughes moved to Las Vegas, hid himself away on the top floor of the Desert Inn, and began buying up great chunks of the town, he set off a fresh flood of stories, long on sensationalism and short on facts. A popular thesis was that he was on a federally approved mission to rid the gambling industry of its long-entrenched mob influence by buying up Mafia-infested casinos. It was a thesis that matched the public perception of Hughes as a kind of innovative, offbeat Daddy Warbucks endowed with the insight, connections, and vast resources that could enable him to do what the Justice Department and the FBI had been unable to accomplish in twenty years. This scenario was supported by his actions—he eventually acquired seven gambling palaces—and by the public pronouncements of Governor Paul Laxalt, who effusively hailed Hughes as having put a sort of Good Housekeeping seal of respectability on the desert Sodom. Hughes, however, did little or nothing to purge mob-connected figures from the casinos he purchased. He retained many of them as casino pit-bosses and gambling overseers because of their invaluable expertise.

There was a parallel story that Hughes had simply decided, because he had always been fond of Las Vegas, to restructure and upgrade his new hometown, the way a wealthy landowner relandscapes a newly purchased estate. Hughes himself lent credence to this speculation. He announced, in a series of uncharacteristic press releases, that he intended to build an enormous new airport for supersonic planes that would make Las Vegas a premier West Coast transportation center. The airport would be built far out of town, he projected, and feed passengers into the gambling capital by a modernistic high-speed transit system. For the city itself, he announced plans for a great expansion of his Sands Hotel into a 4,000-room pleasure dome, equipped with an indoor electronic golf course and far and away the largest hotel in the world.

I made several trips to Las Vegas to try to determine if there was substance to any of this rhetoric. From several well-placed sources, I learned that the primary reason for Hughes's buying spree was more mundane and typical of Hughes than what was being dangled before the public. He had acquired, through the forced divestment of his TWA stock that resolved his battle with the bankers, a windfall of $546,549,771 in cash. For urgent tax purposes, he needed to convert this enormous sum from passive capital to working capital, and was buying up hotels, casinos and land to fend off the IRS rather than cleanse Las Vegas of organized crime. Indeed, although he purchased a number of mob-controlled casinos, the sellers had merely taken his money and bought other gambling palaces, or built new ones. The restructuring of Las Vegas proved equally illusory. The supersonic airport died on paper, and not a shovel of earth was turned on the super Sands Hotel.

His four years in Las Vegas, however, proved to be a pivotal point in his life that thrust him onto a precipitous downhill course into exile, impotence, and terminal disaster. Like the unwinding of a classic Greek tragedy, the forces that undid him were of his own making.

When he had gone to Las Vegas, he had suddenly and unexpectedly elevated Robert Maheu to the top position in his empire, bypassing and deeply offending executives of much longer tenure in Houston and Hollywood. This sudden decision, which Hughes typically made without consultation with anyone, set into motion a bizarre palace revolution that ended up with the effective dethroning of the billionaire himself.

None of this surfaced in the four years at Las Vegas, and the full story did not emerge until after Hughes's death. The first sign of the internal convulsion occurred on Thanksgiving, 1970, when Hughes, without any announcement or explanation, vanished from his closely guarded quarters in the Desert Inn. He was taken, attended by his Mormon aides, to a new hideaway at the Britannia Beach Hotel, on Paradise Island adjoining Nassau in the Bahamas. A team of executives, headed by Hughes's attorney, Chester Davis, and a veteran vice-president, Frank William Gay, came into Las Vegas, announced that Hughes had fired Maheu, and took over the reins of the empire.

Summarily dumped from his $520,000-a-year position without even a word from his employer, Maheu challenged his ouster in court and lost when Gay and Davis produced a proxy from Hughes delegating his powers to them. He was evicted from the $650,000 mansion Hughes had built for him on the Desert Inn golf course and never again heard from his billionaire employer.

This secretly contrived and unruly transfer of power inspired a welter of fresh Hughes stories. While these stories accurately reported the visible tip of what had happened, they gave no inkling of what had actually occurred. Ironically, Maheu himself, who for four years had been closer to Hughes than any other person, was unaware of the anatomy of his own ouster. For several weeks after Hughes left Las Vegas, Maheu remained convinced that Hughes had been taken away by force and was being held against his will in the Bahamas. He even dispatched a team of professional agents, headed by his son, to Paradise Island to rescue his ex-employer.

Having no real information, and aware from experience that almost nothing about Howard Hughes was what it appeared to be, I moved the pieces of this new puzzle around and wrote no stories. I talked to Maheu frequently and picked up some interesting archaeological artifacts. I had been surprised to learn from his court testimony that he had never, in ten years of employment, ever met Hughes face to face. I had assumed, along with most of Las Vegas, that he had had daily tête-à-têtes with the billionaire in his penthouse headquarters, an assumption that Maheu did not discourage.

But now he said that although he had talked to Hughes as many as thirty times a day, it was always by telephone, and that Hughes had consistently put him off when he suggested a personal conference. He also told me, in confidence and not for publication, that Hughes had intervals of bizarre behavior, in which he had proposed outlandish projects, such as million-dollar cash bribes to Presidents Lyndon Johnson and Richard Nixon. "I spent a great deal of time," he told me, "trying to protect Hughes from himself." He also had occasional glimpses into odd phobias that plagued Hughes. Maheu, for example, had employed a personal physician for Hughes at the billionaire's request. Hughes had then refused to let the doctor into his presence when he learned that the M.D. had had psychiatric training.

The first evidence I got that Hughes was no longer in command of his empire came in the summer of 1971, and it came in a roundabout fashion. Hank Greenspun, publisher of the Las Vegas *Sun*, happened onto a stock prospectus for a new issue on the Canadian exchange in Montreal. It offered shares in a company called Pan American Mines, headquartered in Phoenix and claiming to have valuable uranium and other mineral properties.

Greenspun had broken the story of Hughes's secret departure from the Desert Inn and was awash with curiosity about what was happening to Las Vegas's foremost investor. Like Maheu, he was inclined to believe that Hughes had not gone under his own volition. When he got the stock prospectus, he phoned me in California and asked me to do some research for him.

He laid out his reasons for believing that Hughes had not departed voluntarily. He had learned, through his own sources, that

Hughes had been seriously ill only a few weeks before he had left the Desert Inn.

"His weight was down, his hemoglobin count had fallen drastically, and he had required several blood transfusions," Greenspun said. "The doctor who attended him told the Hughes aides that he couldn't be moved anywhere except to a hospital. Now we've got this."

He showed me the Pan American Mine stock prospectus. The mining company was headed by Howard Eckersley, one of Hughes's personal aides, and listed two other aides and their overseer as founding stockholders in the firm. What bothered Greenspun was that the name of Howard Hughes was liberally sprinkled throughout the stock offering. The brochure identified Eckersley as "Chief Personal Staff Executive to Howard Hughes" and gave his address as "C/O Howard Hughes, Britannia Beach Hotel, Paradise Island, Nassau, Bahamas." His fellow investors were also identified as Hughes executives.

"Hughes always had an ironclad rule against any exploitation of his name, except in his own enterprises," Greenspun said. "He also didn't like his people going off on their own projects. Something strange is going on; let's see what we can find out about Pan American Mines."

I wondered how the stock had been presented to Canadian investors, and queried United Press International in Montreal and asked them to relay any financial news stories published there about the stock. They forwarded four in a matter of hours. They not only strongly implied that Pan American was a Hughes enterprise but that Hughes was considering other Canadian projects. Under the headline HUGHES INTERESTS ENTER QUEBEC PICTURE, the Montreal *Gazette* reported: "Emissaries of the mysterious and enigmatic Hughes have been meeting with Quebec government and fiduciary figures on subjects related to their reported interest in becoming involved in the national resources picture in the province." The other stories were similar, and they all prominently mentioned Pan American Mines.

The stock prospectus posed a number of questions, which, given the recent convulsion in the Hughes empire, were entwined with other questions. One question led to another, in circles and arabesques that went nowhere. If Hughes was seriously ill, why had he been taken out of Las Vegas? And why were his personal aides, who served as male nurses as well as business secretaries, chasing about on a mining venture instead of tending to the ailing billionaire? If he was hale and functioning, why had he so precipitously abandoned his Nevada operations, where the bulk of his fortune was invested? If the mining venture signaled a Hughes shift to Canada, why was it spearheaded by Howard Eckersley, a functionary with no business background? And why had Hughes gone to the Bahamas, if he was transferring his operation to Quebec or Montreal?

Over the years I had developed a confidential source in the Hughes organization. He did not yield much information, but he would give a straight answer when he could. I called him and asked him if he knew anything about Pan American Mines. He said he had never heard of it.

Since the company was centered in Arizona, I drove down for a firsthand look. The stock prospectus listed a Floyd Bleak of Flagstaff as vice-president and director of Pan American. I spent a day in Flagstaff and learned that Bleak ran a gravel pit there, which had filed a bankruptcy action the year before.

From Flagstaff I went to Phoenix, where the stock prospectus listed the Pan American "headquarters" at an address on North Third Avenue. The address was the law office of an attorney who had represented Bleak in his receivership action. The attorney wasn't in, but his secretary said she merely forwarded Pan American mail to another address. That turned out to be another law office, which forwarded mail to an address on Indian School Road, where I finally tracked down the international headquarters of Pan American Mines, Inc. It was a dingy little suite in the rear of a neighborhood real-estate office, overlooking an alley. The only person there was a pleasant secretary who was reading *Portnoy's Complaint.* When I knocked on her door and told her I was looking for Pan American Mines, she smiled, gestured with her hands, and said, "Here we are!" She had been employed for only a few months, and had seen Howard Eckersley only a few times. About all she knew about the mining company was that its stock was doing very well in Montreal. It had opened at one dollar a share and was now selling at five-fifty.

The prospectus had listed a Phoenix insurance company as committed to a million-dollar loan to construct a uranium mill on the Pan American mining site. I checked the Arizona State Insurance Commission and found that the company had assets of only $197,000 and was teetering on the edge of losing its state license. At the insurance office, I asked whom they had dealt with at Pan American and how they were going to handle a million-dollar loan, given their meager assets. The head of the company said he could answer no questions without talking to "others involved," and terminated the interview.

On the way north, I visited the town of Payson and asked about the Pan American claim. There had been a minor uranium boom in the vicinity, and some mining men told me the Pan American site had been surveyed by several companies who had walked away from it.

I wrote a five-part series for the *Sun* on the mining company with its offices on a Phoenix alley. Then I requested Hughes Tool Co. for a formal statement regarding the vanished billionaire's connection with the venture. It took two days to pry out a terse communiqué from Nassau, and it was issued not by Hughes or Hughes Tool Co., but by Howard Eckersley. It said: "It has been brought to my attention that some individuals or organizations have implied that there is a relationship between Pan American Mines Ltd. and the Hughes Tool Co. I wish to state categorically that neither Howard Hughes nor the Hughes Tool Co. have any investment, interest, or even knowledge of the business or affairs of Pan American Mines. Certain Hughes employees are merely investors in the highly speculative enterprise."

When the statement was delivered to the *Sun,* I suggested that it should also be released in Montreal, where the stock had soared to twelve dollars a share. Surprisingly, the Nevada Hughes office readily agreed. My source inside the Hughes organization told me what had happened. He said that when the Las Vegas office had queried the Britannia Beach Hotel, they had been unable to get past Eckersley to Hughes himself. "Eckersley is not happy with you, my friend," he said. "He said he would like to invite you to go fishing off Nassau, because he has a leaky boat."

The Pan American Mines story only deepened the mystery of what was happening to Hughes. But it had a spectacular fallout on the Canadian Stock Exchange. The story was picked up by a number of Canadian newspapers and by the Los Angeles *Times,* which learned that one of the Montreal "stock-pumpers" for Pan American was Steve Schwartz, who had been named in a U.S. federal indictment for transactions with a New Jersey mob figure, "Bayonne Joe" Zicarelli.

Shortly after the series was published, I was flown to Toronto by the Canadian television network to review what I had learned about the mining venture in an hour-long interview. This set off several government investigations of the stock which concluded with the removal of Pan American Mines from the exchange, the dissolution of the brokerage house that had underwritten the issue, the suspension of the chairman of the Canadian Stock Exchange, and the resignation of the Canadian Securities Exchange Commission chairman, who flew to Italy at the height of the furore and cabled his resignation.

Several months later I recounted, in a *Playboy* article, the palace coup that had ousted Maheu, the peculiar departure of Hughes from Las Vegas, the persistent reports that he was incapacitated, the mining-stock caper, and the inability of Hughes Tool Co. officials to communicate directly with the billionaire. The title was "Can the Real Howard Hughes Still Stand Up?" Ironically, the article was on the newsstands when Clifford Irving erupted into the news with the McGraw-Hill announcement that Hughes had been flying around the Western Hemisphere for months, covertly meeting Irving and dictating *The Autobiography of Howard Hughes.*" Irving's claims and his Hughes autobiography evaporated within a few months, but the question posed in the *Playboy* piece went unanswered for more than four years.

In those four years, Hughes was moved about, by his Mormon entourage, to a series of new hideouts, always outside the United States. His movements were never announced, but usually acknowledged by the Byoir noninformation official, Hannah, after they had been established by local newsmen. From Nassau, Hughes was shifted to Nicaragua, then up to Vancouver, then back to Nicaragua —where he was driven out by a disastrous earthquake—then over to London, and then back to the Bahamas, where he bought the Xanadu Princess Hotel and seemed to settle in.

Throughout these restless travels, the secrecy machine he had erected around himself functioned efficiently. In fifteen years, only six people outside his entourage were known to have seen him and the normal channels of human communication were kept tightly closed. In Nicaragua he gave brief audiences to the U.S. ambassador and Somoza, the country's dictator, and two investment brokers from New York. In London, he saw Governor Mike O'Callahan and the gaming director of Nevada for an hour in order to break an impasse on the control of his Nevada casinos. Thereafter, the walls closed down around him and the outside world was shut out.

There were occasional breaches through which unrelated pieces of information dripped out. His 1972 telephonic news conference, in which he disavowed the Clifford Irving book, resulted in a defamation suit by Maheu, whom Hughes publicly accused of "stealing me blind." I covered the five-month trial for the New York *Times.* It yielded much about Maheu's experiences with Hughes, but little firsthand from Hughes himself, who did not appear and sent in his company as defendant.

The most revealing disclosure came from a trial exhibit that was not introduced in the case. Wallace Turner, the San Francisco New York *Times* bureau chief, came down at the outset of the trial and together we read all the depositions, exhibits, and legal filings in the case—a collection that filled two long shelves in the court clerk's office. Among them was a tape-recording, subpoenaed by the Hughes attorneys from Maheu's son, Peter. Curious about its contents, Turner and I smuggled two tape recorders into the clerk's office. During the lunch hour, when we were alone, we plugged them in and pulled our own copy of the tape.

It was a telephone conversation, in his final year in Las Vegas, between Hughes and Maheu, and it gave a remarkable insight into the mind of Howard Hughes—in his own words. In a reedy, plaintive voice, he complained that he could not control what went on in the state of Nevada, that people were always doing things he disapproved of, and that he wanted to go somewhere where he had true "freedom."

"It just seems as if we were like somebody trying to move ahead with a mass of seaweed and other entanglements wrapped around him and holding him back," Hughes complained. "I don't pick up the paper one single day that I don't read about various conflicts in which we have a definite stake, a definite reason to be concerned, a definite reason to worry about the outcome . . . Everybody who gets a permit for a well around here and taps the water table is in effect a neighbor whose activities and aims have to be considered along with ours . . . I just wish we could find some place where we could start out with a clean sheet of paper and build a community that would be exactly the way we think it ought to be."

He said he considered buying a tract elsewhere in Nevada "where maybe we could have more freedom than we have here. But I don't think that would be a hell of a lot different . . . it would still be a part of Nevada." He had considered a number of other countries, but they all had their shortcomings. The most likely candidate in his search for "more freedom," he told Maheu, was the Bahamas. But the Bahamas would have to be properly restructured.

"If I were to make this move," he said, *"I would expect you really to wrap that government up down there to a point where it would be —well—a captive entity in every way."*

When I listened to this tape, my mind wound back to my first encounter with Hughes, when he had stalled the California tidelands oil compromise in order to renew his plane-hangar lease. Here he was contemplating turning a sovereign country into a captive fiefdom, in the name of his personal freedom. His deterioration into such megalomania had a chilling historical parallel. Today a state, tomorrow a country.

On June 6, 1974, a short news story in the Los Angeles *Times* reported that the Romaine Street headquarters of the Hughes organization had been burlarized the night before. Four unknown men had overpowered a guard, entered the building, cut open two safes with an acetylene torch, and made off with $68,000 in cash and "some art objects." It was a one-day story, with no follow-up—until seven months later, when it erupted back into the news in a scandal that sent convulsions through the Central Intelligence Agency. As a result of the burglary, the security cover was blown on a major CIA intelligence operation, one of the most closely guarded secrets since the development of the atomic bomb—the Glomar Explorer's recovery of a sunken Russian submarine from three miles down in the Pacific Ocean.

At the time of the burglary, I clipped the story, puzzled over it, and filed it away. The burglary baffled me for reasons that none of the news stories mentioned. The Romaine headquarters, a somber two-story building, was legendary in the Hughes empire for its tight security. For twenty years, until Hughes had shifted his operations to Nevada, it had been the nerve center of his organization, swarming with guards, confidential functionaries, couriers. Noah Dietrich, Hughes's prime minister and financial adviser for thirty-two-years, had been officed there until his ouster in 1957, and Bill Gay, who had masterminded the dethroning of Maheu, had succeeded Dietrich as overseer of Romaine. Here were stored Hughes's confidential files, his deep secrets. The building was reportedly equipped with sophisticated electronic security devices, triple burglar alarms, and devices that would silently zap any intruder. Any burglar, the conventional wisdom went, would be better advised to tackle Fort Knox. And here it had been knocked over as easily as if it were a neighborhood delicatessen.

No one, outside the CIA and the Hughes inner circle, made any connection between the burglary and the Glomar Explorer. The *Glomar,* a huge ungainly vessel with a derrick amidships and a companion submersible barge the size of a football field, had been completed in 1973 at an East Coast shipyard and widely publicized as a new Hughes enterprise. It had been built, the news releases said, with Hughes's money to pioneer the recovery of valuable mineral nodules from the ocean floor. It had been sailed around the Cape of Good Hope and berthed, under tight guard, at Long Beach. Before the burglary occurred, it had left its berth on what was announced as an initial effort at sea mining.

Much later, it became known that the sea mining story was a cover for the *Glomar*'s real mission, to fetch up a Soviet submarine that had sunk several years before northwest of Hawaii as the result of an on-board explosion. Hughes had put no money in the *Glomar,* but had merely agreed—or someone had agreed for him—to front for the operation. The *Glomar* was equipped with a highly sophisticated giant claw with undersea lights and television cameras, lowered to the ocean floor with an extensible pipeline, and capable of locating the sunken sub, clamping a grip on it, and hauling it up and into the *Glomar*'s belly. The project, technically brilliant and innovative, was financed wholly by federal funds that ultimately totaled more than $500,000,000. At the time of the burglary, the *Glomar* was poised over the sub in the Pacific, inching its claw toward the ocean floor. It successfully grasped the sub, hauled it up more than a mile, and then suffered a malfunction and dropped two-thirds of the submarine, recovering only the front portion.

The *Glomar* was trudging back to Long Beach—its cover story intact—when the Hughes officials in Los Angeles made a dismaying discovery. Missing from one of the burglarized Romaine safes was a top-secret memorandum, spelling out the details of the *Glomar* project for Howard Hughes. Word of this loss was relayed to the CIA, which enlisted the aid of the FBI and top Los Angeles police officials in an urgent effort to find the Romaine Street burglars and retrieve the missing memorandum.

None of this became known until the following year, although I got a faint and incomplete whiff of the CIA-*Glomar* connection a month or so after the burglary. It came in a phone tip from a confidential but well-informed source. I was told—in a phone call I subsequently learned was tapped by the CIA—that the *Glomar* was a CIA operation, purpose unknown. That was the total content of the tip. The informant said nothing about a submarine retrieval, or how he knew about the CIA connection, "Go dig on it, and you'll find out," he said. The details were so meager that I did not know how to proceed, having no CIA connections or sources whatever. Shortly later, while in Washington, I passed the tip to Seymour Hersh, New York *Times* investigative ace and their CIA specialist.

In a classic exercise in communication failure, Hersh—who had heard of a mysterious CIA operation called "Project Jennifer" and had been steered away from it by the CIA—did not connect it with my tip on the *Glomar.* On the other hand, I had no inkling about Project Jennifer—the recovery of a sunken Russian sub—and I was no help in tying the two together.

Months went by, and late in January I received another tip. It came from a Los Angeles private investigator whom I didn't know, who was aware of my interest in Hughes. The gist of his information was that the seven-month-old Romaine burglary had yielded much more than the press had reported—two footlockers full of Hughes's confidential memos. He took me to a Hollywood actor, Leo Gordon, who told me a farout story. Gordon said he had been approached by a car salesman named Donald Woolbright, who had asked him to serve as a middleman in peddling the Hughes documents stolen from Romaine. Woolbright had shown him some samples, Gordon said, and they had contained some "explosive political stuff" and some memos—contents unspecified by Gordon—dealing with the Central Intelligence Agency. Gordon had pretended to go along with Woolbright, but had quietly contacted a Los Angeles district attorney's investigator named Frank Hronek. Hronek had passed the story on to the district attorney.

"Then the roof fell in on me," said Gordon. He had been visited by FBI agents and top-level Los Angeles police officials, who told him that the stolen documents involved national security and were the subject of an intense federal search. He was not told how national security was involved. Gordon was drafted into a covert project to recover the stolen papers, under a plan to entrap the burglars by offering them a million dollars for the documents. He was also warned that if the documents were recovered, he was not to read them under any circumstances, but to seal them and turn them over to the FBI. He had agreed, Gordon said, but the recovery operation collapsed when Woolbright suddenly vanished. Several months had gone by, Gordon said, and the whole project apparently was moribund. Throughout his conversations with me, he made no mention of "Project Jennifer," the Glomar Explorer, or a sunken Russian submarine.

The story intrigued me, but it also set up a barrage of warning blips, because of such charades as the Hughes Mata Hari with her fake picture and the Clifford Irving hoax. I checked the story with District Attorney Joe Busch and Police Chief Ed Davis, both of whom froze up when I mentioned the Romaine Street burglary. But I pried out a single fact that gave me a peg to hang the story on. Without telling me anything else, Busch let me know that a grand jury was examining the case and considering the indictment of Donald Woolbright.

I called Wally Turner in San Francisco and summarized what I knew. He got a green light from New York for me to write the story for the New York *Times*. I ran myself ragged in Los Angeles, and put together a long account of the peculiar Hughes headquarters burglary, the cover-up of the stolen documents, and the frantic federal effort to recover them. The only reference to the CIA was a passing mention that some of the documents involved the agency, and there was no reference to the *Glomar* or a Russian sub.

While I was writing this account, for Sunday publication, the Los Angeles *Times*, late Friday, broke the story of the sub recovery, under a massive double-banner headline and tied Project Jennifer to the Romaine burglary. They had got wind that something was up from my trips to the D.A.'s office, had put a four-man team on the story, and learned from their own sources about Project Jennifer. One thing was wrong with their account. They placed the sub recovery in the wrong ocean—the North Atlantic—some 10,000 miles from the actual retrieval site, northwest of Hawaii.

When I read the L.A. *Times* story, I frantically called Turner in San Francisco, who alerted his New York editors, who put a platoon of reporters checking the Los Angeles story. We worked from 6:00 P.M. Friday until 2:00 A.M. Saturday, and came to the smug but incorrect conclusion that the L.A. *Times* was dead wrong on the sub recovery. We reached this conclusion with impeccable logic, by minutely reconstructing the past movements of the *Glomar*. It had never been in—or near—the North Atlantic. Saturday, I completed the story of the Romaine burglary without any submarine, but with an official Hughes denial of the L.A. *Times* sensation.

By Monday afternoon, our smugness was gone. From two sources I learned that the CIA had gone to the *Times* and successfully persuaded Editor Bill Thomas to drop the story because it involved national security. Thomas was told that there had been a partial recovery of a Russian sub in the Pacific, not the Atlantic, and the CIA planned a return trip to try to fetch up the remainder. Pursuing the story, the CIA argued, might enrage the Russians and make the recovery impossible.

There ensued a weird four or five weeks of intense CIA maneuvering, none of which I knew about until later. Sy Hersh pounced on the sub retrieval story, confirmed it and wrote it, only to have CIA director William Colby talk the New York *Times* out of printing it, on the same security grounds the agency had used with the L.A. *Times*. Other publications got onto it, and each time Colby would put a finger in the new leaking dike. Throughout this time, the CIA fretted about what to do about me, since I was a free-lancer only temporarily attached to the New York *Times*, and thus a sort of loose cannon rolling around the media desks. I became the subject of a covert CIA investigation to determine whether the agency should trust me enough to brief me on Jennifer and enlist my aid in suppressing the story. They compiled a twelve-page dossier on me which I later obtained, in which I was referred to under the code of "E-14." It had some remarkably accurate information and a few egregious errors. But the question of my reliability became moot when Columnist Jack Anderson broke—or rather rebroke—the sub retrieval story, whereupon Colby pulled his fingers out of the various dikes and the full *Glomar* story gushed onto front pages everywhere, including a ten-column account by Hersh in the New York *Times*.

All this set off a national brouhaha about the role of the press in publishing the *Glomar* story and the activities of the CIA in suppressing it. People who dislike newspapers railed at them for endangering national security. Newspapermen who believe the press should never get into bed with the government criticized the editors who had briefly ducked under the covers with the CIA.

In all this uproar, no one focused on how the security breach had been triggered. Eventually I got a look at the original police report on the burglary. It noted that the Romaine building had only one old-fashioned burglar alarm and that it was broken. Keeping a top-secret CIA memorandum in such a crackerbox, with only a single guard, grossly violated federal security regulations. Although this laxity led directly to the collapse of a technically brilliant—and enormously expensive—intelligence operation, the Hughes officials responsible were never even publicly reprimanded.

The burglary itself, with its gritty Raymond Chandler overtones, was never solved. But there was a sequel that sounded as if it had been scripted by Woody Allen. After the story of the *Glomar*'s secret mission had come out, the lone Romaine guard who had been seized and trussed up in the burglary came forward with a belated confession. Although he had testified before the grand jury about the burglary, he had omitted one detail. When the burglars had departed with their haul he had loosened his bonds and gone up to the looted office. There on the floor he had found two documents, apparently dropped by the burglars in their flight. He had stuffed them in his pocket and "forgot to tell the police about them." One was the Project Jennifer memorandum. Later, when he had read it, he had panicked when he realized it was laden with federal security secrets. He had torn it up, he said, and flushed it down his toilet.

So all the agonizing by the Hughes and CIA officials, the work by the FBI and the L.A. police, and the plan to bait a trap with Leo Gordon and a million dollars, had been unneccessary. The document they had been seeking had literally gone down the drain, through the sewer mains, and out the Hyperion Outfall, sodden, shredded, dispersed among the kelp and bottom fish, beyond the grasp of even the $500,000,000 *Glomar* and its giant claw.

None of which could be laid at the door of Howard Hughes himself. By the time of the *Glomar* fiasco, he had been in exile from his native land for four years. The decision to phase out Romaine had been made without his knowledge or approval. Although no one in the outside world knew it, he was swirling down a drain himself, in the distant Bahamas. It is unlikely that he could have understood what had happened at his Romaine headquarters, even if it had been explained to him. There was testimony, after his death, that long after the Watergate scandal, someone had mentioned it to him and he had asked, "What was Watergate?"

In his last few years, when Hughes was in the Xanadu Princess Hotel in the Bahamas, the occasional trickle of news about him dried up completely. He had been in exile more than five years and he plainly had no intention of returning to the United States. A Federal grand jury in Nevada had indicted him on criminal stock charges in his acquisition of Air West, and there were platoons of process servers awaiting him in other law suits. Under Bahamian law, he could not be extradited. When a U.S. consul attempted to serve him with a court summons in the Air West case, his functionaries had brusquely dismissed the U.S. diplomat and informed him that there was no way he would be admitted into the billionaire's presence. His wife, Jean Peters, had long divorced him and remarried. On December 24, 1975, he was seventy years old, and apparently determined to live out his days as an alien corn, a man without a country.

In February 1976 he returned to the news, with reports that he and his entourage had abandoned the Bahamas and moved to the Acapulco Princess, a luxury hotel at the Mexican playground of the wealthy. The move puzzled me, because in his taped conversation with Maheu, he had expressed a strong dislike for Mexico. I turned down several editor's proposals that I go to the resort and find out what was behind the move; the prospect of butting once more against his secrecy machine did not attract me.

On April 5, 1976, Hughes died on an emergency flight from Acapulco to a Houston hospital. Within minutes after the news flash, my telephone started ringing and it rang incessantly for the next few days with queries from reporters seeking background information for their final reports on Hughes. Even in his death, his Summa Corp. nonspokesmen kept the information faucet crimped down. On the day Hughes died, Summa issued two brief statements, only one of which was true. Several hours after the news of his death, Summa confirmed that he had indeed died. Late in the day, they announced that he had died of a cerebral hemorrhage, which was wholly false. The formal autopsy gave the cause of death as kidney failure, but only a brief summary was released and the autopsy itself was suppressed. The explanation by Summa was that

Hughes had been an exceptionally private man in life and that his privacy would be honored in his death. And this, it turned out, was the greatest and most dreadful charade of all.

When the calls from newsmen dwindled away, I locked up my files on Hughes, silently said good-bye to the man I had never met, and turned to other things. I rejected several book and magazine proposals; I had written what I knew about Hughes and was not inclined to rake it over.

Three weeks after his death, I had a phone call from an emissary for two men purported to have been members of the tight little inner circle that had attended to Hughes personally in his last reclusive years. A few days later I met with Gordon Margulis, a Cockney waiter-bodyguard for Hughes, and Mell Stewart, a Hughes barber and male nurse. Wary of yet another Clifford Irving hoax, I put them through a series of tests to establish their authenticity. They had passports confirming their travels with Hughes, hotel bills from his various stopping places, and check stubs from his Summa Corp. With this out of the way, we sat down and talked for a long afternoon and into the night.

What they told me was a Gothic horror story, one that in twenty years of writing about Hughes I had only dimly glimpsed. Instead of an eccentric rich man with a peculiar penchant for privacy, Hughes had spiraled down into madness in the early 1960's when he had vanished from public view. He had constructed his own private asylum, retreated into it, stripped off his clothes, and lived for sixteen years like a patient in the back ward of a mental institution—one in which he was in charge and made all the rules. He had become increasingly addicted to drugs, and with the help of private doctors he had employed, had ingested and shot himself up with awesome quantities of Valium and codeine, an opium derivative. He had deteriorated into self-neglect, his hair and beard uncut, his frame plagued with bedsores, and his mind ridden with paranoid fantasies and a variety of phobias. He had survived on a diet that he chose himself, ranging from weeks of nothing but canned soup to weeks of filet mignon. For years he had spent much of his time compulsively watching movies on his own projector, rerunning the same film as many as 150 times.

Throughout, until his last three years, he had been capable of donning a mask of sanity when he had dealt by telephone or memorandum with the executives he had barred from his presence. He seemed to be aware of his cycles of lunacy, and would retreat into inaccessibility when irrational.

His personal madhouse was staffed by six executive aides, five of them Mormon, who had been put in place by Bill Gay, the Mormon Hughes vice-president who had engineered the ouster of Maheu. Margulis and Stewart were lowly functionaries outside this palace guard; they resented what was being done to Hughes, and pitied him. The inner guard were supervised, and reported to an assistant to Gay named Kay Glenn, giving Gay a closed circuit by which he could control both information from the outside, intended for Hughes, and orders and instructions originating with Hughes and intended for his executives. This network had been used to convince Hughes that Maheu was betraying him and stealing his money.

With the ouster of Maheu, the removal of Hughes from Las Vegas, and his increasing dependency on drugs, Hughes had become a willing and unwitting captive of his own private asylum. In his final year, he had plunged deep into madness and drugs. By then he had four doctors on his payroll but had spurned their treatment and advice and kept them at arm's length. His lead doctor, and chief source of drugs, was Dr. Wilbur Thain, Bill Gay's brother-in-law.

In his last days, he had stopped eating, was drastically dehydrated, suffering from malnutrition and kidney failure, his weight down to ninety-two pounds. His entourage, fearful of exposing him to outside view, had refused to take him to a hospital until a scant hour before he expired.

When I had the bare bones of this story, I flew to New York and contracted with Random House to write a book about the Margulis-Stewart disclosures. Aware that the project involved what was basically breaking a sensational news story in a hardcover book, we enveloped it in such tight security that only the editor and the chief executive officer at Random House knew of the forthcoming book.

I secluded Margulis and Stewart in an apartment in Seal Beach, California, under false names and spent four weeks debriefing them on what had gone on in Hughes's final years. They then returned to their homes, and in the next four months I wrote *Howard Hughes: The Hidden Years,* making only one copy of the manuscript and locking it away every night.

The security held, and when the book was published, *Time* magazine made a cover story from it, with twelve pages of excerpts. It was serialized in the London *Express, L'Express* in Paris, and other foreign publications from Copenhagen and Turkey around to Japan and Thailand. While I was pleased with its best-seller success, I took more lasting satisfaction from putting together the final major piece of a human puzzle I had worked on for twenty years.

By the time the book was published, Bill Gay had elevated himself to president of Summa Corp.—the successor to Hughes Tool. Co. —a position that Howard Hughes himself had never held. But within a year, Gay and the tight little group that had run the Hughes organization—the executive triumvirate of Gay, Chester Davis, and Nadine Henley, the Mormon aides who had operated his traveling asylum, their overseer, Kay Glenn, and two of the doctors who had supplied Hughes with drugs—were all gone from the Summa organization, by dismissal or resignation. Control of the empire was taken over by a Houston attorney, Will Lummis, a cousin of Hughes and his closest relative.

After their departure, Lummis, on behalf of Summa Corp. and the other heirs, filed a $50,000,000 lawsuit naming Gay, Davis, Henley, Glenn, five of the personal aides, and Dr. Norman Crane and Dr. Wilbur Thain as defendants. The suit charged that they had betrayed their positions of trust, controlled and manipulated Hughes and his enterprises, wrongfully converted his assets to their own uses, negligently mismanaged his businesses, and neglected his proper medical care, all "through a series of self-dealing schemes and conspiracies."

The suit loosed a flood of affidavits, testimony, and depositions. As with the Watergate scandal, once the stone walls were breached, past loyalties and fears were swept away, tongues were loosened, and the hidden story came pouring out. Four years after publication of the Margulis-Stewart disclosures, I spent two weeks reviewing more than 2,000 pages of new revelations about old secrets.

When Lummis had been summoned to a Houston hospital on the day Hughes died, he had been shocked at the deterioration of his cousin, whom he had not seen in forty years. He had looked at the ninety-two-pound corpse and exclaimed, *"This* is Howard Hughes?" When he had moved over into the management of the empire, he had discovered that the Hughes holdings had suffered from comparable mismanagement and neglect. In the six years— from the ouster of Maheu until the death of Hughes—Summa Corp. had suffered an aggregate loss of $132,000,000 under the management of the Gay-Davis-Henley triumvirate. Even the seven busy

Nevada casinos had collectively lost money. While the Hughes empire was bleeding red ink, Gay's salary had been increased from $110,000 a year to $412,000 a year. Attorney Davis, originally retained at $90,000 a year, had billed Summa for $8,082,907—more than $1,300,000 a year—after the palace coup.

The most poignant of these revelations was that Hughes himself, in his final year, became aware that he had effectively become a captive of his own asylum. In an affidavit, Jack Real, a former Lockheed executive Hughes had brought into his organization and his last window on the outside world, told of a conversation with Hughes during one of his last periods of lucidity.

"Mr. Hughes was afraid that Gay would attempt to have him declared incompetent or committed to a mental institution," Real declared. "He expressed that fear to me in mid-1975. I stood by Mr. Hughes's bed in the presence of John Holmes while he told me he thought Gay planned to have him committed so that Gay could assume total control of his enterprises. Mr. Hughes then cited evidence of his strange life style as the means Gay could use in court. He referred to his lack of cleanliness, refusal to dress, fear of germs."

Shortly before the $50,000,000 conspiracy case was due to go to trial, Summa dropped its suit and made an out-of-court settlement with Hughes's caretakers. They went their way, and Lummis and the other Hughes heirs went theirs.

It was a conclusion, bare of sentiment, that eerily befitted his autistic existence. In the end, his lifetime of manipulating others, his capricious misuse of wealth and power, his callousness to friendship, funneled down to no lessons other than the banalities that money can't buy happiness, and that monstrous power can corrupt monstrously. He was like some being from outer space, acutely attuned to all our human weaknesses and blind to all our faltering virtues. And in the end, after all that study and research, I knew and understood no more about him as a fellow human than I knew at the beginning.

10

The Assassin, the Impersonator — and Others

Because I am drawn to offbeat and difficult stories, I have encountered more than my fair share of offbeat and difficult people. My telephone tends to ring frequently, late at night, with calls from utter strangers recounting strange tales. I have been alerted several times to the imminent end of the world, to people who are constructing atom bombs in their garages, and to new disclosures about the murder of John F. Kennedy, including a recent call from a man who identified himself as Lee Harvey Oswald. The simple solution would be to get an unlisted telephone, but unlisting one's phone, for a reporter, is akin to having one's eardrums punctured. There is also the certainty, from years of experience, that now and then amid the fevered paranoia and fantasies, there is someone out there, desperate and sane, with an authentic story. I have learned to listen quietly, to be skeptical but not cynical, to say "Hmmmm" a lot—and not to accept collect calls from far places.

I had one such call after the Reverend Jim Jones took the members of his cult down to Guyana. The caller put me in touch with some of the anguished people in California who had been futilely trying to get their relatives out of Jonestown. They gave me a thick dossier documenting their efforts, plus their unsuccessful attempts to interest the U.S. State Department in what was going on deep in the Guyana jungle. We devised a plan whereby I would fly to

Guyana, and they would arrange transportation for me into Jones-town to confirm their contentions that the cult leader was holding some members of his flock against their will. Then I got hung up on the complexities of an article I was writing for *Fortune* magazine and my trip to Guyana, which depended upon some precise timing, had to be scrubbed.

Some months later, Congressman Ryan and a group of reporters made the trip I had contemplated. Their foray to Jonestown touched off the mass suicides and murders there, in which some nine hundred people, and the congressman and a number of reporters lost their lives. Had I gone down there alone, I doubt that I would have got out alive. When the first word of the Jonestown atrocity was flashed to the United States, it sent a convulsive shudder through me. I called Bill Stout of the CBS outlet in Los Angeles, and gave him the dossier I had acquired. Within hours, CBS put him on its national network with the first account of the State Department's gross mishandling of Jonestown and the Americans who perished there.

On the basis of another tip, I flew to Paris in 1963 and spent a month—and several thousand dollars of my own money—trying to track down the man who had assassinated Leon Trotsky. He was a Stalinist agent named Ramon Mercader, and he had infiltrated the heavily guarded compound in Coyoacán, Mexico, where Trotsky had lived in exile, and sunk a mountain-climber's ax in Trotsky's head in 1940. After a twenty-year prison term, he had been released and flown to Castro's Cuba and then on behind the Iron Curtain. I learned from Isaac Don Levine, who had chronicled Mercader's chilling career, that the assassin's mother, a veteran Stalinist *apparatchik* named Caridad Mercader, was living in Paris. She had become disillusioned with Stalinism, Levine had been informed, and was embittered at having raised, trained, and abetted her son in his role as executioner for Stalin. Stalin was then dead and his policies repudiated by Khrushchev; I was curious about what had happened to Stalin's murderous agent, since the assassination of Trotsky had appalled and alienated world opinion. The new Soviet regime owed no loyalty to Mercader. When he had been released in Mexico, Trotsky's widow had posed an intriguing puzzle. "The murderer of my husband," she said in a public statement, "now goes to his reward—or his execution."

I consulted several magazine editors on the idea of trying to learn

Mercader's fate. They agreed that the answer would make a fascinating story, but doubted that anyone could get it. I was so caught up with this puzzle that I financed myself, on a commitment from *Collier's* that they would reimburse me and pay a handsome fee if I got the answer.

I found the apartment where Caridad Mercader lived, about a mile from the Arch of Triumph. It was in a high-security building, inhabited by Soviet diplomatic functionaries, and I was turned away when I tried to get up to her apartment. I then wrote her a letter, identifying myself as an American journalist, and requested an interview. When I got no reply, I staked out the building from a café across the street and waited for her to emerge. I had several pictures of her and she was easily identifiable—a stocky Spanish woman with a distinctive broad-cheeked face. On the second day of surveillance, she emerged from the foyer with a husky male companion, and headed for a car that had drawn up to the building. I crossed the street, approached her and said, "Senora Mercader, I am the American journalist who wrote you a letter . . ." That was as far as I got. She looked me up and down with icy contempt, lowered her head and spat near my feet, then got into the car and sped away.

I returned to the United States with my psychic itch unrelieved. The project had been highly quixotic, but on the other hand, by Lew Gillinson's axiom, one never knows what can be learned unless one goes and looks. Fifteen years later, a Reuters dispatch dated November 20, 1978, answered the question that had sent me to Europe. It reported that Ramon Mercader had died in Havana, where he had gone the year before for treatment for cancer. It said that he would be cremated and his ashes flown to the Soviet Union for burial "in a place of honor in Moscow."

After Howard Hughes died, I was swamped with appeals from people assuring me that they were the illegitimate offspring of the billionaire and asking my help to establish this. I counted up to twelve of them before I lost track. Some wrote, most telephoned, and one showed up in person. Among the former was a very black man, who sent a picture of himself wearing what appeared to be a native dashiki. In arguing his Hughes descent, he pointed out that he was very tall. "I'm six ft. four inches" he wrote, "the same height as my daddy." He needed help because he was writing from prison, put there by cunning men who wanted to deprive him of his fortune.

There was also an illegitimate daughter who telephoned me frequently from Oregon. I asked when she had learned that Hughes was her father. "When the FBI hypnotized me," she replied. She wanted to know if I had heard from anyone else claiming Hughes as a father and I said I had. "The world is full of greedy, dishonest people," she complained.

The best of the new Hughes's came up from Texas to meet me at my Long Beach home. He had an astonishing resemblance to Hughes. He was tall, lean, and had the same face and bone structure, enhanced by a gray Van Dyke beard and hair down over his collar. He said he was born in Ohio and that his mother had revealed his true father's identity shortly before her death. He claimed to have a 1934 birth certificate listing Hughes as his father and a handwritten document from the billionaire acknowledging paternity, written in the early 1950's. He wanted me to test his claim and, if satisfied, to help him establish that he was no fraud. He had sought me out, he said, because I had exposed Clifford Irving and was a man not easily taken in by rascals. I told him that the quickest and best test would be to have a laboratory examine his documents, establish the age of the paper on the birth certificate and the age of the paper and ink on the Hughes admission that he was his father. "That is exactly the kind of expertise I need," he countered, with apparent enthusiasm. He said he would retrieve his papers from their hiding place and then went off, after sticking me for our dinner check, and I never saw him again.

To suspend one's disbelief amid such encounters sometimes required unusual efforts. When I first heard of a man who called himself Pierre Lafitte, my credulity was strained beyond the most elastic boundaries. Even after I met him, I had difficulty believing that he was even semireal, or that he had done any of the things that he said he had done.

He was a short, bald man with cold blue eyes and a French or Italian accent. He could affect either, and could thicken them up to incomprehensibility when he needed time to think—which happened often in his line of work. He had served for several years for the Federal Bureau of Narcotics and the FBI as an undercover agent —on an independent contractor basis, not as an employee—specializing in infiltrating mobs, organized bands of thieves, and narcotics operations. When he had nailed down the case, he would pull the flush-chain and send the wrongdoers down the legal drain, sometimes by appearing in court as a surprise witness against them. He was a sort of premature, one-man Abscam.

He had at least forty names, and the one he used when he was impersonating himself was Pierre Lafitte. By the best evidence, his true name was Jacques Voignier, which he stubbornly denied. He had once served in the French Foreign Legion, from which he had deserted, or so he said. He had worked as an ocean-liner steward, and entered the United States by jumping ship in New York, where he became, among other things, the maitre d' in a midtown French restaurant. He was an excellent artist and caricaturist, a superb cook, and late in life became manager of the posh Plimsoll Club in New Orleans. He was a man for all seasons—the stormier the better—and the most remarkable adventurer I ever knew.

I first heard of him in the mid-fifties, in Las Vegas, where he had bailed out the Las Vegas *Sun* and its rambunctious, free-booting publisher-editor, "Hank" Greenspun, from a million-dollar libel suit. The local sheriff, Glenn Jones, had filed the suit when Greenspun had accused him in print of being on the take from a notorious brothel operator named Roxie Clippinger. Greenspun had a witness with firsthand knowledge of the bribery. He was so confident of his facts that he had reprinted his original story after the sheriff sued for libel—with the provocative comment to the *Sun*'s readers: "This is what a million dollars worth of prose looks like." But when Greenspun had taken his witness to the district attorney, the fellow had suffered sudden amnesia and refused to repeat his charges. Greenspun was left in the deplorable position of the journalistic gunslinger who strides into a bar, tosses a glass of whiskey into the sheriff's face, goes for his gun—and finds his holster empty. As Greenspun described his plight, "I was left naked to my enemies."

Fortunately, he had a well-connected reporter on the *Sun* staff, Ed Reid. Reid, an émigré from New York, knew the man who called himself Lafitte, and got in touch with him. Financed by Greenspun, Lafitte had come out to Las Vegas in a rented Cadillac, posing as a wealthy East Coast mobster and using the name of "Louis Tabet." As "Tabet" he had put up at a posh suite at a Las Vegas Strip hotel. He had fared forth, dropping Eastern mob names in the right places, and intimated that he was going to invest his racket fortune in various local enterprises. This *persona* established, he had sought out Roxie Clippinger—with a tape recorder strapped to his leg—and discussed buying her prosperous brothel. Roxie, upset by all the newspaper notoriety, was eager to sell. In a single two-hour conversation, in which Lafitte had convinced her that he had run a nonexistent string of whorehouses in Havana, he got some incriminating admissions from her on his tape recorder. He told her he wanted to run "a quiet joint, with no trouble" and asked her, "Who do I have to grease?" Roxie had obligingly told him that she paid off Sheriff Jones every month and offered to introduce "Tabet" to the sheriff via her lawyer. With such an impeccable introduction to "Tabet," the unsuspecting sheriff had come out to his hotel suite and agreed to continue the brothel's immunity in return for cash— unaware that reporter Ed Reid, an assistant district attorney, and a tape recorder were concealed in a capacious nearby closet.

When "Tabet" had fourteen hours of incriminating tape, he had quietly disappeared from Las Vegas. Greenspun then broke a sensational series of articles by Reid with verbatim and devastating quotes from "the mysterious mobster, Tabet," the madam, the sheriff, and various other local characters. The stories sent the *Sun*'s circulation through the ceiling, with citizens queueing up every morning for the next chapter. Throughout the series, there was no indication how the *Sun* had managed to acquire the material.

When the series broke, I was out in Las Vegas on a routine "Sin City" assignment from *True* magazine, and was intrigued by the *Sun*'s sensation. I sought out Greenspun, who told me the story behind the story, and offered me the tapes for an article in *True*. I was eager to do the story, but needed to meet with Lafitte. Greenspun told me that Lafitte operated under such stringent security that he hadn't even informed Greenspun where he was going when he slipped out of Las Vegas.

"Every now and then he telephones me," said Greenspun. "I'll try to get him to call you." With the enthusiastic approval of *True*, I dropped what I was doing, and went home to California and waited for Lafitte to call.

I waited two weeks before his first call. When I told him what I had in mind, he let out a string of English, French, and Italian obscenities and hung up. With some pressure and reassurances from Greenspun—who was eager to get some national recognition of his Las Vegas coup—Lafitte called me again and finally agreed to an exploratory conference. He would set up the arrangements, at a time and place of his choice. "There are a dozen Vegas guys who would like to blow me away," he said, "and I don't take no chances. I'll tell you how we meet and you don't tell nobody or play no games."

A few nights later he called, at 11:00 P.M., and told me to drive at once into Los Angeles and register at the Biltmore hotel under a false name that he gave me. I followed instructions, and sat in my Biltmore room until 3:00 A.M., when there was a tap on the door and I opened it and met the short stocky man with the cold blue eyes. We talked until far into the morning, the beginning of a cautious friendship that lasted some seven years.

I did the "Tabet" caper for *True* under the title "The Man Who Took Las Vegas." When the editor, Doug Kennedy, got the manuscript, he urged me to try to get Lafitte to recount some of his other cases. We worked out the arrangements and I flew to New York and lived with Lafitte for three weeks in his home in Riverdale, where he resided under yet a different name. We wound up doing a series of seven articles, under the tag line of "The Incredible Impersonator."

He had been recruited—or roped—into his unusual occupation by Colonel George Hunter White, the legendary dope-buster for the Bureau of Narcotics under Commissioner Harry Anslinger. Lafitte had been in jail in New York, awaiting deportation as an illegal alien, when White had struck a deal with him. Among Lafitte's cellmates was a major Sicilian heroin dealer, also awaiting deportation from the United States. He was the head of a large distribution network in New York, and White wanted to nail the Sicilian's colleagues. In return for Lafitte's help, White agreed to intervene in his behalf with the Immigration Service and help Lafitte stay in the States.

Lafitte proceeded to con the Sicilian mobster so convincingly that, when Lafitte told him "my lawyer is springing me," the Sicilian had designated Lafitte as his surrogate in the heroin operation. The mobster had a large stash of heroin in Marseilles, awaiting shipment to the United States, and needed the money from its sale. The Sicilian advised several of his colleagues, when they visited him in jail, that Lafitte would oversee the shipment and distribution, and that, "When this man speaks, he speaks for me." Lafitte took over the mob and at the critical juncture of the heroin operation, White, tipped by Lafitte, rounded up the members. To keep Lafitte's role concealed, he arrested Lafitte with the others. Not until they went to trial and Lafitte took the stand as a government witness, did they learn how they had been done in. In this one case, eleven members of the Sicilian group were convicted and imprisoned.

When Lafitte told me this story, I began to understand the stringent security precautions he took. I also acquired my own apprehensions, by osmosis. I would talk to him during the day and work on the series at night. His home in Riverdale had a wooded lot behind it, and I began to hear footsteps and twigs being broken by murderous and nonexistent Sicilian gunmen intent upon blowing the head off their nemesis. What made things worse was that I am bald, like Lafitte, and was working in a study with French doors looking out on the wooded lot. I began to suffer nightmare visions of a gunman putting my head in the center of a rifle's cross hairs. When I confessed this to Lafitte, he moved me to an upstairs bedroom out of firing range—with a wry joke. "Look at it like this," he chuckled. "For you, it's just a few weeks. For me, it will be the rest of my life."

He had pulled off some fascinating operations. I restricted the series to cases where there was either a court record or a federal file to support his story, because he was not wholly forthcoming. Sometimes I would ask, "How did you get in with *that* guy?" and he would brush his chest in the classic French "my-fingers-are-burning" gesture and say, "On that I don't tell you nothing." On occasion, he would go to great lengths to convince me, as in one tale involving the Detroit Mafia capo, Pete Licavoli. I asked if he really knew Licavoli or had just read about him. Lafitte withered me with a glare, pulled out a little black book, and dialed Detroit. "Hey, Pete," he said, "this is Louie Monaco again. I got some more stuff on that thing we were talkin' the other day"—and went into a cryptic conversation with the Detroit capo. When he hung up, he grinned and said, "Yeh, I know Pete Licavoli."

He used dozens of different names—and occupations—in dealing with mobsters around the country, and somehow kept his identities straight in his mind. Years later, he sent me a birthday card from the Belgian Congo—where he was engaged in God knows what. It had forty of his names— like Orsini, Monaco, Tabet, Shillitani—on it, but not the name Pierre Lafitte.

One of the stories we did involved his recovery of a fortune in stolen antiques in Cicero, the mobster hangout west of Chicago. In the raid, the FBI had picked up a convicted Greek killer named Pete Montos, who had escaped prison in Georgia and was guarding the

stolen antiques for the thieves. Lafitte had not had to testify, and
Montos had not learned how he had been sent back to prison—or
by whom. After weighing the pros and cons of telling the full tale,
Lafitte had agreed because Pete was safely back behind the stone
walls.

The article in *True* was on the stands when I picked up the
morning paper and read that Montos had broken out again and was
a fugitive. Not too long after that, I had a phone call from Lafitte,
who had moved from Riverdale to a new hideaway in Westchester.
He asked if I had seen the news about the escape, and I said I had
indeed.

"I hope he don't read *True* magazine," said Lafitte. "If he read
that story you wrote, he's gonna find out for the first time who
dumped him back in the can. But he don't know where to find the
son-of-a-bitch Lafitte, right? So I am sitting here, thinking how
Montos is gonna think. He calls *True* and says he has a good story
for this writer, Phelan, and gets your address. Then he goes out to
Long Beach, rings your bell, and puts a gun against your head, and
he say, 'Tell me fast, where I find that nasty man Lafitte.' "

He let this sink in on me, and then laughed. "But I don't worry
none, Jeem, until something happen to *you,* hey? You have a good
night sleep now, okay?" And he hung up.

They recaptured Pete Montos four days later in a motel near
Washington and put him back in prison. That night, I had a good
night's sleep.

Lafitte had a good grasp of criminal psychology, a quick mind,
could improvise under pressure, and knew how to get people who
don't talk to talk. "You take a guy who has pulled a big job—like
this guy in New York I made who stole two million dollars in
bonds," Lafitte said. "He's real proud, like a ball player who hits
three home runs in one game. But nobody knows this guy has hit
three home runs. He's got nobody he can tell how great he is. I hang
out in the bar where he likes to drink and we get to know each other.
After a while we get friendly and I tell him about a big score I made,
smuggling stolen paintings to Europe. He tells me I think *that's* big,
he could tell me something a lot bigger. He's drooling to tell me
about the bonds, and I'm drooling to listen. But I shove him away.
I tell him everybody in New York is a big man and full of shit, and
I got too many earsful of their stuff. So now he's *gotta* tell me all

about the bonds, and so I say 'okay, tell me about your fucking bonds.' "

Somehow he survived and retired, under yet another name, in a small town far from New York. Two years ago, John Crewdson of the New York *Times* and I tracked him down, after Crewdson learned that both Colonel White and Lafitte had been used by the Central Intelligence Agency in their ill-considered experiments with LSD on private citizens back in the 1950's. When I phoned him and told him Crewdson was coming to talk to him, he cut loose with the same string of obscenities he had adorned me with, twenty years earlier, back when he was "Louis Tabet." But he wound up talking, minimally, to Crewdson, and sent a message back to me—to forget that he had ever existed. As much as I would like to accommodate him, I don't think I'll ever be able to erase him from my mind.

There are two kinds of stories that Seymour Hersh, the well-known investigative reporter, refuses to work on—Kennedy assassination plots and flying saucer tales. He objects that they are equally unproductive, and that their adherents become hostile if one does not readily accept their accounts as graven in stone from Mount Sinai. I agree with him about the Dealey Plaza fanatics. Ever since the Jim Garrison fiasco in New Orleans, they have dismissed me as a tool of some far-flung Establishment that is intent upon concealing the truth about November 22, 1963. It does no good to point out that the conspiracy buffs have derived so many "truths" about Dallas that they cannot possibly be reconciled. Like the hot-eyed followers of the late Joe McCarthy, they have a simple litany to separate the forces of good from the forces of evil: "Are you now, or have you ever been, a believer in the Warren Report?" To respond that one still maintains an open mind is to confess heresy or worse and the vats of boiling oil are wheeled up.

The people who embrace flying saucers, I have found, are more tolerant of journalistic scepticism. If one does not accept their holy truth, they tend to pity you rather than detest you. They see themselves more as benign missionaries among the heathen, not Inquisitionists among the infidels. And unlike Sy Hersh, I have resided many years in UFO country and have learned to live with the natives.

There are so many people in California who have ridden on flying saucers, or at least talked to their crew members, that they hold an annual convention on these close encounters of the third kind. I attended one, at a remote airstrip in the Mojave desert, that attracted over eight hundred of the faithful. The airstrip was owned and operated by a man named George Washington Van Tassel, who literally lived under a rock. He had contrived comfortable living quarters in a kind of cave under a giant boulder alongside the airstrip.

My favorite among the faithful was Orfeo Angelucci, a thin, intense man who told his UFO tale with the down-to-earth details that some of the other sagas lacked. He had been walking down Sunset Boulevard one Saturday night, he related, when a modest-sized saucer—"a little bit larger than a delivery van"—had landed in a parking lot. Angelucci, a man of ingrained curiosity, had gone over to examine it up close. The entrance had whirred open and he had gone aboard. Although it was empty, it had promptly taken off on an aerial tour of the Los Angeles basin. The saucer had flown itself, or had been flown by a control saucer, known among UFOites as a "mother ship."

"What interested me was that there was a jukebox aboard," said Orfeo Angelucci, "and it had all my favorite records on it."

Flying saucers dropped out of the news when stories about them became commonplace and no one produced any verifiable hardware. The national UFO fever began to wane when a West Coast housewife told an inquiring reporter, "I don't understand all this excitement about flying saucers. They come through our backyard all the time."

But they reemerged in 1976 with a bizarre story out of Oregon that made the national news wires, a full page in *Newsweek*, and a long report by Walter Cronkite on the CBS news broadcast. He reported that a score of persons had disappeared from a small Oregon town on what they believed to be "a trip to eternity" on a flying saucer. Terry Drinkwater then gave the details.

"Rocket ships from outer space; Buck Rogers fantasy, or is it? Today there is a group of earthlings who believe they're on their way to a rendezvous with such a ship for a trip to the unknown. Here along the cloud-covered coast near Newport, Oregon, a mysterious couple appeared three weeks ago, circulating a flier proclaiming a UFO would soon be ready to take whoever would follow them to another world." He quoted a local newsman that the vanished people "gave away everything, including kids, all of their material belongings—property, automobiles, boats and money, and just left. Twenty or more faithful are now apparently headed for the lonely prairie of eastern Colorado."

None of the news reports identified the mysterious two, except by their UFO names of "Bo" and "Peep." The editor of the Sunday magazine of the New York *Times* assigned me to track them down, interview them in person, and see if I could get an earthly identity for them.

Having no idea of their whereabouts, other than "the lonely prairie of eastern Colorado," I made inquiries among outer-space fans in southern California, and lucked out with a Beverly Hills psychic named Joan Culpepper. She had been one of the original Bo and Peep recruits, and had wandered with their space sheep for several months before becoming disillusioned. She put me in touch with some of her friends, who still believed in the space shepherds, and I tracked down a congeries in San Diego. Their subleader said no one knew the whereabouts of Bo and Peep, but he occasionally would get a phone call from them. I told him that the prestigious New York *Times* wanted to document all the outer-space news that was fit to print, and gave him my phone number. Within a week, Bo telephoned me and agreed to an interview if I would fly to Little Rock, Arkansas.

I met them in a motel there, and tape-recorded a two-hour interview—which they counter–tape-recorded in the interest of accuracy. They turned out to be a pair of middle-aged Texans, "Bo" an ex-professor of music in Houston named Marshall Herff Applewhite, and "Peep" a professional nurse and astrologist, Mrs. Bonnie Nettles. Neither, they said, had come directly to this planet from outer space, but had come down in previous reincarnations. When they had met in Houston, they had instantly realized that they had known each other in earlier lives on the "next level," as they referred to the outer-space Heaven. They had compared notes, and decided that they were the two heavenly messengers whose appearance on earth was predicted in the Bible's Book of Revelations. They were sent here, according to the Good Book, to preach their gospel, for which they would be killed by disbelievers, and then, after their bodies had lain in the street for three days, would rise from the dead and be summoned up to Heaven in what the Bible called "a cloud" but which was actually a spacecraft. They would take all their faithful followers with them. At the present time, they told me, they were patiently awaiting their assassination. They were also, like almost everyone else here below, writing a book.

They were gentle, rather down-to-earth people, and they told me all this, and much more, while sipping Coca-Colas from paper cups. When I had a tape recorder full of their marvels, we shook hands, and parted friends. "I suspect that you don't believe all we have said," said Bo. "But that is all right. You'll see."

I flew back to UFO home country and wrote their story. The New York *Times* magazine used it as a cover article, under the title, "Do You Sincerely Want to Leave This Planet?"

In our Little Rock interview I told Bo and Peep that some of their followers had fallen away and were saying unpleasant things about them.

"I know," said Bo, sadly. Then he embarked on a short dissertation about the human condition, with which I found myself in total agreement.

"Some people are like lemmings, who rush in a pack into the sea and drown themselves. They join any movement—self-discipline, *this* kind of meditation, *that* kind of meditation, *this* kind of strict diet, *that* kind of diet. Then they go halfway around the world to try another movement, and it is just look, look, look, *look.*"

He shook his head at human gullibility. He concluded with an observation that sums up, in one sentence, just about everything that I have learned in my years as an overly investigative reporter.

"Some people," said the former music professor who claimed he would rise from the dead and take his followers to Heaven on a UFO, "will try anything."

About the Author

JAMES PHELAN has been a newspaperman and magazine writer for more than forty years. He was a staff writer for the *Saturday Evening Post* for six years and has contributed to dozens of other magazines, including *Forbes, Fortune, Playboy, Penthouse, The Reporter, True, Paris Match*, the New York *Times* Sunday magazine, *Cosmopolitan, Parade*, and the *Columbia Journalism Review*. His first book, *Howard Hughes, the Hidden Years*, was a 1977 international best seller and the subject of a cover story in *Time* magazine. He resides in Long Beach, California, with his wife, Amalie, a clinical psychologist, and has two daughters. "If I could choose any line of work in the world," he says, "it would be the one I got into." He is working on his third book.